THE PROFESSION
OF POETRY
AND OTHER LECTURES

OXFORD UNIVERSITY PRESS
AMEN HOUSE, E.C. 4
LONDON EDINBURGH GLASGOW
LEIPZIG NEW YORK TORONTO
MELBOURNE CAPETOWN BOMBAY
CALCUTTA MADRAS SHANGHAI
HUMPHREY MILFORD
PUBLISHER TO THE
UNIVERSITY

THE PROFESSION
OF POETRY
AND OTHER LECTURES

BY

H. W. GARROD

Fellow of Merton College, formerly
Professor of Poetry in the
University of Oxford

OXFORD
AT THE CLARENDON PRESS
1929

10-29-47

Printed in Great Britain

To
DAVID NICHOL SMITH
MERTON PROFESSOR OF ENGLISH LITERATURE

and

GEORGE GORDON
PRESIDENT OF MAGDALEN
WHO LATELY HELD THE SAME PROFESSORSHIP

and to the memory of

WALTER RALEIGH
WHO FIRST MADE THE PROFESSORSHIP ILLUSTRIOUS

THREE FRIENDS FROM EACH OF WHOM
I LEARN SOMETHING DAILY

PREFACE

THE greater part of this book consists of lectures delivered during my five years' tenure of the Chair of Poetry in Oxford, 1923–8. Not all the lectures, however, were professorial. That upon Massinger was made for a private and almost domestic occasion, the nature of which appears sufficiently from the lecture itself. *How to Know a Good Book from a Bad* preserves a discourse to a summer-vacation audience of elementary teachers. Its aim was of the humblest; but it was in demand several summers running, and it seems more decent to print it than to grow old declaiming it. The lecture *Milton and Oxford* was written for the same audience. It contains nothing that will be new either to students of Milton or to the scholars of the Oxford country-side; but enough, perhaps, that is not too old to interest a less sophisticated public.

To the lectures I have appended an 'Appreciation' of an Oxford man who was the principal literary figure of my time. It is not a studied portraiture. It was written within a few days of the death of the person whom it commemorates, with the printer, almost literally, waiting at my door. At the time, it gave pleasure where I had hoped that it would; and I think that it has, perhaps, more truth than a more laboured composition would have hit. I have left it just as it was, though one or two of its sentences need straightening, and there are phrases which I could easily improve.

In one of my lectures I have quoted an eminent French critic, who speaks of the Oxford Chair of Poetry as 'one of the glories of England'. He had read the lectures of Matthew Arnold, and he had heard those given by

Mr. A. C. Bradley. That during my tenure of the Chair I should often have reflected 'in whose seat I sat' goes without the saying. Nor was this reflection the only embarrassment of my five years' period. That period coincided with conditions of criticism which, in some at least of their connexions, were new. When Matthew Arnold lectured in Oxford, neither in Oxford nor anywhere in England was there a 'School' of English Literature. When Mr. Bradley lectured, if there was an English School in Oxford we were hardly aware of it. There was a professorship,[1] indeed, of 'English Language and Literature'; but it was held by Mr. Napier, a distinguished philologian, who limited the range of his criticism to Early English. To-day, every University in the kingdom has its School of English Literature—in Oxford there are three professorships of English, and four professors. Small wonder if I sometimes asked myself whether I was a sheep among wolves or a wolf among sheep.

However, what I am concerned to notice is that this immense extension of English studies must necessarily affect powerfully the whole character of literary criticism; of literary criticism both within and without the universities. The age of elegant amateurism is either dead already or dying. Very soon, it will be no longer possible for any of us to escape the duty of knowledge. Some of us will know more than others, and either be, or pass for, 'dons'. If we know less than we should we shall be called 'journalists'. These are two honourable professions; and there is no reason why they should call one another names. It will still be true that the criticism of literature is valuable only by the depth of its perceptions.

[1] I have heard the late Mr. George Brodrick say that he made efforts to secure Matthew Arnold for this professorship; but that Matthew Arnold had pleaded that he was made, not for use, but for ornament.

Be that as it may, the character of criticism has changed greatly in the last twenty years, for the reason which I give; and its new direction is not yet complete. My immediate predecessor was the late W. P. Ker. Ker's two volumes of *Collected Essays* are a notable monument of the new criticism. How new it is may be seen by placing those two volumes side by side with Matthew Arnold's two volumes of *Essays in Criticism*. You cannot explain the contrast—you do not even name it truly—by saying that Matthew Arnold was a man of letters, Ker just a scholar. Certainly Ker was a scholar, one of the finest which this country has produced. Yet he had a depth of feeling and perception which has nothing to do with scholarship.

I do not know that Ker (though he had an interest in almost everything that was interesting) ever much interested himself in, or occupied himself with, what is called 'the new poetry'. But here was another of my embarrassments. This new poetry was about me and around me like the air. Sometimes I was reproached with neglecting it, sometimes with paying more attention to it than was proper. My Inaugural Lecture was thought 'Victorian'. Yet, though I was born in the Victorian Age, I like it less than most; and I sometimes wonder whether Matthew Arnold was not its best poet. I gave some offence, again, when I lectured upon Mr. Humbert Wolfe —I remember being asked whether I would not lecture next time upon Mr. P. G. Wodehouse (a thing I should delight in doing, and could do, I believe, better than most people). Whither shall a man turn?

For the new poetry I have, let me say here, a very real respect; and if I knew it better I fancy that I should respect it even more. But I confess to being a bad scholar in it, and indeed ill-read beyond what I can easily excuse.

What I like best about it is its determination to supersede what went before it. There at least is something worth doing. I speak seriously; for we had lived too long, I believe, on stale forms. A new experimentation was due, and indeed overdue. Some parts of recent experimentation—the experiments in diction, especially—have been, I think, in a true direction; and the technique of verse, generally, is, I should be inclined to suppose, better understood to-day than ever before. Perhaps it is too well understood, and used, as a consequence, rather wantonly and to effects self-consciously grotesque. Much of the new poetry, accordingly, I find it difficult to read with pleasure. Nearly all of it, again, seems to me to proceed from an inadequate spiritual discipline.

For permission to print some poems which are still copyright I have to thank Mr. Robert Bridges, Messrs. John Murray and the Clarendon Press; Mr. A. E. Housman; the Executors of Rupert Brooke and Messrs. Sidgwick and Jackson; Mr. Humbert Wolfe and Messrs. Benn.

H. W. G.

November 1928.

CONTENTS

I do not altogether think the worse of a book for having survived the author for a generation or two. I have more confidence in the dead than in the living. . . . The dust and smoke and noise of modern literature have nothing in common with the pure, silent air of immortality.—HAZLITT.

THE PROFESSION OF POETRY[1]

'And therefore here I stand forth, only to make good the place we have thus taken up, and to defend the sacred monuments erected therein, which contain the honour of the dead, the fame of the living, the glory of peace, and the best power of our speech; and wherein so many honourable spirits have sacrificed to memory their dearest passions, shewing by what divine influence they have been moved, and under what stars they lived.'—SAMUEL DANIEL: *A Defence of Rhyme.*

IN a history of more than two hundred years, it has happened, I think, only twice before—and in living memory once only—that the Chair of Poetry should become vacant by death; and accordingly, though there are still living and working among us scholars whose names have added lustre to this Professorship, I feel obliged, breaking, I fancy, with precedent, to say a few words of my immediate predecessor. Few words they shall, and should, be. Ker was himself a man who hated the waste of words, and he would better have liked that we should remember him here with kindness than speak a panegyric upon virtues which his shyness made always some study to conceal. Moreover, to many of those here, he was better known than it was my fortune to know him—it is not for *me* to cry the last hail and farewell. And yet again, and above all, there was that in the manner of his death which would make it poor in us to lament and knock the breast. Let no man deceive us; nor our own hearts. It is a good thing, to die in the profession of poetry. *Felix ille quem in hisce litteris meditantem mors occupat.* It is a good thing, to die amid the great spaces of sky and mountain, the everlasting consolation of poets. And once more, it is a good thing, to die young at seventy. I think, indeed, that in saying *that*, I have said already all of Ker that there needs. He was a man full of poetry; and it is to the poetry

[1] An Inaugural Lecture, delivered before the University of Oxford, 13 February 1924.

B

in them that men and nations for ever owe the renewal
of their youth.

> Trust to good verses, then;
>   They onely will aspire,
> When pyramids, as men,
>   Are lost i' th' funerall fire.
>
> And when all bodies meet
>   In Lethe to be drown'd,
> Then only numbers sweet
>   With endless life are crown'd.

This is a very old nation; and there are many causes
which operate at the present time to oppress it with the
sense of age. The years just gone have been fraught with
loss beyond precedent in history; and the years which wait
are shadowed with difficulties to expedite which there will
need, not genius only and courage, but, if I may borrow
a term from an allied profession, grace. Perhaps to some
I shall seem to be speaking academically; and yet I feel
myself to be touching deep realities, when I say that I find,
in this disquiet of the times, no circumstance of happier
augury than the fact that more than at any other season,
as I think, in our history, poetry and the study of poetry
engage interest and inform action.[1] The causes of this
I will not venture here to explore. Let me only say, in
parenthesis, that I am not much inclined to credit the
facile generalizations of those who believe that literature
is either made, or made better, by the operation of great
wars. Indeed, if we were either able to read poetry, or
willing to read history, more truthfully than our habit is,
we should find some reason, as I fancy, for thinking that
the God of Battles is three parts of him a Philistine. For
myself, at least, I mistrust in literary history that temper
which awaits, from the issues of battle, with equal complacency economic distress and spiritual affluence, worse

[1] In saying that they 'inform action' I am thinking especially of their
share in the formulation of the new and large demands for political and
moral liberty which, whatever justice they have, are an important activity
of the times.

homes and better poetry. Such conjunctions are, when they occur, at least more mysterious than our easy comment upon them. That there is at the present time more poetry written and read, and more experimentation in poetry, than there has ever been at any other time—that is, I believe, true, and important; but just because it is both, it behoves us to be circumspect in our comment. That all this poetry, or most of it, is good, or this experimentation as new as it seems, I should not like to affirm. To one of his friends Lamb ascribed the amiable quality of being unable to believe 'that there could be anything bad in poetry'; his friend, indeed (it was George Dyer), had carried this temper so far as to greet with joy the *Epigoniad* of Wilkie on the ground that 'there must be some good things in a poem of 8,000 lines'. That is not a proper temper, you will, I hope, agree, in a Professor of Poetry; yet it is certainly a better temper than a bad temper—by which I mean a criticism ungenerous and inexpectant. One quality the new poetry has without which great poetry cannot be: it has immense faith in itself; and not to believe that from this high confidence, infused through so wide a range of youth, there must necessarily ensue great consequences for the national life and art is to be either very old or seriously deficient in poetry. The directions taken by a large part of this poetry are interesting in themselves and significant beyond themselves. Of that part of it which is either most interesting, or interesting to the greater number of students of poetry, some of the characters are written plain. It is for the most part lyrical, and its verse vindicates a freedom believed to be new. Its language affects an extreme plainness; and its content is informed by the dogma that whatever is is good enough for poetry. Its purposes are whatever may be its results; or at any rate its final cause does not stand in ethical theory. Its conception of the character of the poet is different, perhaps, from any that has hitherto had wide currency. I know not how better to hit this difference than if I say that the race of long-haired poets is dead.

The bardic has gone the way of less noble affectations; and our makers of music and dreamers of dreams seem almost intolerably trim and brisk. That with all these characters of the new poetry I feel equal sympathy, I will not pretend. I have that innocent trust in 'good verses' which makes me like them better when they scan; and I am too scrupulous to call either new or free types of verse which, in truth, repeat some of the oldest metrical pedantries known to me. I confess, again, to a sneaking liking for what great poets, I know, have decried, 'poetic diction'. I am tempted, indeed, to borrow the comment of a poet who, though he employed a diction notably vicious, was an excellent critic of all poetry except his own. 'As to prosaicalness in general', says Leigh Hunt, 'it is sometimes indulged in by young writers on the plea of its being natural; but this is a mere confusion of triviality with propriety; and is sometimes the result of indolence.' Upon the subject of the purposes of the new poetry, I could say much, but nothing in a spirit not diffident and perplexed. You will divine already that I have been bred in a very stick-in-the-mud poetics; and I find myself still stuck in two of its dogmas: the one, that among the purposes of poetry, is pleasure; and the other, that there is very little, in literature or life, that affords permanent pleasure which has not some hold in ethics. The most famous of my predecessors in this Chair was thought in nothing so much to have abused its authority as when he hazarded the dictum that 'poetry is a criticism of life'; nor much to have mended matters when he added that it is a criticism 'mainly upon the side of morality'. I may be forgiven perhaps, if, in this 'home of impossible loyalties', I am so far loyal to a critic who caught my youth, and a poet whose poetry I grow old in admiring, as to pay to this half-forgotten dictum the proper homage of a truism —which is, not to argue it. It was a part of Matthew Arnold's nature that he rather enjoyed being misunderstood. What, indeed, should it profit a man to have founded a society for the promotion of Sweetness and

Light—of which he was the only member—if he were
readily intelligible to the dark and sour souls who constitute the great body of his countrymen? I will not to
that degree vex his ghost as to try here to make him understood; but I will content myself with observing that he
was certainly not commending didactic poetry, and that
he was careful to lay it down that the term 'morality' was
as wide as life. What is the matter with didactic poetry,
of course, is not that it is didactic, but that it is not—
there is nothing to be learned from it. All other poetry
is didactic; just as life and our friends are, though in a
fashion nobler, less obtrusive, more ingenious.

I hope that I shall not, to youth aspirant of immortal
garlands, seem to hold out injurious deterrents, if I suggest that, of the great mass of students and practitioners
of poetry—never before so numerous—not all, or not
enough, have figured to themselves how difficult the business of poetry has become. I am not sure, indeed, that
the poetry of to-day sufficiently asks itself what it would
be at. Mainly lyrical, it is content to depict moods; and
that these are important moods, moods that matter, or
that they are the moods of men who matter, of this we
are given often, I think, only imperfect assurance. Poetry
seems ill-paid, indeed, but easy. Yet never, I fancy, was it
harder. Easy, no doubt, it was, once upon a time. Once
upon a time, the world was fresh, to speak was to be a poet,
to name objects an inspiration; and metaphor dropped
from the inventive mouths of men like some natural
exudation of the vivified senses. Life was a rhythm, a
magical flowing, and every motion was untaught metre.
Poetry was not a criticism of life, but life itself. That
youth of man and nature has gone; and only by some
critical labour of poetry can we either recapture it or even
believe in it. The world and its life grows every day harder
to express: no day but, as our newspapers record it for us,
is big with omens of defeat for poetry. So intractable has
our material become that already one part of our poetry
is dead altogether, and almost without our knowing it;

that part, I mean, which consists in the union of speech and music, and which we call song. Once the poet greeted easily with song all seen things. But to-day a song wants two men's work, and one of them does it badly. Where among the songs of the last two centuries, if you except perhaps portions of Burns and Blake, will you find that vital union of music and words which you feel in the songs of Shakespeare? For Shakespeare, his songs still sang themselves as he made them.

> What is love? 'Tis not hereafter;
> Present mirth hath present laughter;
>   What 's to come is still unsure:
> In delay there lies no plenty;
> Then, come kiss me, sweet and twenty,
>   Youth 's a stuff will not endure.

There are words made, not for, but with, music; and the art is dead, and it is a chance if anything like it will again revisit literature. The body of our joy has sensibly shrunken. From the old Greek, and the old human, unity of words, music, and dance, we have dropped to mere verse; and already we are asking whether it need scan, and yet again, whether poetry need be in verse at all. About the answer, I have no doubts. It need not; perhaps one day it will not. But the soul of man will have lost, in that day, something of its lilt. Of the fortunes of poetic speech, of the actual words which poets employ, the account is more difficult. Words wear out faster than numbers, than tunes; quicker cease to be vital, and pass into convention. Hence periodic revolutions in diction; when some great and original poet takes us back to simpler elements, to a more human speech; and perhaps with the *naïveté* of his class tells us that the speech of poetry and of prose is one and the same thing. Between the language of prose and the language of poetry there is, in fact, no difference at all—save a difference of poetry; and that is why, so long as there is poetry, there will be poetic diction. None the less poetry works here, still and always, overshadowed by

its deadliest peril, the peril of custom. Sick and fevered
it respires after freshness, and reaches arms towards eloquence, but

> Custom lies upon it with a weight
> Heavy as frost and deep almost as life.

These pains of poetry which its forms reflect are part
of a deeper embarrassment. That poetry is a particular
manner of expressing life, or (what is the same) moods of
living persons, will probably be conceded by any criticism
not entirely captious. The expression which it achieves is
more or less adequate according as it can effect adjustments between its means and its material. Its trouble proceeds in part from the mere multiplicity of life, its tangle
of connexions. Each day there happen to all of us, and to
the world, things that the soul does not need, things that
will not fall into their places, that jar a postulated rhythm
of the spirit; until first the world refuses to be sung,
presently it can be *versed*, if at all, only with difficulty,
insensibly driving us down to forms of speech and rhythm
not much above prose. 'I look in vain', says Emerson, 'for
the poet. . . . We do not with sufficient plainness, or sufficient profundity, address ourselves to life, nor dare chant
our own times or social circumstance'; and he goes on to
commend, as unexplored themes of poetry, log-rolling,
political cabals, negroes, Indians, repudiations, the wrath
of rogues, and the pusillanimity of honest men, trading
and planting, Texas and Oregon. That poetry should deal
with life courageously, God forbid that I should question.
But there are many kinds of courage; and these monstrous
and bizarre elements of our developing civilization go not
out, I fancy—they do not come into poetry—otherwise
than by some high courage of prayer and fasting. It is no
good being free and easy with them. The glory of poetry
is in proportion to the greatness of its strife; and that
these elements do not, or may not, multiply themselves,
and their combinations, swifter than poetry—which has
already abandoned to them song, and some wealth of

speech and rhythm—swifter than poetry can adjust itself;
that they are not, in fact, gaining on poetry; this is less
certain, perhaps, than we suppose. And yet, of poetry,
when it endeavours to express life, these are probably not
the most formidable trouble. As the world becomes older,
and the springs of human consciousness less elastic, the
desolating trouble of poetry is, not the things that jar, but
the things that do not. Each day, I said, there happen to
all of us, and to the world, things that the soul does not
need. But equally each day, and in part as a consequence,
nothing at all happens; there happens only that cyclic
relapse into ordinariness which is so much a part of our
lives that, save for the critical admonitions of poetry, we
die in living. 'Custom lies upon us with a weight' which
only poetry—only that frail efficiency—can lift.

This homily has a purpose humble and practical; which
is no more than to suggest that the problem of poetizing
the complexity of our material civilization is less easy than
a good deal of modern practice might seem to imply. I am
even disposed to believe that poetry might be made better
by an increased attention to the theory of it. That is only
academic innocence; or it may pass as such—I am not sure
that, in what follows, I shall not carry my academicism
into guilty and sinister connexions. I have spoken of
poetry as expressing life, and of some poetry as doing so
in a fashion which I think a degree too free and easy; but
if you ask me to hint to you a better fashion, I can offer
nothing that will not expose the beggarly character of
my critical elements. For I own to a long pupilage
to that rather crabbed father of all poetical criticism,
Aristotle.[1]

Aristotle is credited, as you know, with the dictum that
poetry is an imitation of life. All that he wrote upon
poetry was, in fact, directed to the refutation of this
dictum. Plato had called poetry an imitation, or copy, of

[1] I should like the paragraphs that follow to be read in connexion with
the lecture *Poets and Philosophers* (pp. 15–29), where what is here said is
amplified, and the emphasis of it qualified.

life, or things; of sensible things, themselves only copies of meanings; condemning the poet as three times removed from meaning, a creature not only unphilosophic, but anti-philosophic, whom he exiles from his perfect state. Aristotle, more content with a world of imperfect men and half results, brings back the exile, at least partially vindicated. The poet, he says, does not copy life. It is the historian who copies life; the business of the poet is more philosophical, and better worth while. Literature, or at any rate poetry, is not worth while if it merely repeats the fault of a large part of life—if it throws together unrelated happenings. The end of poetry is, truly enough, to present life; but to present it in such a manner as to eliminate what is unessential, unrelated, inorganic; to present it as a whole of which all the parts are seen to be co-operative. It does what life does not—what, because we cannot do it for our lives, makes them so hard: it eliminates the unessential. It hunts the true connexions of things; and in so far as it finds them, its picture of things is a criticism of life.

A great deal of this—which is not difficult—is expressed by Aristotle in language more technical than need be. It was not easy for him to persuade himself that the criticism of art is itself an art; and hunting through art connexions other than those of life, he assumes, more lightly than we feel to be proper, that these connexions are logical. In occasional parentheses of that kind by which nature entraps great minds into more than they mean, he supplies corrections of himself which it is venial in us, I think, to seize over-greedily; as when he puts first among the gifts of the born poet an eye for metaphor; or hazards—rather surprisingly—the doctrine that the poet is a maniacal creature. The gift of metaphor is, as he says, the power to see resemblances which escape the observation of common men, to seize connexions other than, and in some sense truer than, those of life. Let us make the most of these, and other, oracles. Life, for Aristotle, is matter striving after form. I am tempted to carry that with some reck-

lessness beyond Aristotle, and to say that it is prose
struggling into poetry—

> The mortal and the marble still at strife,
> And timidly expanding into life.

This desire of everything that is for self-expression, for
meaning, only philosophy, and philosophy only on that
unattained eminence from which it beholds all time and
all existence, can completely interpret or satisfy. But God
did not make man barely philosophical, any more than
barely two-legged. He threw in 'mania'; and to a small
order of 'maniacal' men, men ecstatic, enthusiastic, possessed, as the Greeks variously called them, he gave eyes
divining hidden connexions, the vision of obscured likenesses, the power to recognize things and name them; a
faculty of imitative magic, summoning at will, and sub-
duing by spells, the rebellious elements of the world's life.

The poet is, in fact, the prophet of the world's final
causes; the interpreter, vexed often and hesitant, but still
the only present interpreter, of a creation groaning and
travailing after its proper meaning. He, more fully than
any other, shares, and is 'possessed' by, the desire of things
for good and for intelligibility. It is his art, or talent,
or mystery, 'to give' (in Bacon's phrase) 'some shadow of
satisfaction to the mind of man in those points wherein
the nature of things doth deny it . . . submitting the shews
of things to the desire of the mind'.

That not all of this is free from difficulty, I can hardly
be ignorant; perhaps, indeed, I came here to-day to
make difficulties; nor do I think that, in the conditions
of the time, I can be better employed than in insisting that
both poetry and the theory of it *are*, at all points, hard.
I do not know that there has, in fact, ever been a theory
or a practice of poetry which did not conceive the poet as,
in some sense, the master of connexions other than those
of common life, connexions, if not more true, at any rate
more important. To what, in himself and the world, he
owes this mastery, and in what sense the connexions which

he seizes, and which he fixes for us, are real—these are
questions to which there have been many answers; and
that none of them illustrate their subject more than
partially—this may at least serve to remind us of what
is more important about the poet than anything else: he
is a being essentially mysterious. I spoke just now of the
new order of trim and brisk and closely cropped poets; and
the bardic, I said, had gone from our lives. I am willing
to unsay it; for I hope that, in the deeper sense, it is not
so. The trustee and repository of the world's hidden connexions is, truly, bardic; and in that spirit, if I may say so,
it is his business to regard himself. Upon the veracity of
his report of the world, the world, so far as it is beautiful
and fit to live in, depends; and the guarantee of his veracity, to him and to us, is himself. It was said of old that
poetry is 'the resonance of greatness of soul'; and Milton
has told us that 'he who would not be frustrate of his hope
to write well hereafter in laudable things ought himselfe
to be a true Poem'; and not this only; but I think it worth
insisting that the same dogma is the coping-stone of the
theory of poetry propounded and practised by the great
poets of the romantic revival. Those poets were certainly
not a school of Tupperish piety; and they certainly did
not believe that it was the function of poetry to moralize;
save, of course, in that wide sense in which I have called
all poetry didactic. Yet they stand, their work stands, in
this dogma; and if you take it from them the whole arch
of their poetic theorizing falls in.

Will you yet bear with me if I end in illustrating this?
and indeed, to all that I have said, it is relevant that I
should insist upon the intimate connexion throughout the
period of the romantic revival, of theory with practice.
Of Wordsworth, Coleridge, and Shelley, it is the paradox
that, though they were before all else poets, yet each of
them, before he was a poet, was—that abject thing—a
professor of poetry. Each and all, they wrote to, and from,
theory. The beginnings, at least, of their theorizing they
fetched not from Aristotle, but from a source even more

unromantic—from the English experiential philosophers. The debt of Coleridge to Hartley has always been recognized—it was one of the few intellectual debts which Coleridge acknowledged with some approach to common honesty. A recent writer, again, has shown how much the famous Preface to the *Lyrical Ballads* is infected at once with the ideas and the phraseology of the 'sensationalist' philosophy. Such a philosophy had no place for the 'universals' of Aristotle. Its primary endeavour was towards a rehabilitation of the senses. For Wordsworth the true report of the world is given by the senses and by their unimpeded combinations; combinations unimpeded, that is, by the logical reason. There is no trouble in the world, and no untruth, but thinking makes it. Why all men are liars, and not poets, is because the average man imports into his perception of nature relations and connexions which are not truly there. The impressions of sense received by an unspoiled and purely passive sensibility begin poetry in us—or in the poet. These lie in the mind, submitted to that modifying process which Wordsworth calls 'recollection in tranquillity'. They lie there awaiting the summons of creative passion; for all creation works in passion. The mood of poetic creation may be described as a storm of association; of such a storm poetry is the reverberation.

The obvious difficulties of so bold a sensationalism could not escape the notice of its originators. It is all very well to call the creative activity of the poet a storm of association; but who, or what, rides the storm? And again, over that modifying process by which the impressions of sense order themselves in tranquillity, what power presides? What answer Coleridge had to these questions in the years in which he was a partner in the *Lyrical Ballads*, we have no means of knowing. Later he escaped into a German idealism of which he may be called indifferently the prophet or the charlatan. But in the momentous period of his partnership with Wordsworth, he was still under the exclusive domination of the English sensationalists. We too much forget that Shelley and Wordsworth began their

philosophy at the same source—Godwin; and from the
spells by which that impossible Pretender—the *archimagus*
of a metaphysic quackish beyond redemption—bound
the most exalted spirits of the time they escaped, by tracks
not now clearly discernible, into one resting-place. Both
find the ultimate principle of poetic creativeness in what
Wordsworth calls 'Spiritual Love', and Shelley, more
barely, and more consistently, Love. Thither, for Wordsworth, 'the affections gently lead us on', the every-day
affections of common men; thither Shelley is more tumul-
tuously swung or sung, as winds lift the leaf, as light the
mists. But examine either for the guarantee of his
safety, his ground of assurance; and his only passport
is that of the pure senses. All men are naturally free,
naturally good, and in them dwells a natural truth. In
my reason dwelleth no good thing. But the senses are
naturally pure. If the poet differs from other men, it is
because, first of all, he has, indeed, 'a more lively sensibility'; and secondly, he has been, from whatever cause,
better able than other men to save this sensibility from the
contamination of reason, or, what is the same, the infection of custom. Accordingly, he sees things, or feels them
—and he says them—not indeed as they are, but as they
matter. Poetry describes things, Wordsworth says plainly,
not as they are, but 'as they appear to the senses'. Its
descriptions are at once less real, and more true; its
effects supernatural, because natural. The purposes of
Wordsworth's poetry are excellently defined by Coleridge
in the fourteenth chapter of the *Biographia Literaria*.
They are 'to give the charm of novelty to things of
every day, and to excite a feeling analogous to the supernatural, by awakening the mind's attention from the
lethargy of custom, and directing it to the wonders of
the world before us; an inexhaustible treasure, but for
which, in consequence of the film of familiarity and selfish
solicitude, we have eyes yet see not, ears that hear not,
and hearts that neither feel nor understand'. To Coleridge goes back, you will notice, Shelley's famous phrase,

by which he selects as the peculiar function of poetry that it 'makes familiar objects to be as though they were not familiar'.[1] And that is, indeed, its peculiar function, its redeeming office. It redeems us out of life into ourselves; out of all that seems not to matter into a world vital, organic, pulsating.

That is why, in the phrase of a great writer whom I have already quoted, 'the world is always waiting for its poet'. But not for any poet, but for one bardic, daemonic, possessed: possessed, in the purity of his senses, by that colour and rhythm of life, which our mean vision misses, which escapes common hearing, which, only through him, our dull hearts catch at all. No wonder, when so high the office, so fine the endowment of character, and requiring so long and so subtle a discipline of heart—no wonder if 'the world is always waiting for its poet'. But always the vigil is worth while: for upon the issue of it hangs the world's life.

> Strange vigil of eyelids wan and worn!
>   What thing is this we wait to see?
>   Shall Christ of Cain begotten be,
> Out of our baseness beauty born?
>
> And yet, not idle utterly
>   This watch the anxious ages keep.
>   If ever once we close in sleep
> Our waiting eyelids, lo! we die!

[1] Elsewhere, in the same context, Shelley borrows Coleridge's actual words 'the film of familiarity'; and the *Defence of Poetry* was clearly written when the influence of the *Biographia Literaria* was fresh upon him.

POETS AND PHILOSOPHERS

UPON the 'ancient wrangle', as Plato calls it, of poets with philosophers, it is perhaps permissible to observe that it is a pity that two classes should quarrel who have otherwise so few friends; and perhaps for me, who may regard myself as the paid, if not very well paid, *advocatus poetae*, it may be thought not only permissible, but proper, that I should remind you that the quarrel began from the side of the philosophers. Of the two classes, these have always been, I should suppose, the less popular with the man in the street. To the man in the street either is a kind of man in the moon. But, upon the whole, I take it, he has more tolerance for the poet; not, perhaps, because he understands him any better, but because to understand him at all is less necessary. Mr. Robert Bridges recently, protesting finely and effectively against poetry for children, against the dogma, that is, that the best poetry cannot be appreciated by children, even by the worst children, has emphasized the fallacy of supposing that we only find meaning in what we understand. You can carry that to paradox, and, perhaps, are meant to; even so I should not forbode for infant years any irreparable harm from the experiment of changing *Jack and Jill* for *Antony and Cleopatra*. But of philosophy the situation is less enviable. It must be understood before it can be loved.

In these contrasted circumstances the wrangle, we may suppose, took its origin; and, by the time of Plato, it was aggravated by conditions which, while they permitted the poet to philosophize, imposed upon him no particular obligation to do it well. Plato and the Platonists took upon poetry a revenge more worthy priests than philosophers; seeking to stifle by a political sentence enemies whom it was not in their power to subdue by argument. But poetry is too like nature; you may drive it out with a pitchfork, but it comes running back. The world whistled it back, the world which never, over any long period, forgets its sentimental needs; and between poetry and philosophy Aristotle, a philosopher who, in his youth, or his second childhood, I know not which, had been guilty of poetry, was successful in effecting an accommodation more enduring than he had, perhaps, any title to anticipate. The practicality of his peace-making is worthy of all praise. Perhaps any poetry is better than none; but not all poetry is equally good; and it is the merit of Aristotle that he was the first thinker seriously to explore the conditions which determine good and bad in poetry. He had his reward: he was able, upon the one hand, to persuade the philosophers that their quarrel was, not with good poetry, but with bad; and upon the other to allay the irritation of the irritable race of poets, of whom each supposed that a criticism directed only against bad poetry hit every one but himself.

By profession Aristotle was a teacher of youth; and of the passions of youth, none perhaps is so overmastering as the enthusiasm of poetry. If poetry can be taught, there will never want young men ready to learn it; and if you live by teaching, there will always be the temptation to teach anything. I say this, not to the moral disparagement of Aristotle, but to emphasize the rather practical character of what, in his *Poetics*, he undertook to do. Of the modern professor of poetry I do not know that practical effects are often, or at all, demanded. But Aristotle was more deeply committed; he undertook to teach poetry beyond the point of mere appreciation. Those who attended his lectures expected to go away poets.

But if poetry was teachable, it was some kind of knowledge; nor to 'the master of them that know' was such a conception of it unnatural or inacceptable. Alike the prejudices of Aristotle, and his studies in poetry, prepared him to conceive of poetry as a kind of philosophy. A man unemotional, or emotional only with a very close-lipped emotionalism, none the less, in effect, though nowhere in so many words, he defines poetry as philosophy touched with emotion. The difference between good poetry and bad is a difference, ultimately, of philosophy; and, indeed, Aristotle's poet would be a philosopher outright save for that in him of which Aristotle, though he uses of it terms of guarded compliment, seems anxious to say no more than he is obliged: he is a kind of maniacal man, says Aristotle. It was left to the neo-Platonists to investigate at large this maniacal quality in poetry. Aristotle labels it, as he labels, conscientiously, all the parts of nature; but he conceives it no part of his business to put it on the train.

We must take him as we find him. To the masterpieces of Greek literature he brought an analytical acumen probably unsurpassed in the history of criticism. By a dispassionate analysis of the best examples of Greek art, above all Greek poetry, he convinced himself that what more than anything else marks off a good work of art from a bad is a certain unity. The good work of art is, before all else, a whole of parts; all of its various elements are necessary to each another, and exist for the sake of the whole. That is easily said, and simple; and for Aristotle it was, no doubt, easy to say it; he had a flair for these grand simplicities. For us it is easy to speak of it as a commonplace of art; but I could wish that we always lived up to our commonplaces. A commonplace is a part of our necessary and obvious beliefs. But in art, as in religion, we only believe as deep as our practice; and I am not wholly happy in a world which reads the *Oedipus* of Sophocles in order to clap—shall I say?—the *Abraham Lincoln* of Mr. Drinkwater. But what Aristotle says of the unity of a work of art is, in any case, less simple if we take it in its connexions. The unity of a work of art is proportionate to the thinkableness, or reasonableness, of its subject. Poetry is *about* something; it says something *about* things. So much almost any criticism will concede. But in the way in which it speaks of things there is something distinctive, something which marks off its discourse from most other discourse. In the discourse of poetry, or art, what is distinctive is, Aristotle believes, its power to express its subject as a whole of parts. Poetry expresses, or imitates, its object by saying something, not about a piece of it, nor about all the pieces of it, but about it as a whole; and a whole may be conceived as at once more, and less, than its parts. A whole is so much of anything as is relevant to it; so much of it as can, in thought, be made to work together. What there is in anything which will not work in with everything else in it, is, for poetry, not really a part of it; and this, poetry leaves aside. Poetry expresses things in their connexions, and no further. This, and nothing more difficult, is what Aristotle means when he says that poetry 'imitates' 'in a universal fashion'. Poetry expresses things in their connexions; of any piece of life which it expresses all the elements are essentially inter-related and co-operative; nothing is without its proper relevance and meaning. If we speak of poetry as the study to express the ideal relations of things, we shall be straying outside the Aristotelian phraseology, indeed, but not outside Aristotle.

For Aristotle, then, that unity of a work of art which makes it art, and not nature, reflects a way of thinking things, not as they happen, or are, but in their connexions. The demand for unity is the demand for intelligibility, for ideality; and the concern of poetry, as of philosophy, is not things, but meanings.

Of what Aristotle says, the most effective illustration is to be sought where, of course, he seeks it, in Greek tragedy. Of a tragedy of which the incidents follow upon one another without necessary connexion, or of which the actions are not essentially dependent upon the character of the agents, we say that it lacks unity. But the same criticism is equally well expressed by saying that the plot, or the characters, are 'unintelligible'. In his practical fashion, Aristotle insists that the subject of any tragedy must be something that the audience, or the reader, can easily 'take in'. In a sense, this is to explain the unity of art as the response of the artist to the demand made by mere human weakness. Yet in fact it is in this weakness that the strength of men is made perfect. All discourse, all reason and speech, that is, implies that, in reasoning and speaking of things, we make things more intelligible; implies that things are susceptible of a greater intelligibility than, without discourse, they have or present. To demand unity from a work of art is only to demand from one form of discourse what we demand from all discourse. That we demand it especially from art, is because art has always been pre-eminently characterized by it. Indeed, that high expectation of truth which we entertain in respect of art is in large part created, we may believe—certainly Aristotle so believed—by the unity which its works in fact have.

Let me pass by for the moment some of the difficulties which Aristotle may be conceived to have created for himself. Of these I take the principal difficulty to be Greek tragedy itself: a practical difficulty. What I mean is this. It is no good to tell me, what I know by a calculation of dates, that the masterpieces of Greek tragedy were not written by poets who had the *Poetics* of Aristotle open in front of them. Aristotle's theory of poetry is deduced from the practice of the great tragedians. But you can only deduce from practice the theory which, consciously or unconsciously, lies behind it. Consciously, or unconsciously—I am inclined to think more consciously than not—Greek tragedy *is* dominated by the belief that poetry hunts universals, that it must present, not particular things and men, their actions and passions, but the meanings of these; that it must separate realities from their accidents, and give them to us in such degree of abstraction from the casualty of life that only what is essential to the thinking of them remains. At least the shadow of this theorizing lies across the whole of the Attic drama; and I will say frankly that I think it a somewhat dark shadow. This is not the place to speak of the deficiences of the Attic drama. Of some of them I have my own opinion; and it at least has the advantage that it is not tinctured by cant. That the circumstances of my profession—I have been teaching classics for a quarter of a century—may have induced in me some degree of prejudice, I would not deny; and from the finest successes in criticism they may have debarred me altogether; for they have made it impossible for me to talk of the Greek drama without knowing something about it. The Greek drama is, to my mind, dominated by theory, by theory false and partial. Theory, false theory, the same false theory, has affected in varying degrees other poetries; but no other poetry that I know has been so consistently true to its theory. 'It was likely that Iphigenia would do so-and-so', says Aristotle. It was likely, not because she was Iphigenia, not for the only dramatic reason; but because she is a type, because she has a pattern to which she must conform.

When Aristotle spoke of poetry as an 'imitation' of things, he meant, that it was a particular way of speaking about things. That the business of poetry is to let things speak for themselves was a rejoinder too obvious to be missed. The best poetry, it was urged, never comments. It reports life, without any impertinence of criticism. Certainly this promise of 'no chatter' is heartening. Yet that the theory towards which it conducts, or encourages us, the theory of aesthetic realism, has not itself some quality of chatter, I have always taken leave to doubt. Chatter about chatter is as bad as thinking about thought; and what I have to say about the chatter of realism I can say briefly. For it presents a type of aesthetic theory which I conceive, in fact, to have been exposed before it was born. Whatever the defects of Aristotle, he had at least made untenable, before they occupied it, the position, if they have one, of the so-called realists. I say, their position, if they have one; and if they have, we may suppose the heart of it to lie in the dogma that poetry describes things as they are, omitting nothing, extenuating nothing, and setting down almost nothing in malice. 'The

dull catalogue', it is supposed, 'the dull catalogue of common things' ceases to be dull if only it be sufficiently
complete. The type of poetic invention is the inventory;
and, not to imitate, but to ticket, nature is the business
of poetry, and, everywhere, of a really consistent realism:
to put in everything, and to let things speak for themselves. But just this is the trouble of realism. If you let
things speak for themselves, they will never be done talking. They perish of their own volubility. The only way
of describing things as they are is to leave out, from what
they are, the greater part. I speak of 'a consistent realism';
but in fact there is no such thing. What the realist means
is, not that he puts in everything, but that he refuses to
leave out what he should. He believes in putting in the
ugly; and he fails to see that, in so doing, he is presenting,
not objects as they are, but a particular theory of them.
He asserts his own idea of things against things; and is
thereby an idealist without excuse.

Sharply opposed both to the intellectualist, or univer-
salistic, theory of Aristotle, and to the realistic theory, is
the theory of what I will call romantic sensationalism. It
cannot be too often said, because it has been so much
forgotten, that, in this country, the poetry of the romantic
revival has its philosophic origin in that materialistic
explanation of experience which, from Hobbes to Mill,
has dominated English metaphysic. Dryden says of
Hobbes that he began the study of poetry too late for
success in the art. But for a distinguished success in the
theory of it, Hobbes was certainly in time. In his letter
to Sir William Davenant, which belongs to the year 1650,
he outlined a theory of poetry which, to the exclusion
of any other, dominated English thought for a century
and a half. The source of all experience is the senses.
'Experience (sense-experience) begets memory; memory
begets judgement and fancy; judgement begets the
strength and structure; and fancy begets the ornaments'
of poetry. This conception, in part the effect, and in part
the cause, of contemporary conditions, remained a kind of

practical gospel of poetry throughout the second half of the seventeenth and the greater part of the eighteenth century. The poetry of that period has its champions; but I should be sorry to cry mew among them. Of that poetry I conceive Hobbes to be the evil genius, but if others like to figure him as its guardian angel, I shall not demur; for it is no good being unreasonable with the Age of Reason. The sensationalist philosophy of Hobbes found distinguished continuators; but I do not know that, save with one exception, any of them exercised upon the theory or the practice of poetry an appreciable influence. The exception is David Hartley, who represents English materialistic philosophy in its extremest form. By his theory of the association of ideas Hartley sought to explain the whole of experience and knowledge as the result of a purely mechanical combination of the impressions of sense. Reason is no more than what results from a kind of mechanical habit of sense-impressions to associate themselves in particular combinations. Reason is, in fact, just an effect of custom.

Both Wordsworth and Coleridge owed much to Hartley. Yet a recent writer,[1] who has properly emphasized this, has failed, I think, to see that it is just where they diverge most from Hartley that they begin to be poets. The importance of Hartley, for both of them, lies, not in the questions which he answers for them, but in those which he makes them ask. A very few words can, I fancy, make this clear.

Reason is an effect of custom; and the poetry of the Age of Reason was another of the effects of custom. Just what was the matter with it was that: it was utterly customary, utterly reasonable. Was it possible to interfere with that bad custom of the senses by which their impressions combine into reason? That was the question which an intensive study of Hartley suggested to Coleridge and Wordsworth; and their poetry draws its life from the answer which they gave to it. That they answered

[1] See A. Beatty, *William Wordsworth, his Doctrine and Art in their Historical Relations.*

it over-gaily, and with a disposition to think the problem
simpler than it was, is likely enough. But it was the very
gaiety of their answer which made them poets. Or was it
the poetry of them which made them thus gay? In any
case, in the flight from reason and custom, from what
Wordsworth calls 'the meddling intellect', and from that
custom of which he speaks as lying upon us with a weight

Heavy as frost and deep almost as life;

in the flight from these to nature and the senses, English
romanticism was born, or reborn. Of the passionate addic-
tion to the senses, on which Wordsworth's poetry is based,
of his faith that truth, the only truth worth having, the
truth of poetry, is in the keeping of the senses, and may be
won by perfect self-surrender to them, by such a baptism,
such a total immersion in them as shall wash us clean from
the infection of reason, so purifying us from the effects of
custom that the familiar face of the world takes that
'freshness and glory' of the unfamiliar which is poetry,
romance; of all this I have said something elsewhere; and
pleasant as it is to make what one has said seem true to
oneself by saying it again in slightly different language,
I forbear. From this gospel of the senses, Coleridge, at a
later date, withdrew into a Schellingesque theosophy
never intelligible, I think, even to himself, and of which
it may be said that, if it gave him a theory of poetry, it
incapacitated him finally for the practice of it. He is only
a poet in the years in which he and Wordsworth shared
the passionate sensationalism in which they both began.
In those years he is, of all our poets, Keats only excepted,
the most purely sensuous; the effective poet of *all five*
senses—the poetry of Wordsworth ends, I should be inclined to say, with the eyes and ears.

With the German metaphysicians, who were the tutors
of the romantic movement in Germany, I need not here
further concern myself than to remind you that German
romanticism stands rooted in a philosophy diametrically
opposed to the materialistic explanations of experience

from which the English romantics take their departure; and that between the poets and philosophers of the period there was in Germany a closer rapport than the two classes have ever at any time achieved in this country. Of the pure sensationalism towards which Wordsworth strives the difficulties had been exposed in Germany in such a fashion that not the merest tiro could miss them. Of some of them Wordsworth himself hardly failed to be conscious. Though he never, I think, abandoned his faith that the senses, unvexed by reason, are the source of poetical truth, there are passages in his writings where he tells us plainly that the senses point us always—always, that is, where there is that surrender to them which makes poetry—beyond themselves. In the intuition of the poet, the light of sense, he says, is itself extinguished 'with a flash which has revealed the invisible world'. The impressions of sense, in some sort, die to live. They die into meanings.

It will not do, therefore, to contrast naïvely a pure sensationalism of the romantics, of the English romantics, with a pure intellectualism, or universalism, of Aristotle. It is easy to say that, for Aristotle, the poetry of things consists in a certain thinkableness in them; and that, for Wordsworth, it consists in a *flight* from the thinkableness of them; that, for Aristotle, poetry is the search for form, for Wordsworth a kind of relapse into matter. Yet both hunt meanings; and when you have called the Aristotelian meanings logical, and the romantic meanings emotional, they are still meanings.

For the moment, let me leave both Aristotle and Wordsworth, and make some endeavour to be a little more in the fashion. The Waynflete Professor of Moral and Metaphysical Philosophy—once my teacher, a teacher to whom I owe so much of either philosophy as I am capable of being taught—addressed to me recently an 'open letter',[1] which some of you may have read: a letter in

---

[1] *The Nature of Art: An Open Letter to the Professor of Poetry*, by J. A. Smith, Waynflete Professor of Moral and Metaphysical Philosophy: Oxford, Clarendon Press, 1924.

which, with something of the fervour of Lucretius plead-
ing with Memmius for his soul, he begged of me that I
should remember that it was not possible for me to speak
of poetry without having a theory of the nature of it. And
not that only; if I had not a true theory, it was ten to one
that I had a false one—indeed, it was more than ten to
one, it was a certainty. It was neither likely nor seemly
that upon such earnest adjuration I should retort mere
flippancies—as that, it seemed to me possible to like my
food without a physiology of the digestive processes. It
was neither likely nor seemly. Nor perhaps necessary, I
reflected; for Professor Smith was ready there and then—
as I had known him in my youth—to hand over the true
theory.

For this theory, if I understand it, poetry consists, not
as Aristotle supposed, in the hunt for universals, but—
quite the opposite—in a kind of hunger and thirst for
that which is individual. To exhibit objects, not in their
universal connexions, but in their individuality, by disengaging them from the connexions of logic, reason, custom; to see them, not as parts of a whole, but as wholes, as
momentary perfections, as arrests of chance and the stream
of appearance, each of them a something cogent in itself,
a *that* and not a *what*, its own logic, its own living body—
this is what all poetry is after; the success, not of an apo-
deictic art, but of a deictic moment, unique, compulsive.

Something like this I understood Professor Smith to say
to me; and towards something like this I felt strongly
allured, because something like this I had long fancied
Wordsworth to be saying to me. That I should call the
Waynflete Professor of Moral and Metaphysical Philosophy a mere romantic, God forbid. Yet I did feel him
to be, in some sense, on the side of the angels.

As I got into detail with him, however, I grew less
cheerful. For one thing, I seemed to see a threat to my
own profession. I had supposed naïvely that the arts were
five, or more; and that I myself professed one of them.
But not so. I now learned that there are, in fact, no arts,

but only art. The arts are a unity. The essential character of all of them, in which they are all one, is that they apprehend what is individual. Wherever we have this apprehension, we have art, and nowhere else.

This sounds easy; but if I tried to tell you all the difficulties which I felt in connexion with it, the sun would go down upon your wrath, and the stars see me still perplexed. Let me speak only of what chiefly troubles me; though it is difficult for me to put my trouble into words and at the same time to seem to you a serious person.

The arts, whether five or, as I had fondly hoped, more, disappear. Wherever we have the individual, we have art, and wherever we have art we have the individual. But did it need, I asked myself, did it need that Professor Smith should send me Croce, or some one from the dead, to tell me that *A* is *A*? Art, as you see, becomes, upon this theory of it, a casual emergence, as it were, of the individual from a mixed context—a context as wide as the world. But to recognize this fitfully emerging individual is possible only to art. Only art can discern art, and it can say no more of it than that it is art. It is open to any one, in respect of a given example of art, to affirm 'Here is the individual; I have had the aesthetic experience': and the positive statement is in no case refutable. All aesthetic judgements are true, and all of them affirm nothing except themselves.

Alike of the critic of art, and of the artist, the function becomes, upon this showing, somewhat absurdly limited. They may coo ecstatically over their imaginations, they may wail high or low; but articulate they cannot; to say something to you and me, to mean something, is *beyond* their art.

Let me leave art, though I leave it speechless, and come back to poetry; about which I often speculate whether it is so much like other arts as the common name implies, whether it may not, in fact, be *sui generis*. Let me leave art, and come back to Aristotle and Wordsworth; for both of whom it is part of the essence of poetry that it means something. And that surely is why poetry says something. It is essentially a saying, and not a being; and a saying which is not a mere talking to oneself. If you ask what poetry says, and in what sort what it says reflects things, you will not, I fancy, get the answer unless you first inquire to whom it says it. We sometimes speak as though it were not only the practice, but even the duty, of the poet to talk to the clouds. If he so conceived things, then, indeed, it would suffice for him, as for Croce, that he should coo. But he, in fact, not only uses words, but is above all men the insatiable amorist of words. He speaks to men; and he has stood doing so for so long a period that I should suppose him to know his public. Now, as I have already hinted, the very existence of speech implies that things, by being spoken of, become more intelligible. If you leave them as you found them, you help nobody, and you interest nobody. The public which the poet has to satisfy is a public passionately convinced that things are, in fact, intelligible: that they are, in some sense, intelligible as they stand. Therein lies the contrast with philosophy. We look, indeed, to the philosopher to explain things to us; but the expectation which we have of him is consciously limited in two directions. We know, and he tells us, that the philosophical explanation of any-thing is possible only by an explanation of all things; the flower in the crannied wall involves, philosophically, the universe. We know, again, what the philosopher tends not to know, that effective assent to any proposition involves an act, not of a part of us, but of the whole of us. Things will not be intelligible so long as they present any elements against which there are parts of our nature, passion, desire, or what not, which protest; there is even something in us which protests against being told that, to understand any-thing, we must understand everything. This is the oppor-tunity of the poet; he is the prophet, or evangel, of our mixed desiring nature; and it is his office, essentially, to make a this or a that intelligible here and now, and let the universal connexions of it go hang. He does things like that because, if he does them otherwise, he is a philosopher, or he babbles. This is not to preclude him from philosophy; what of philosophy he can use, he takes; remembering only that he can use no material which is not adjusted to his only purpose, that of convincing here and now a mixed human nature. What the philosopher tells us we can test—he is content that we should—by the rules which he himself supplies to us. But the poet supplies no rules; of the truth of what he says the only criterion is the effective assent of this mixed human nature. Dare I say that I know no theory of poetical truth more satisfactory than what I have heard called the 'Click Theory'? If it has connexions with the spinal shiver theory, that is not my fault, nor a fault of the theory. The spinal shiver which follows something consummately said, all save the coolest natures know well. It is the comment of the emotions when the hand of the master is laid upon them. The 'Click Theory' goes a little further. Something is said; and all the intricate wards at once of the infinitely mysterious mechanism of our human nature, turn; all the parts of us meet decisively, yet softly, falling into place with that swift noiseless *click* which is the unresisting assent of the totality of what we are. You may say a trick has been put upon us, that this is not truth but persuasion. And the only answer is that you cannot put a trick upon the whole of what we are. Only the supreme hand can move so the marvellous mechanism, can thus deftly turn the key in the oiled wards,

And seal the hushed casket of the soul.

But there are other clicks in the world; and none more monitory, as it beats out the little life of a lecture, than the clicking of clocks and watches. If I am driven to end in the middle, I may at least plead that it is the fate of all honest thinking. If a man comes to a conclusion, look to your spoons and forks; for there is no truth in him. I am left with the half of Aristotle and Wordsworth, of intellectualism and sensationalism, still on my hands. I

have some hope to come back to them at a later date; and
yet a half-hope to be tired of them. For a quarrel about
emphasis is always tiresome; and I am not sure that this
may not plausibly be so conceived. Of our mixed human
nature, Aristotle emphasizes one side, the desire for form
and for the apprehension of connexions; *so* it was natural
for him to conceive intelligibility in things. Yet that the
connexions which he demands in poetry may be, at least
in some examples of it, emotional connexions, he is hardly,
when he calls the poet 'a maniacal creature', wholly un-
aware. It was natural, again, for Wordsworth, reacting
against the age of reason, its formal poetizing, and the
trim connexions of all its thinking, to conceive of poetry
as a mere explosion of sense, throwing up truth in its
radiant coloured mist. Yet that in the shock of the
explosion sense itself perishes, this Wordsworth knew, this,
as I have already noticed, he himself tells us in terms
sufficiently precise. It is easy to speak hard words of
the bloodless universalism of Aristotle; and in the Greek
drama which is, if not as he made it, yet as he beheld
it, pronouncing it 'very good', I miss myself the warm
flesh which better protects from criticism poetry of less
pretension. Yet that poetry, like all other thinking,
universalizes, remains true. It remains also true that it
universalizes something, or is itself nothing; and true again
that it is this something which is, for poetry, everything;
hold this something, and that which universalizes it is at
once nothing. It is the conviction of this something which
is the supreme postulate of our mixed nature; and of this
conviction poetry is the consummate expression. That it
is possible for the poet to analyse his processes, I have never
thought; for I have thought them always to be the processes of inspiration. Yet that the heart of these processes
is to be found where Wordsworth finds it, in some cutting
loose from universals, some flight from things as thought—
this, when poets ask me to believe it, I am more ready to
believe than to believe a philosophy more fully articulated.

'PURE POETRY'

WE are none of us as famous as we should be; and I dare say the name of the Abbé Bremond is unfamiliar even in Oxford.[1] If so, we are foolish and ungrateful; for it was among the Oxford Jesuits that this distinguished scholar received his education—or a part of it. A good many Englishmen will know, perhaps, his essay on Newman; and a few special students his principal work, a six-volume *History of Religious Sentiment in France*. But M. Bremond, years since, either listened to, or read, the lectures given in Oxford by Mr. A. C. Bradley. His memory of them makes him so bold as to say that 'the Oxford Chair of Poetry is one of the glories of England'; and not so long ago[1] he delivered at the Institute of France a lecture of which I understand him to give the glory to Newman and Mr. Bradley. He gave to it the title of 'La Poésie Pure'; and 'never had the French Academy', says M. Robert de Souza (himself both a poet and a critic of poetry), 'never had the French Academy heard anything like it'. The lecture was printed, at the end of 1926, with a number of supplementary essays, in a volume which contains also a long essay by M. de Souza. When he does not talk about the rhythm of the universe, M. de Souza is readable. The Abbé Bremond is readable everywhere. He has a vigorous Chestertonian style; and is perhaps somewhat more gay with those who disagree with him than need was. Of one of his antagonists, for example, he is moved to say that 'he is, after all, only a symbol; a sort of Behemoth, anti-poetry made flesh. If it had not been my good luck to meet him living and laying down the law, I should have had to invent him.' Even so, M. Bremond's book is too long. The lecture alone would have done. But

---

[1] This was written at the end of 1927. In the summer of 1928 the University of Oxford conferred on M. Bremond the honorary degree of D.Litt.

the explanatory pages run to near 150. It is true, they
keep gay. 'Fools will ask me', says the Abbé, 'When are
you going to end? and sensible people, When are you
going to begin? To the first, I answer, By-and-by; to
the second, Not yet.' Not content, I may add, with
writing too long a book, M. Bremond has lately issued
a sequel to it, and—to my mind—a rather dull one:
dull, I mean, for M. Bremond. Under the title of *Prayer
and Poetry* this sequel has lately been translated into
English. If, instead, some one had been at pains to
translate *La Poésie Pure*, he would have been better
employed.

I come back to M. de Souza's remark upon the lecture.
'Never had the French Academy heard anything like it';
and M. de Souza wonders how the audacity of it will take
an English audience; what we in Oxford, I suppose he
means, will think of a critic—and a cleric at that—who
talks of Baudelaire and Mallarmé in the same breath with
Shakespeare and Wordsworth and Keats: Baudelaire, a
reprouvé, a *maudit*; Mallarmé, so long laughed at, but
behold, he lives! Indeed, he is as living as Lycophron;
for so long as human nature is what it is, it will never be
difficult to make a living by not being understood.

The primary interest of M. Bremond is the psychology
of mysticism. If he is a literary critic, it is because poetry
is a manifestation of the mystical spirit. It is not that
there is a poetry which is mystical, and some other poetry
which is not mystical. To M. Bremond *all* poetry is
mystical. Commenting on Pater's dictum that 'all art
constantly aspires to the condition of music': No, he says,
all art constantly aspires to the condition of prayer. So
far as Baudelaire is a poet, he is trying to pray. Nor is
that so absurd as it seems—

> Lovely and loved, by whose light shine
>   Our lights, the spiritual eye,
> To thee, Life's Angel and Divine
>   Idea, be immortality!

Like airs whose salt makes sickness whole,
    Through all my powers thy power spreads,
And on my never-satiate soul
    The zest of life eternal sheds.

O scent of roses, still perfuming
    The lorn hold of thine anchorite,
Forgotten censer, still reluming
    The secret silences of night!

How may my lips, O Love, unblamed
    Thy life express that cannot lie?
Seed shaping hid and half-ashamed
    That all of me not doomed to die!

Lovely and loved, in whose joy mine,
    And in thy health my health, doth lie,
To thee, Life's Angel and Divine
    Idea, be immortality!

Well, that is Baudelaire—so far at least as any character survives in my inadequate Englishing of it.[1] It is not the Baudelaire of whom we commonly think. But if M. Bremond is right, there is no other Baudelaire. If M. Bremond is right, and if I understand him rightly, poems like *La Chevelure* and *La Charogne* are as much prayers as this Hymn. Indeed, if they are as truly poetry, they are more truly prayers. For the Hymn seems so far not pure poetry that it carries the contagion of ethical preoccupations.

Even from so much, you can guess the order of controversy in which M. Bremond's lecture involved him. 'Once again in France', says M. de Souza, 'the theory of poetry has been found to excite an interest which poetry itself cannot claim.' If I were clerically minded, it would be natural in me, I suppose, to be disappointed in a cleric who insisted that poetry had nothing to do with morality. But my chagrin would be nothing to that which I should feel if, having taken the pains to be anti-clerical, and to affect poets like Baudelaire quite as much because they had nothing to do with morality as because they were poets, I

[1] The version is reprinted from my *Poems from the French* in Messrs. Benn's *Augustan Poets* series.

were then to be told that, not only all poetry, but that of
Baudelaire in especial, 'aspired constantly after the condition of prayer'. I understand accordingly the kind of ani-
mosities which M. Bremond's lecture seems to have aroused.

M. Bremond, of course, has not taken Baudelaire from
mere caprice or mere paradox. The modern theory of
'pure poetry' in fact begins, he tells us, or is supposed in
France to begin, with Edgar Allen Poe, Baudelaire, Mallarmé, and M. Paul Valéry. I feel obliged here to say that
I think that French criticism will begin again to be what
it should be when it finds out that in the history of
aesthetic theory Poe has no place. He does not count;
and that is bare truth. That he should have had upon
Baudelaire, a great poet, that influence which he had, will
surprise no one who remembers from what inferior French
poetry some of our Elizabethans took fire. Let me say
further that the line of descent, Baudelaire-Mallarmé-
Valéry, offers perplexities which I am not equipped for
expediting. It takes two swallows to make a summer; but
in France, as you know, it does not always take two poets
to make a school of poetry. If it did, we might have come
to rest in Symbolism, and never know anything of the
naturists, the integralists, the unanimists, the Jammists,
the intimists—schools of poetry which, if they keep
nothing else, keep, I must suppose, first-class dictionaries.
However, the school of pure poetry did, in fact, M. Bremond says, not begin with Baudelaire, Mallarmé, Valéry.
These were merely the continuators of a tradition sufficiently venerable. The father of the tradition in France
was, it pleases M. Bremond to note, a churchman, the
Abbé Dubos, in the early part of the eighteenth century.
Dubos, in his turn, derives from the Italian humanists.

'Let us take the notion (of pure poetry)', says M. Bremond, 'at the moment when it moves, tiptoeing timid
and uncertain, across the Vergilian cell of P. Rapin.[1] That
excellent man of letters has just been enumerating, in

---

[1] René Rapin (Renatus Rapinus), a French Jesuit of the seventeenth
century.

accord with the teaching of Aristotle, the essential characters of poetic beauty. It was his business to stop there.
But he was a poet himself, and he has a dim feeling that
there is a good deal left for him to say. "There are still",
he suggests, in rather sleek fashion—and his "still" is capital
for us—"there are still certain things that are beyond
expression, and which do not admit explanation. They
are a kind of mysteries. There are no rules in accordance
with which you can explain these secret graces, these un-
seizable charms, and all those sweetnesses hiding in poetry
which find way to the heart".'

Rapin, says the Abbé, is at once very far from us, and
very near. 'To-day, we do not say of a poem that it contains lively pictures, sublime thoughts, sublime sentiments, that it has this or that quality, and then, over and
above, something beyond expression. We say that, first
and above all, it contains something beyond expression,
albeit closely bound up with this and that excellence.
Every poem owes its character, its strictly poetical character, to the presence, the radiation, the transforming and
unifying action of a mysterious reality which we call *pure
poetry*.'

So much appears innocent; and this air of innocence
M. Bremond studies to preserve as he goes along. He
proceeds to invite our attention to a 'common experience';
an experience so common that we hardly attend to its
significance. 'In order that the poetic condition should
adumbrate itself in us, it does not need that we should
acquaint ourselves with the whole of a poem. Three or
four verses stumbled on by the accidental opening of a
book, often no more than just fragments of a verse, are
enough. *Primum Graius homo.... Ibant obscuri....* The
phrase is unfinished, we don't know what is to come; but
already the spell is on us. . . . The action which certain
verses produce upon us, thus detached from all context,
is . . . immediate, sudden, sovereign.'

I suspect that I am being taken here further than I am
prepared to go. Mr. Bridges made not long since a trans-

lation of a part of the sixth *Aeneid*; and his book when he published it bore for title just those words which M. Bremond quotes—*Ibant obscuri*. Mr. Bridges knew what he was doing; but he knew for whom he was doing it. He knew that there were persons for whom the sentiment of that 'tag', if I may so call it, would be 'immediate, sudden, sovereign'. Rich with infinite associations, it would come over them like a summer cloud. But did he reckon, does M. Bremond reckon, with the casual hearer of the word, with such a student of poetry as I, in fact, recall, who, taking Mr. Bridges's book in his hand, asked me, in his innocence, 'What's all this Abracadabra, then?' M. Bremond avers—and should know—that a well-bred peasant girl has no difficulty in appreciating the poetry of the Psalms in Latin,[1] even when not sung. I will not question it. But both here, and with M. Bremond's *Ibant obscuri*, surely both the disposition and the capacity to be spellbound is as much as the spell itself. For these spells to be successful you need, not only a poet educated, or inspired, to make them, but a recipient educated to receive them, in the one case a scholar, in the other a 'well-bred peasant-girl'—well bred, that is, in the simplicities of the Catholic faith. The recipient must be well educated for spells; must bring to any spell the associations which makes its operation effective. The spell of *Ibant obscuri* neither begins nor ends in itself. The emotional response is not to those words, and out of a neutral disposition; not to those words, but to all Vergil, or the half of Vergil, to the half of antiquity and the half of other poetry; and out of a disposition in which these have established associations of a character diversely sensitive.

Of all this M. Bremond is too subtle a psychologist not to be aware. But he leaves it aside, and hurries on; content to notice that we must, of course, 'read poetry as it should be read, that is to say, poetically'. To the average undergraduate, he says, when he takes his degree, all that remains of Vergil is some eight or ten misinterpretations—

[1] See the note at the end of this lecture.

the dictum comes in the first instance from M. Jules Lemaître, a priest turned journalist, with whom M. Bremond has accordingly certain affinities. Identifying himself with these 'bachelors' so lightly dipped in Vergil, 'After all', says M. Bremond, 'the exact sense of the fourth eclogue, if it has one, is no great matter. We, more Vergilian than Vergil—but thanks to Vergil—we realize the poetry unexpressed which inspires his obscure lines. . . . There is misinterpretation; but on the other side, there is intuition infallible; victory of the pure over the impure, of poetry over reason.' Is it thus that they read their Vergil in Campion Hall?

As with Vergil, so with Shakespeare. 'A man of taste will not ask the meaning of this or that song of Shakespeare, how exquisite so ever.' Still less of a song of Burns. M. Bremond quotes with approval some remarks of Angellier on certain of Burns's songs. 'There is nothing there at all. The pieces are emptied of any shred of intellectual content. They are void. All trace of content is lost, of image, idea, colour. They quiver with some invisible flame. The effect of them penetrates without being able to be held.' The sonnets of Nerval, again, have no more meaning than Hegel has; and if they had, the charm of them would be gone. And once more: the popular poetry of all countries loves to be a poetry of no-sense. That is why Béranger was, not a poet, but only a very clever man.

Poetry comes to us in poems. The problem is to disengage the poetry of the poem from the impurities, the contagions, that it carries with it. M. Bremond enumerates these. They are all that in the poem which occupies immediately our superficial activities of reason, imagination, sensibility; all that the poet expresses or suggests, or tries to express or suggest; all that the grammarian or the philosopher isolates for consideration; all that survives translation;[1] the sum and subject of the poem; and also the meaning of individual phrases, the logic of ideas, the detail of description; instruction, narra-

[1] See the note at the end of this lecture.

tion, painting; and even all that makes the flesh creep or draws tears. Not these things, not the impression that they make, but the expression given to them, is what matters.

'Yet what are we to say', M. Bremond continues, 'what are we to say of this expression, which is sometimes void of meaning, sometimes carries meaning, but very little, but which, even when rich in noble sense, yet reserves for us pleasures unknown to the reason? These words of every day and every person, by what unheard-of metamorphosis do they find themselves of a sudden vibrate with new light and new power, a light and power divorced from prose, married to poetry?' Shall we say, as M. Valéry would have us say, that poetry is just music?

To say that, M. Bremond thinks, would be, in any case, to define the unknown by the unknown—music seems even more mysterious than poetry. But it cannot be true. If poetry is merely music, then, what a thin and monotone music is it in comparison with real music! If Baudelaire is only music, what a poverty-stricken music he is in comparison with, say, Wagner. All poetry is verbal music; but it is something else. And there is verbal music outside poetry; in prose,[1] often enough. If you compare some poetry either with some other poetry, or with prose, the more musical is not always the more poetic. The truth is that, though there can be no poetry without a certain verbal music, yet it is so special a kind of music that it would probably be better to find some other name for it. That the verbal music that there is and must be in all poetry is the principal element in it seems after all unlikely. So far as it is music, it is of a quality and compass so meagre that it cannot carry the deep experiences that poetry does carry. 'Mere bells of rhyme, the flux and reflux of alliteration, cadences in turn answering expectation and baffling it—all this assemblage of pleasant sounds cannot carry to the deep regions where is the seething of inspiration. . . .'

[1] See the note at the end of this lecture.

The criticism here seems to me both subtle and good; though I do not know that I understand M. Valéry to say what the Abbé Bremond attributes to him. I understand him, in fact, to emphasize, just as M. Bremond does, the musical inadequacy of verbal music. I recollect him as saying plainly that the richest and most resonant harmonies of Hugo fall, as music, far short of Berlioz and Wagner. He does say, however, that the whole direction of 'Symbolism' (a movement of which, in his unregenerate days, *pars magna fuit*) was towards music; and that the first of the French poets to invoke and interrogate music was Baudelaire. Neither of them mentions Verlaine; but with him first, I should suppose, this verbal music becomes the primary article of a reasoned *Art Poétique*:

> Music, music, still and ever;
> And be your verse that thing enskied
> The soul's wings let slip as they quiver
> Heavenwards, lovewards, deified.

For Verlaine, just that mystical music is poetry; 'et tout le reste est littérature'.

I agree with M. Bremond that it is no good calling poetry music when it is quite plainly something else. But if we are not to call it that, we are hard put to it, when M. Bremond has disconnected it completely from so many other things with which we had supposed it intimately associated, meaning and feeling, reason, morality, and the rest of it—we are hard put to it, when all these are taken away, to relate it to anything at all in human experience. How comes it that words in order, rhythm, and rhyme do in fact open out to us an access to the spiritual grandeurs that we know poetry to reveal?

M. Bremond will not say with Baudelaire that the process is one of 'suggestive magic'—for the power to suggest addresses itself to our superficial faculties, and belongs to pure prose. He prefers to call the process one of infection, or radiation. It is a veritable creation, or magic transformation, by which we reproduce, not the ideas or the sentiments of the poet, but that state of soul by which he

is a poet; a state of soul which is a 'confused massive
experience, inaccessible to the logical consciousness'.
Poetry is a 're-collective magic', inviting us to a quietude
where we have nothing to do save to allow ourselves to
be worked upon by a power greater and better than ourselves. M. Bremond takes refuge finally in a phrase of
Keats: 'an awful warmth about my heart, like a load of
immortality'. That is what poetry is. This load of immortality, whither will it precipitate us?—why, 'to those
august retreats, where awaits us, whither calls us, a presence more than human. Walter Pater has said, that all
the arts aspire constantly towards the condition of music.
No, they all aspire, each by the mediation of its proper
magic, words, notes, colours, lines—they all aspire to join
prayer.'

I will not call that a lame and impotent conclusion. It
is not a conclusion at all. The truth is, if I may be allowed
to be sensible upon a subject which is usually better kept
upon another plane, some poetry is very like prayer, and
other poetry as little like it as could be.

> O my love 's like a red, red rose
>   That 's newly sprung in June:
> O my love 's like the melodie
>   That 's sweetly play'd in tune!

Is that like prayer? or is there any sense in saying that it
is? Is it more plausible to call it prayer than to call it
music? To which side run all the analogies? I take those
lines because of the remark of Angellier about Burns which
I have already quoted. But take something else. Take
almost at random this—from a graver poet than Burns:

> Sah ein Knab' ein Röslein stehn,
>   Röslein auf der Heiden,
> War so jung und morgenschön,
> Lief er schnell, es nah zu sehn,
>   Sah 's mit vielen Freuden.

Already, I would say, before Schubert or Reichardt
touched it, that was not far from music. But is it, in any
sort, near to prayer? Does it take us into a world of the

same order as the world of prayer? Some poetry does;
perhaps the highest poetry does; and that poetry should
do so seems to me hardly at all strange. What is strange
is just what M. Bremond refuses to notice; namely, that
so much poetry, equally poetry with that poetry which
seems most like religion, carries us to, or keeps us in,
connexions which it is mere levity to correlate with the
mysticism of prayer. In the introductory pages of his
Prayer and Poetry M. Bremond sighs amiably for the old
days when the poet was recognized as a seer and a prophet,
the repository of an essentially religious knowledge. But
what has brought about the changed point of view? Not,
as M. Bremond thinks, the badness of men's hearts, the
refusal of the modern world to take great poetry seriously;
but the facts of poetry, surely, and a more intelligent
study of them. If Burns were Orpheus or Musaeus, or
even Vergil, or if, save in the single circumstance of being
a poet, he were the least like any of these, the theory of
poetry would be plain sailing. It might anchor then
securely in that haven of prayer where M. Bremond would
have it be.

There are prayers that happen to be poetry. Not from
any affectation, but because I was bred in these studies,
and because classical antiquity seems to me so often to
furnish a standard by which to correct easily the extra-
vagances of our modern aesthetic, I will take the Prayer
to Beauty, which opens the eighth Nemean Ode of Pindar.
And I will take it the more readily in that it cannot be
translated. If M. Bremond is right in saying that a well-
bred peasant girl has no difficulty in appreciating the
Psalms in Latin, I need not hesitate to try even the Greek
upon an audience in which, if there are some persons not
bred in that tongue, there will be none that are not better
bred than to show it:

Ὥρα πότνια, κᾶρυξ ᾿Αφροδίτας
  ἀμβροσιᾶν φιλοτάτων,
ἅτε παρθενηίοις παίδων τ᾿ ἐφίζοισα γλεφάροις
τὸν μὲν ἀμέροις ἀνάγκας χερσὶ βαστάζεις, ἕτερον δ᾿ἑτέραις.

ἀγαπατὰ δὲ καιροῦ μὴ πλανα-
θέντα πρὸς ἔργον ἕκαστον
τῶν ἀρειόνων ἐρώτων ἐπικρατεῖν δύνασθαι.

As I say, that is a prayer. So far at least as it is not poetry but a prayer, I can do what I said could not be done. I can translate it to you—I can paraphrase it, that is; and I will. I will even ask you to remember that, in my third line and my last line, I have preserved the metrical character of the original.

> Sovran Flower of Youth, of Aphrodite
> Forerunner, and those ambrosial felicities,
> Thou that hast thy seat in kindled eyes of boys and maidenly eyes;
> Some, compulsion uncompelling, some, thy mighty
> Hands necessitous bear, the way of love;
> Be it mine to hit (nor let thy saint's eye rove!)
> Thy seasons, and nor heart nor eye lack straightness:
> Mine to know and mine to cherish love that lifts man's life to greatness.

Now of the original, if I were asked what distinguished it as poetry from other poetry, I should say, I think, three things. First, its effects of rhythm are such that I know nothing in any language, ancient or modern, comparable to them. These no version can render. Then secondly, there is what is equally lost in translation, the mere beauty of the words, a beauty (in this example of it) something between sound and colour. The vocabulary of Greek lyric, let me say, has always seemed to me the greatest creation of the Greek genius:

ἅτε παρθενηίοις παίδων τ᾽ ἐφίζοισα γλεφάροις

—significant sound is carried to a point where the fact that it is significant hardly seems to matter. And yet, with this beauty of sound go beautiful meanings. That these meanings are a part of the poetry M. Bremond will not allow. Yet as the third element in the poetry of this poem, which makes it stand out among other poems, I should feel obliged, if I were commenting, and regarded it as the business of a commentary to deal in essential matters—I should be obliged to signalize a certain ethical

quality. And it is no good for you to go with me about
the beauty of the words and the rhythms, and then to jib
at ethical quality; as though I had committed an aesthetic
offence by introducing a moral consideration. For the
truth is that this ethical quality has infected already the
words and the rhythms. I suppose this prayer to have for
its subject (so far as the subject of it is separable from its
form) the typically Greek ideal of temperance, temperance
in respect of all that class of pleasures which are furnished
to eye and heart by what Pindar calls 'Hora', the beauty
and freshness of youth. Let us say simply that a moral
idea is here treated poetically; and for the moment let us
leave it at that. If any one likes to say that we do not
go to poetry for morality, at least I understand what he
means; I understand it, I believe, better than he does.
But to that I will return.

   That we do not go to poetry for morality no one is
more fully persuaded than M. Bremond. He has persuaded himself, indeed, if I understand him rightly, that
we do not go to poetry for anything that we find there.
Poetry, he says, aspires after the condition of prayer. Yet
it is no good to take him to any actual prayer—this of
Pindar that I speak of or any other. For him a prayer, so
far as it means something and says something, is not yet
poetry. It is, in truth, not even a prayer. Pindar's words
and music alike, and the sum of his intellectual and moral
content—all these things, however much they seem to
convey a truth of their own, are simply what M. Bremond
calls 'conductors'. They are the conductors, so far as they
are poetry, not of their own truth, but of a truth which
neither significant sound nor music has power to render.
They are conductors traversed by a current of knowledge
both supersensual and outside intellection. If we are to
take great poetry seriously, says M. Bremond, we must
'make the *salto mortale* of admitting the legitimacy, the
value, of a kind of knowledge which does not and cannot
express itself, which words cannot render. We must believe that such knowledge is not a myth, that of old there

were men who had it at their service, that to-day there are
still such men; and that by the very fact of their having
such knowledge these men are our superiors, are more than
we are'.[1]

With some of that I can sympathize. I should be sorry
to think that we knew only what we understand. I agree
with M. Bremond, again, in accepting frankly the fact of
poetical inspiration. I have said often that we shall only
understand poets by believing what they tell us. And
when they tell us, as they for ever do in one way or
another, that they are inspired, I take it for what it is
worth; and I suppose it to be worth everything. The
value of their testimony is, I think, not at all diminished
by the interpretation put upon it by Plato, who classed
together as 'inspired' poets and politicians—for the reason
that both classes were occupied in talking about what they
did not understand. But some of M. Bremond's paradoxes—the consequential paradoxes of his main position—
are too hard for me. Let me but barely mention two of
the difficulties that I feel.

First, though I believe that poetry and art do in fact
open up to us a world of knowledge not opened up by the
ordinary processes of judgement and inference, yet between the life of that world and the life of our world,
between the awareness, if you like, the mystical awareness
of things which comes by poetry—between that and our
ordinary knowledge M. Bremond seems to me to break
down all the bridges. Secondly, the analogy that he makes
between the poetical condition and the condition of religious mysticism, his identification of the knowledge which
belongs to the one with that which belongs to the other,
ceases to be plausible the moment that we inquire how
the conditions are attained. Is it plausible, or is it in
God's providence, that the ecstasy of the saint should
follow so hard a discipline—fasting and loneliness and
every renunciation—and that the ecstasy of the poet,
the same ecstasy, the same vision and knowledge, should

[1] *Prayer and Poetry*, p. 2, E. T.

demand nothing of this spiritual preparation? Does a
just God, or some ridiculous accident, equate in the long
run Baudelaire and St. Theresa? Is it equally easy to die
into life and to lounge into it?

The two difficulties which I put are interconnected.
The old faith in poetry and poets to which M. Bremond
is so anxious to recall us, the belief in their inspiration,
the will in us to take their greatness in a serious and great
spirit—of old that rested, surely, on two things with which
M. Bremond will have nothing to do. It rested, firstly, on
the belief that what the poet said meant something in *our*
lives. Yet for M. Bremond, what the poet says or means is
no part of his poetry. It rested, again, on the belief that
what the poet said meant something out of *his* life. Out
of some holiness in him he spoke things worth hearkening.

I am back again, you perceive, upon the ethical connexions of poetry; and if you ask me, when am I going to
end, I shall say, At once; if, when I am going to begin,
I shall answer, Very likely never, but perhaps next term.
Let me have here none the less the satisfaction of saying
something which, unless I qualify it at some later date,
will certainly be misunderstood. I have never supposed
that it was the business of poetry to make men better—
as that business is commonly understood. On the other
hand, firstly, I have never supposed that the winds of the
spirit could blow through a poet and take no infection of
character. Secondly, I think we too much neglect, when
we consider what the reading of poetry means, the element of interest. Even if there were such a thing as pure
poetry, we do not come to it pure. We bring to it interest:
the interest of all that we are, all that we aspire to be.
Poetry only lives by answering the demand of that interest.
A paramount interest of the human soul is, I am so old-
fashioned as to believe, its own salvation. All the implications of that phrase, I am not prepared to tabulate. But
if, as Milton thought, a poet's life must be a true poem,
equally, I believe, must a poet's poem be a true life: and
the highest poem will be the highest life.

NOTE

'Une paysanne bien née [writes M. Bremond] s'épanouit sans effort à la poésie des psaumes latins, même non chantés.' I have not ventured to question this statement. It is not altogether clear what the phrasing of it in fact means—the expression 's'épanouit' is accommodatingly vague. But however we take it, what is said creates difficulties. The Latin Psalms are, in the first place a translation, and in the second place a prose translation. I do not know whether M. Bremond anywhere explicitly and finally commits himself to the position that poetry can as well be in prose as in verse. He certainly, however, allows that some prose is indistinguishable from poetry; and the general trend of his criticism is to break down the barriers between metrical and non-metrical composition. But he nowhere explains why poetry tends to occur more often in verse than in prose. On the other hand, among the impurities and contagions of poetry as we know it he reckons 'all that survives in translation'. Of the Psalms, accordingly, and of any successful translation of a poetical original, we must suppose him to believe that the success is due to a new act, or condition, of inspiration on the part of the translator. The Psalms, and others of the sacred writings, are in the happy position, it would seem, that they have never, or almost never, failed, among civilized nations, to find inspired translators. They remain, or become again, inspired, in a Latin which is not the Latin of the greatest Latin poetry (or of any great Latin literature which is not like themselves), and in the English of more than one translator; and again in German, and in other languages—the French I will leave to M. Bremond—where I cannot judge the merit of the versions offered. I should suppose, again, that many parts of the New Testament are poetry. Yet I think that any person who can be regarded as a scholar in, say, both the English and the Greek tongues, will find that these poetical parts of the New Testament are, in fact, more like poetry in English than they are in Greek. Not much of the meaning, I take it, is lost; and the language is, in our version, a truer language of poetry than it is in the original. Does the best Greek scholar, in fact, that ever was, reading the original Greek, derive from it one tithe of the *poetical* emotion which is aroused in him by the English? Yet, to give the full emotion, the *poetry*, of Homer, of Pindar, of Plato, what translation suffices? And if this is not due to the circumstance that, of some poetry, the *expression* counts little, the meaning, the feeling, much—almost everything—to what *is* it due?

I could wish that the Abbé had pursued further this problem of translation. That for a perfect rendering of any inspired writing—I use 'inspired' in the widest sense —there is needed a new act, or condition, of inspiration, is, I am sure, true. But is it not equally true, and perhaps more remarkable, that it needs a considerable degree of non-inspiration, a genuine gift of spiritual fumbling, so to render poetry in some other medium as not to leave *a great deal of it* still poetical? I am tempted to set out here a few sentences of Joseph Warton which, however much they exaggerate the truth that they have, do put squarely facts which M. Bremond blinks:

'Nothing [says Warton] can be more judicious than the method *Horace* prescribes, of trying whether any composition be essentially poetical or not; which is, to drop entirely the measures and num-bers, and transpose and invert the order of the words: and in this unadorned manner to peruse the passage. If there be really in it a true poetical spirit, all your inversions and transpositions will not disguise and extinguish it: but it will retain its lustre, like a dia-mond, unset, and thrown back into the rubbish of the mine. . . . Take ten lines of the Iliad, Paradise Lost, or even of the Georgics of Vergil, and see whether by any process of critical chymistry, you can lower and reduce them to the tameness of prose. You will find that they will appear like Ulysses in his disguise of rags, still a hero, tho' lodged in the cottage of the herdsman Eumaeus.'

As I say, there is a good deal of exaggeration here. Yet it remains true, I think, that of poetry, when translated, even of great poetry (perhaps of great poetry especially), there does struggle through enough to assure us of the greatness of it. And what struggles through so is not the music, the rhythm, the words, the *idiom* of thought, but just the poetry; that subtle something or nothing which Pope, defining what translation must not lose, is content to call 'the fire'. Are there not some things poetically said of which the poetry not merely is not, but cannot be, lost in any language? As when Priam says to Achilles, 'Remember thine own father, an old man even as I am'; or as when Michal was taken from her husband, 'and her husband went with her, weeping as he went, and followed her to Bahurim. Then said Abner unto him, Go, return: and he returned'? [1]

I could wish that upon the subject of yet another kind of translation M. Bremond had said something, when he was speaking of the relation of poetry to music. You may doubt whether it is worth while rendering verse into some other kind of verse, or into prose—though so long as we live under the shadow of Babel poets and scholars will continue to essay both these exercises—but I have never heard anything said about the futility of setting verse to music. Yet the act of doing so implies a philosophy of translation the dark places of which would be well worth exploring. M. Bremond, rightly, as I think, refuses to call poetry music. Yet some of the greatest parts of poetry were born under conditions in which words and song were not two things but one. This is true of some very simple, even primitive, forms of poetry. It is also true, in varying degrees no doubt, of some highly complex forms—of many of the forms of Greek lyric. When the musician to-day 'sets to music' the words of Burns or Goethe, he performs some act of translation. Is 'what survives in translation', there too, everything except the 'pure poetry'?

I will note finally that, breaking down, as he has found himself obliged to do, the barriers between poetry and prose (i.e. metrical and non-metrical composition), M.

[1] 2 Sam. iii. 16.

Bremond involves his theory of 'pure poetry' in a difficulty which comes near to making it absurd. If we can have poetry in prose, we can have it in ordinary speech, in unwritten speech. At any moment any one of us is liable to 'talk poetry without knowing it'—as the Bourgeois Gentilhomme talked prose without knowing it. But, *ex hypothesi*, the poetical character of what we say is divorced wholly and entirely from meaning, morality, sentiment, &c. In any speaking, therefore, we may lapse at any moment, without knowing it, into the highest form of speech, stumbling into the very life of life. But between this high speech, this poetry, into which we lapse, and the context, or environment, of it—which is *what we are trying to say*, an environment of human meanings and feelings—there is, so far as this high speech is poetry, no relation: no relation, at least, which is ascertainable and definable. In the beginning was the word; and we meant it to mean something. But it has fallen upon the divine life, it has become incarnate Logos, by an accident which seems to leave human intercourse a business hardly worth study.

BYRON: 1824–1924

THE magic of round numbers is justly alluring; and among what Dr. Johnson calls the 'anfractuosities of the human mind' there is a proper place for the superstition which greets kindly bakers' dozens and golden weddings and any greatness that can knock up a century. To have lived for a hundred years is a somewhat rare achievement; but the class is very wide indeed among which nature has distributed the distinction of having been dead for a like period. Whether, within this wide class, there are spirits of just, or great, or interesting men departed, whom it pleases, upon the great secular occasions, to catch, from this side the barrier, some murmur of felicitation, some weak note of our human goodwill, it were difficult to say. But I would rather think it, and act upon it, than that their posterity should seem to them churlish; and upon the centenary of Byron's death, I should be sorry to have no gesture of acclaim, and no generous word, with which to hail the ghost of one who died in the creed of liberty, and of whose life, if vanity and egotism and sensuality were the dress, yet the body was genius and courage.

Young men, ever the most magnificent and, it may be, the most discerning patrons of poetry, no longer, it is said, read Byron. Whether this is true I have not the means, that is the youth, to discover; but what is certainly true is that, of the poetry of the last half-century, or more, Byron has not been among the formative influences. We have almost forgotten how great he once seemed, how marvellous he, in fact, was; and we figure to ourselves only with difficulty the emotion of those days when he bore,

> With haughty scorn which mocked the smart,
> From Europe to the Aetolian shore
> The pageant of his bleeding heart,
> And thousands counted every groan,
> And Europe made his woe her own.

H

It is exactly a hundred years ago to-day[1] that the news of Byron's death reached London. Hazlitt was putting the last touches to the very lively portrait of Byron which he has included in *The Spirit of the Age*. 'We had written thus far', he says, 'when the news came of the death of Lord Byron, and put an end at once to a strain of somewhat peevish invective. . . . We think it better, and more like himself, to let what we have written stand. . . . Death cancels everything but truth; and strips a man of everything except genius and virtue.' Those are lofty words, snatched from platitude by the impressiveness of their occasion; and among the temptations to which centenary commemorations expose judgement, they are perhaps worth recalling now. It is the peril of such commemorations that they enlarge charity beyond the point of literary health; and it is salutary at such times that we should be reminded that the business of criticism is truth, and that a man can leave to live after him only his genius and virtue.

I emphasize these elementary pieties because, though I do not think that the time has come when we can relegate Byron to the limbo of obsolete fashions, I have no wish to be accomplice with any class in a Byron 'boom'; and, what between journalists seeking wisdom and Greeks desiring a loan, I am not sure that we are not threatened with one. Perhaps the republication, three years ago, of *Astarte* began it to us. Let me add at once that the book was, in my opinion, a book proper to be published, and that the persons responsible for it would have acted wrongly if they had suppressed the material which it contains. About the same time we were given two new volumes of Byron's letters; and a renewed interest in the man was natural and legitimate. It was in some degree reinforced by the general conditions of artistic criticism; by the disposition, I mean, of a good deal of modern criticism to estrange art and morality. Something was added, perhaps, by the War, and that minor calamity, the

[1] May 14, 1924.

Peace. Both quickened an internationalization of taste to which other causes had been already conducting us; and the Europe of 1918–1923 offered in politics specious analogies to the conditions of what may be called, not inappropriately, 'Byronic' Europe.

> Yet, Freedom, yet, thy banner, torn but flying,
> Streams like the thunderstorm, *against* the wind.

Our new continental ties disposed us to a more sympathetic consideration of what we had long used ourselves to regard as a superstition of foreigners; and this spirit of complaisance was even enlarged by a calculation of interest. While we were all endeavouring to screw our Puritanical courage to the sticking-point of April 19, were we not admonished by one of our leading journals that, whatever might be the truth about the genius or the virtue of Byron, his repute was one of our international assets?

God forbid that in these evil days we should gamble with our few remaining assets; and yet among them I should wish to reckon our dignity and good sense. I am not sure that all that has been written about Byron in the last few weeks consults either; and I should not be greatly surprised if presently a reaction from it swung us all back to Swinburne, in whose extravagantly perverse dicta upon Byron there is a good deal of rough British sense. Swinburne, indeed, has staked to us his word as a poet that Byron is read upon the Continent because he is readable only in translation; that the best of him is his prose; that in verse his highest praise is, in the Bernesque genre, to have been better than Berni; that it was by his politics, and not his poetry, that he captured the fine soul of Mazzini; and that the elaborate encomium of Goethe meant no more than that Germany's greatest poet was the world's worst critic. All of this is, no doubt, plumply insular. Yet if I am to speak my mind, I am not sure that it should not be. I am sure at least that there is more truth in two pages of Swinburne than in twenty of Taine;

and I would hazard a guess that something of insularity is a proper qualification for speaking about Byron at all. When all is said and done, there was never any man of us more insular than Byron himself, insular in his very continentalism. If the Elysian fields have an English quarter, his ghost, it is true, haunts by preference all other solitudes, nursing apart his immortality of wounded pride —and thereby confessed a most English ghost.

At the least, Byron is much more English than foreign criticism can believe; and indeed, I sometimes think that if Nature had designed him expressly for a typical Englishman of his time and place—the time Georgian, and the place the House of Lords—she would have hit her mark, save for one particular wherein she was culpably careless; one of the ingredients she omitted—she forgot the phlegm; and her creation strayed from a talented Whig into an ineffectual Titan. Of this new Prometheus, all the world was the Caucasus, and all the men and women in it vultures; and the part of first vulture was taken by a preposterous mother.

Like every other Englishman, Byron was descended from ancestors who drank and fought, and made, or forgot to make, imprudent marriages, and in general lived faster than is proper to men who can do it only once. He was born on January 22, 1788—the day of the month was marked to him in our almanacs until an age of milder virtues appropriated it to the passing of Queen Victoria. At twelve he insisted on being allowed to be educated; not, as most of us, from love of learning, or because he was a prig, but 'else', he writes, 'I shall be called, or rather branded with, the name of dunce; which you know I could never bear'. At thirteen, he threw a missile at the head of Lord Portsmouth, but had the misfortune to break the window instead. Attempts were made to give to the incident a better colour than it wore. But Byron was, more often than not, truthful. 'I did mean it,' he screamed; 'I will teach a fool of an earl to pinch another noble's ear.' The same consideration for truth, an equal

want of consideration for other people's heads, and the
same sense of what was due to a noble, pursued him to
Harrow. For a public school, as schools then were, he was
made. He liked fighting and rebellions and 'rowing'; not
ro-ing, he says, but rowing, making a row. He played
cricket against Eton; a circumstance which would be be-
neath the dignity of history save that, firstly, by a pretty
accident, the names of Byron and Shakespeare jostle one
another in the team; and secondly, though Byron was
often truthful about other things, he lied about his
score. To physical pain he was insensible; but it was
a title to his love that a boy was, like himself, lame. He
used to thrash big boys for thrashing little ones; and
thrash little ones who failed to thrash those as little as
themselves; but it was distasteful to him, he protested, to
see a 'brother peer' put down on the punishment list to be
thrashed by a commoner. At seventeen he weighed close
upon fourteen stone. His head master, Dr. Drury, he has
made immortal, in one of the notes to his poems, as 'the
only man who was ever kind to me as a boy'. 'Strict too',
he adds grimly, in one of his letters. But he never forgot
this, or any, kindness. If he could have had no mother,
and Dr. Drury for a father, he would have been as happy
as is, perhaps, necessary. The sting of Harrow was the
holidays. These had to be passed mostly at Southwell;
and at Southwell sat 'Allecto'; for it was by the name of
the least amiable of the Furies that Mrs. Byron was known
to her son and step-daughter. In Southwell, Byron used
to pray that a volcano would swallow him up—but he was
never quite easy that he would not find Mrs. Byron in
the heart of it. Many men have been ruined by women;
few by their mothers; but for this bizarre experience fate
destined Byron. Perhaps there is something to be said
for Mrs. Byron; but I cannot read Byron's early letters,
and then wish to say it—I find myself always siding passionately with the boy against his mother, an unlovely
partisanship, God knows. Her sudden death filled Byron
with remorse; while she was being buried, he boxed.

At Cambridge, he made the mistake of not having been at Oxford. 'I must own, I prefer Oxford', he writes. However, 'College improves', says a later letter; . . . 'nobody here seems to look into an author, ancient or modern, if they can avoid it.' 'College', he says elsewhere, 'is not the place to improve either morals or income.' He was still a freshman when the full truth about colleges flashed upon him. 'Improvement', he writes to his mother— 'Improvement at an English university to a man of rank is, you know, impossible, and the very idea of it ridiculous.' Having paid his debts at Cambridge by the simple, if rather antiquated, expedient of contracting new ones elsewhere; and after partially redeeming a bad start in sentimental poetry by what, silly as are the individual judgements which it expresses, must yet be called a good start in satire, he discovered that a pilgrimage to Greece and the Aegean would enable him not only to live more cheaply than his vanity allowed him to do in England, but also, under the guise of avoiding the world, to escape, in fact, from his mother. That he was endeavouring at the same time to flee from a deep dissatisfaction with himself, he both knew well and advertised well. If he liked the advertisement better than the knowledge, he probably divined what, from Horace onwards, is a commonplace of the moralists, that when we ship overseas our characters book passage with us. For two years, up and down those regions where he was one day to bring his wandering spirit to its only possible rest, Byron carried the burden of his unnatural self; and if he looks now like a man hunting his own grave, perhaps the figure is not much short of the fact. For two years he hobnobbed with brigands and Pachas, and in one and the same spirit, from danger, women, and antiquity, plucked material for *Childe Harold*. That he formed any just estimate of the value of the material or of the use to which he had put it is not likely from his character; and he was, indeed, more interested, when he got home, in his second-rate *Hints from Horace*. This latter work was not destined to see the light until after its author's death; but in March 1812, the discernment of Murray, a discernment neatly compounded of poetical and commercial, gave to the world the first two cantos of *Childe Harold*, after they had been refused by two publishers. When Byron says that he 'awoke and found himself famous', it is the first part of the phrase which is chiefly noteworthy. The great soul, of course, never sleeps; but its tossing may be out of all relation to the environing realities. That he stood in some relation to the world, to society, other than that constituted by the impact, upon an unyielding material, of thoughts flung or slung outwards with no better intention than the wrath of their recoil upon self—this it had not occurred to him to conceive; and that, of a world of which he had figured himself as sometimes the Timon, sometimes the Tamerlane, he should suddenly discover himself the *pet*, this, truly, was to 'wake', either from a dream or into one. Painfully from childhood, he had built himself into a melodrama which had no action save the spectacle of the world's malice aimed unrelentingly at the exposed front of a shadowy ironic Titan. And lo! all London was taking the Titan to its breast; petting and fondling what a true instinct perceived to be, not an alien creation, but the very epitome of its own tastes in romantic fiction: the Tale of Terror made flesh and dwelling in the Albany.

Of Byron's 'reign', as Scott calls it, as he himself called it, I have no intention to rehearse the brief and monstrous annals; nor to stage again the drab peripety of that wilful abuse of power. Still less do I mean to ply a critical muck-rake among the confused elements which make the tragi-comedy of Byron's Italian exile. Over that 'expense of spirit in a waste of shame' which genius in action so often is, it is base to cry our cheap pieties; and silly, when fate or character overset in the dust this precious wine of human greatness, to indulge the peevish hysteria proper to spilt milk and small accidents. Let me add that, from the cant which so easily besets us, we only escape, I suspect, into a different kind of cant, when, against the rest of Byron, we plead the redeeming months at Missolonghi.

While it is true of all men, that they are not like ordinary people, it is especially true of poets; and perhaps only in their case has the circumstance any particular importance. Yet precisely here, it may be, we are apt to forget it. Particularly do we forget how early in some natures the process of not being ordinary begins. I could wish that Byron, who was interested ultimately only in himself, had followed the example of a greater poet, who had some touch of the same ailment, and had left us a *Prelude.* He was capable of being quite as truthful as Wordsworth, though he brought to the business an inferior industry; and it is never easy, it requires application, to be wholly truthful. Most of what in Byron, as man and artist, is justly charged with falsity, is to be imputed, I fancy, to laziness. Scraps of a *Prelude* lie embedded in such poems as *The Dream*; and a great deal of reject material is strewn across his journals. What might a less lazy talent not have made of those memories of Mary Duff which the journals have not wholly succeeded in lifting out of vulgarity? To what effects would not the author of *Wilhelm Meister* have employed this scrapped material! At eight years old, at a time when, he says, he 'could neither feel passion nor know the meaning of the word', Byron conceived for Mary Duff, a child of his own age, a love that, throughout his life, remained an ineffaceable memory. When he was sixteen, the news of her marriage, though he had not seen or spoken to her since they were children, threw him into one of those convulsive fits to which violent emotions subjected him. At twenty-five, when the world at least detected in him not much softness of sentiment, he still recollected vividly 'every word, every caress' which had passed between them; and 'my misery,' he writes, 'my love for that girl, were so violent that I sometimes doubt whether I have ever been attached since'. She 'still lives in my imagination at the distance of more than sixteen years'. He was still the merest boy

BYRON: 1824-1924 · 57

when he fell in love with Mary Chaworth; and to the end he always persuaded himself—and I see no good reason for questioning his sincerity—that the circumstances of that attachment had made impossible for him any subsequent happiness. We all know how, at his marriage, as he stood beside his wife at the altar, there intervened between him and her the vision of the 'one beloved face on earth', the embodied ghost of this dead passion. One of his school-friends was Lord Clare; in later life they were separated; but nothing ever, he says, came between them save distance. They never communicated; but he records that at no season could he ever so much as hear the name Clare 'without a beating of the heart'. In 1821 he met Clare by accident wandering among the Italian hills; they met for just five minutes; but 'the meeting', says Byron, 'seemed to annihilate all the years'. 'I hardly recollect an hour of my existence which could be weighed against' those five minutes. Remember that in all this a man speaks who knew the world, who at least had had those contacts with it which brush off school-boyish sentimentalities. There is a good deal else in Byron, in all his periods, which matches this unpredictable tenderness; and I could sometimes think that there were patches in his heart as pure as Shelley.

This is no more than to think with Shelley. How many persons have quoted Shelley's famous *dictum* about the poets—

> Most wretched men
> Are cradled into poetry by wrong;
> They learn in suffering what they teach in song,

and forgotten that, in the poem in which it occurs, the speaker is Byron? It is a queer grandiloquence, no doubt, when Shelley salutes Byron as 'the Pilgrim of Eternity'; and it is characteristic of Byron that what he chiefly liked about Shelley was that he was so completely a 'gentleman'. Yet perhaps these seeming misfires of judgement hit real effects. There was something Byronic in Shelley;

and perhaps what makes Byron so little like Shelley is a
point of difference quite as much intellectual as moral.

When we have tired ourselves of finding in Shelley
qualities which either were wanting to him or are not in
themselves admirable, we shall have leisure to recognize
that characteristic of his spirit which marks him off from
spirits most his kin: I mean his fearless logicality. It is in
the terrifying innocence of his logic that he is greatest and
most himself. All other men stop somewhere short of the
just inferences of their own individuality. Shelley alone
is never afraid of himself, alone of men he is in all his
actions unremittingly reasonable. He starts back from
none of the conclusions of nature. An ingenious French
writer has recently observed, I think with perfect truth,
that to Shelley, when he and Byron were in daily intercourse at Geneva, it neither occurred, nor could occur,
to think it blameable in Byron or out of nature that he
should have lived in an incestuous relation with his half-
sister. The innocence of a perfect logic knows no taboos.
This is why both Shelley and Shelley's poetry are to
those who understand either utterly simple. It is only
our superstitions that make us difficult.

Shelley had no superstitions. What is the matter with
Byron is that superstition shadows all his thinking. Bold
to translate into action the gospel of revolt common to
himself and Shelley, acquiescing cynically in that disease
of action which habit is, adroit to assume the air of a
perfect intellectual conviction—yet he starts at his own
shadow. The fear of himself is audible in his poetry: be
his Pegasus never so gaudy in its trappings, behind perches
Superstition. There is, indeed, no end to the medievalism
of this most modern of men. If he did not believe in God,
he believed in ghosts. Of those conventions by which
society endeavours to regulate the relation of the sexes, he
exhibited always a disregard brutally gay; yet perpetually
the phantoms of wronged women kept watch over his
terrified sleep. For doctors he had a supreme contempt,
but for quacks, like Spurzheim, a solid respect: when that

eminent phrenologist divined from the bumps on his head
that he had a spirituality 'antithetically mixed', he was
profoundly impressed; that everything about him, from
his behaviour at a dinner-table to his worst poetry, cried
the precious secret everywhere, it never occurred to him
to reflect. Nature had deformed his foot; and (just as
when she made Richard III crooked) she had aimed at the
mind. The moral corollaries of it haunted him; and with
the obsession of them you may see him playing fearfully
in the *Deformed Transformed*. His conviction of the
efficacy of curses, which he laid freely and formally upon
his mother-in-law and Sir Samuel Romilly, is the sublime
of servant-maidishness. The suicide of Romilly was an
intellectual satisfaction—the curse had worked. 'It was
not in vain', he says solemnly, 'that I invoked Nemesis in
the midnight of Rome from the awfullest of her ruins.' [1]
He threatened to haunt any one who, when he was dead,
should uncover his deformed foot. When he lay dying, he
was heard muttering the consolations of the Christian
religion. So at least his half-sister persuaded herself; and
whether it be true or not hardly matters. She knew him
better than any one else; and it did not seem to her an
impossible inconsistency. Indeed, she hoped that it had
been so: woman-like she believed that men are saved by
their weakness.

Of the motive of his own poetry he has given us an
account which I take to be entirely truthful; and it lies,
put plainly, in a superstitious terror of himself. 'To with-
draw from myself', he writes, 'has ever been my sole, my
entire, my sincere motive in scribbling at all.' [2] Poetry
affords escape in action from 'a mind which else recoils
on itself'.[3] 'In rhyme', he writes in another place, 'I can
keep away more from facts; but the thought always runs
through, through . . . yes, yes, through.' [4] In the agitation
of the last words it is difficult to miss the accent of naked
fear. They should be read in conjunction with the well-

[1] *Letters*, iv. 269.   [2] Ibid. ii. 351.
[3] Ibid.   [4] Ibid. 323.

known sentences about the genesis of the third part of
Childe Harold. 'I was half mad during the time of its
composition, between metaphysics, mountains, lakes, love
unextinguishable, thoughts unutterable, and the night-
mare of my own delinquencies.' [1] In a superstitious flight
from the consequences of his own mind nearly all Byron's
poetry begins. He is seeking always to get free of himself; and his poetry is a kind of frightened magic. Like
some *magus* wreaking his will upon waxen effigies of the
powers whom he would control or destroy, he sets up
in rapid succession one image after another of his self-
dreading mind; all of them like, but the truth of all of
them waxen and without health. He sets them at distance,
and standing at vantage leers fearfully upon a material
over which he exercises only precarious domination.

The creative impulse is, as I say, a kind of superstitious
terror: to confuse this with the nobler sentiment of
remorse is to credit Byron with an emotion of which no
part of his writings exhibits so much as the shadow. There
is a *pleasure* in fear, moreover; Byron plays with his fears,
and the play of fear is cruel and lascivious. To project
the image of himself was a recurrent necessity to him;
I would even say that it was a disease: of which the revela-
tions of *Astarte* have done much to assist the diagnosis.
Of the *Bride of Abydos* Byron writes that it 'wrung his
thoughts from reality to imagination'. The theme, as he
first essayed the story, is plucked from his own experience;
and when I say that, you will divine that I find the
evidence of *Astarte* compelling. What is notable is that,
in this poem, where he handles the theme for the first
time, he shrinks back; fear, not of the world, but of the
implications of his own nature, makes him turn aside in
the very act of embodying his creation; and he wrests the
narrative to a kind of maladroit innocence. Yet at once,
in *Parisina*, he is driven back to the same *motif*, though
here the guilt is that of wife and step-son. In the very
next year, in *Manfred*, for those who had either knowledge

[1] *Letters*, iv. 49.

or that crueller instrument, suspicion,—and they were half London—he does everything save name the act and the actors. In 1821 he wrote *Cain*; and in that drama you may see him make straight course for the old tyrannizing theme, and then swerve. And all the while Augusta Leigh sat in London and shook. Certainly Byron had, in respect of her, no wish to add torture to torture. But there she sat, never knowing what he would not say next. She had refused to allow Murray to publish the lines which Byron had addressed to her when he left England. When *Don Juan* began to appear, she dared not open it—though, in this respect, it was in fact harmless. But fear consumed her. In truth it consumed her and him; but he could live only by giving body and shape to the ghosts of his diseased imagination. *He must tell.* Superstition has its heights and depths; but it is one creature, whether it dresses itself in Byronic terrors—real terrors of poetry, remember—or merely scrawls obscenity on the street-doors.

That a Byron hunted into poetry, and pursued through it, by superstitious terror is necessarily therefore a truthful poet, I am not deluded into affirming. In poetry, as in other things, it is easy to be genuine without touching truth. That the images of himself which Byron projects in each of his more considerable poems have a correspondence with real, and not feigned, conditions of mind and circumstance; that correspondence, namely, which constitutes truth to fact—I do not doubt. But that they are real in the only sense that matters, that they possess truthfulness for, and from, the imagination, this does not, I think, follow. I am not sure, indeed, that Byron ever gives us better than mixed truth; and it is just this jostle of true and false that has so much injured the repute of his poetry, and has caused it, in recent years, to be so diversely judged.

Like Wordsworth, Byron believed himself to write most truly when he wrote at a distance of time from his object; there must intervene some period of 'emotion recollected in tranquillity'. 'My first impressions', he writes, 'are strong and confused, memory selects and reduces them to order.'[1] 'As for Poesy', he says elsewhere, 'mine is the dream of my sleeping passions. When they awake I cannot speak their language.'[2] The concurrence here with Wordsworth is interesting, and unexpected. But, unlike Wordsworth, Byron could never wait. Hunted into poetry by the disquiet of his own mind, more often than not he 'cannot speak the language of his own passions', he fumbles his own realities; and the deeper he feels, the more falsely he writes. Nearly all of his best in lyric looks *back*.

> Time tempers love, but not removes,
> More hallowed when its hope is fled.
> O what are thousand living loves
> To that which cannot quit the dead?

In verse of that kind lie Byron's truest effects; and too often they are miserably shortlived.

> The love where Death hath set his seal
> Nor age can chill nor rival steal
> Nor falsehood disavow.

How well it rings! But almost at once he wakes out of the dream of his sleeping passions'; and the rest is verbiage. A perfect lyrical whole—such a piece as (in the same mood) the lines beginning 'O snatched away in beauty's bloom'—he almost never accomplishes. His most characteristic successes in lyric owe their strength, in fact, to the same quality as that which constitutes their weakness— the restless energy of a temperament devoid of artistic conscience. That this conscienceless temperament should retain the superstition of Augustan forms is not out of character.

Matthew Arnold supposed it possible to stop the holes in Byron's decaying repute by anthologizing him. But the remedy, as the event showed, is worse than the disease. The trouble of Byron is that the best of him is

---

[1] *Letters*, iv. 119.   [2] Ibid. iv. 43.

the whole of him, true and false together. That posterity
will willingly let live so much that commingles so
wantonly good and bad, true and false, is perhaps doubtful. Under the unloved compulsion of the man, of his
personality, she may be brought to keep more than some
of us expect; for be he never so much a pseudo-Titan, she
will hardly get away from the shadow of his stature. For
myself, I think his best poetry to be all of it. But posterity
has ever had a passion for scraps, and she is mostly too
busy for exact justice. I should not be surprised, therefore, if she held to *Don Juan*, and let the rest go.

In *Don Juan* Byron first finds himself—or loses himself.
I will not call *Don Juan* 'after *Paradise Lost*, the greatest
long poem in our language', however intriguing it may
be so to juxtapose two distinguished compositions; for
myself, I would rather have the *Prelude* or the *Faerie
Queene*. Be it remembered that, when he began *Don Juan*,
Byron had barely turned thirty. He had just finished the
last canto of *Childe Harold*—where you will find more of
true poetry, and less of false, than in anything that he had
till then composed. Already there, from whatever cause,
the poison, I think, was beginning to work itself off and
out—perhaps the cause was not more subtle than that
Byron was growing up—I had almost said 'growing *down*'.
At twenty-five he had felt himself, as he says, fifty. Now
suddenly the half of his gloomy abnormality falls from
him; and he begins to evince for the first time some promise of a settled strength. He had written already poetry
sufficient, as his age believed, for an immortality of fame.
But, except for the fourth canto of *Childe Harold*, he
despised the whole of it; and was very honestly convinced
that none of it would live. He was now to write a poem
in which his contemporaries were to detect the decline of
his powers—and we their maturity. The other great poets
of the age—if we except Keats and Shelley—lived to write
themselves out; Byron died just as he was writing himself
in. What might have come to Keats and Shelley, had
they lived longer, it is always entertaining to speculate.

There are critics who can detect in Shelley the promise of a staid mid-Victorian old age, and can conceive him delivering to Swinburne just such priggish lectures as he himself had listened to from Southey. There are critics who can divine in Keats that most tiresome product of poetical sensuosity, an elderly voluptuary. For myself, I have not this debauched acumen; yet I can catch in *Don Juan* what I sometimes fancy that I miss in, say, *The Triumph of Life*, or even in *Hyperion*, the hint of a procession from strength to strength. The real tragedy of Byron lies, not in his early period, but in the period from 1818 to 1824;[1] for there is no such tragedy as virtues brief and unfortunate.

In *Don Juan* Byron's deeper passions were not engaged; and the motive of the poem is his perfectly genuine persuasion that the moral beliefs of the great mass of mankind are cant. That persuasion is not inconsistent with the superstitious terror in which, as I have suggested, his more serious poetry takes its origin. Perhaps indeed some fundamental genuineness presented to him the disquiet of his own superstition, the intellectual faltering of his libertinism, as itself a kind of cant. Out of some such paradox, sufficiently felt as such to be enjoyed, springs the masculine gaiety of *Don Juan*. The rest of Byron is spoilt, I feel inclined to say, by its bad moral logic; it carries the burden of a responsibility to which Byron was intellectually not equal. But *Don Juan* from first page to last is the most irresponsible poem in our language. The

[1] The period contains, I know, *Cain* and *Heaven and Earth*, that is to say (though great men have praised these pieces), some of Byron's worst rubbish. But even here he is moving, I fancy, towards self-recovery—the vehement theological prepossession is a part of the effort to get free of superstition. The argumentation is not good—the best of it is not better than Hyde Park; and the verse is as bad as it could be. Of *Sardanapalus* and the *Deformed Transformed*, which belong to the same period, the versification is almost equally bad; but both have other merits, and are interesting in so far as they foreshadow something of the internal struggle in which Byron engaged himself before he took the final resolution to go to Greece.

luxury of Italian skies has got into it; and perhaps also, if I may hazard a guess, something of the redeeming influence of the Guiccioli. When I call it a redeeming influence, I am, once again, only echoing Shelley. It was an influence of which Byron finally grew tired, as he did of all others. Yet it was the only influence of which chivalry forbade him to break the ties. *Don Juan*, let me plead, has its own chivalry, its quite genuine Quixotisms. What is the matter, at least, with most other Quixotisms is that they shy at anti-climax, and have no stomach for a bad rhyme. All beauty is, we know, irresponsible; and perhaps there are parts of our morality of which the appeal would be wider if they were a degree gayer. Whether in an age which prefers to the golden silences of Victorianism the cheap metal of a perfectly frank speech, *Don Juan* may be regarded as apt for youths and maidens, I am neither old enough nor young enough to say. Contemporary judgements upon it varied a good deal. 'The only sincere thing you have ever written', said an anonymous critic; 'it will live many years after your humbug Harolds have ceased to be.' Other persons thought it 'execrable', 'even as a composition'. It was hard to persuade Murray that there was either morals or money in it; and Byron, when he had finished five cantos, sat and sulked. 'The highest of all poetry', he had said (and believed), 'is the ethical, as the highest of all earthly objects must be moral truth'; [1] and it was in the faith of this paradox that he resumed his interrupted task. Let people say of *Don Juan* what they would; Byron had found that ease which comes from moral conviction. The rest might go; but in *Don Juan* he really believed. He believed that it would make men better—and that that was why it bored them.

[1] *Letters*, v. 554.

COLERIDGE

THE publication of the *Lyrical Ballads* furnishes one of those dates in literature by which it is convenient to mark epochs. The 'ignoramuses and Pope-admirers'[1] were until 1798. Thereafter poetry is recalled to those elements of speech and feeling which are primary and underivative, and relies for its power upon its truthfulness. To the volume of 1798 Coleridge contributed, not only that poem which is commonly accounted his master-work, the *Ancient Mariner*, but three poems in blank verse which are greater than anything else which he achieved in the same kind. But the book was 'not liked at all by any'.[2] It fell flat—it is possible, indeed, that any curiosity which it excited was due to the suspicion that Coleridge was its author. It was, in fact, Coleridge's first failure in poetry. Two and a half years earlier he had achieved a notable repute by his *Poems on Various Subjects*.[3] Upon this work the reviews had 'cataracted and cascaded panegyric'; a new edition had been called for within a year; and a third was already in preparation before the *Lyrical Ballads* went to press.[4] Moreover, in the spring of 1798 Coleridge had written, and in the autumn, before the publication of the *Lyrical Ballads*, had published, *Fears in Solitude*, *France: an Ode*, *Frost at Midnight*—a quarto volume, brief but golden. In the joint-venture, therefore, of the *Lyrical Ballads*, he staked a good deal more than Wordsworth—for he staked a reputation already achieved. Wordsworth was unknown, or known unfavourably: it needed Coleridge himself to discover in the *Evening Walk* and *Descriptive Sketches* what no obtusity of criticism could miss in *Poems on Various Subjects*, 'the emergence of an original poetical genius'.[5] The bargain of the *Lyrical Ballads* was,

[1] Coleridge, *Letters*, p. 313.
[2] Letter of Mrs. Coleridge, Dykes Campbell, *Life*, p. 93.
[3] Published in April 1796.   [4] Dykes Campbell, *Life*, p. 89.
[5] *Biographia Literaria*, i, p. 56 (ed. Shawcross).

in fact, inequitable, save that either poet had that easy
confidence in himself and in the other, and in the greatness of their common enterprise, which made the calculation of interest impossible. We can see now that this
confidence was not merely noble but reasonable. Yet a
contemporary observer, it is likely, would have judged
differently, and would have credited to Coleridge some
degree of quixotism.

Before he formed that friendship with Wordsworth
which, if friendship may be known by its fruits, is probably
the most notable in literature, Coleridge had in fact accomplished in poetry work of which the sum and quality
are alike remarkable. A good deal of this work carries a
diction plainly derivative; in particular, the earlier pieces
show traces of the influence of Gray and Collins—the *Song
of the Pixies* is only one example among many. In 1794[1]
begins a period of conscious 'Miltonizing':

> Fair the vernal mead,
> Fair the high grove, the sea, the sun, the stars;
> True impress each of their creating Sire!
> Yet nor high grove, nor many-colour'd mead,
> Nor the green ocean with his thousand isles,
> Nor the starred azure, nor the sovran sun,
> E'er with such majesty of portraiture
> Imaged the supreme beauty uncreate,
> As thou, meek Saviour! at the fearful hour
> When thy insulted anguish winged the prayer
> Harped by Archangels, when they sing of mercy!
> Which when the Almighty heard, from forth his throne
> Diviner light filled Heaven with ecstasy,
> Heaven's hymnings paused; and Hell her yawning mouth
> Closed a brief moment.

Religious Musings, of which those lines form part of the
exordium, was called by Lamb 'the noblest poem in the
language next after *Paradise Lost*'. The praise was exaggerated; Mr. Swinburne, indeed, in his plain fashion, has
called the poem 'damnable'; and certainly not all of it

---

[1] *Religious Musings* was begun on Dec. 24, 1794.

sustains the high Miltonic note of the exordium. Yet if a good deal of the matter and manner of the poem is weak, or offensive, it remains a composition in which the discerning reader will scarcely miss the presage of a talent capacious of sublime effects. In the fragmentary *Destiny of Nations*, again, an unbribed judgement will certainly find those merits and defects of which mediocre talent is commonly sterile. This is, after *Religious Musings*, the most considerable of Coleridge's 'pre-Wordsworthian' pieces; and the casual student will note with surprise the degree to which portions of it, perhaps the best portions,[1] anticipate that manner which we recognize as distinctively Wordsworthian.

Yet, when this has been said, it remains true that nearly all of what is supreme in Coleridge's poetry was written when he was with, or near, Wordsworth. Far the greater portion of it dates from the years at Nether Stowey (1797–8); when Coleridge and Wordsworth (and Dorothy Wordsworth) met daily; when, in Coleridge's phrase, they were 'three persons and one soul'. The next most considerable portion belongs to the years 1802–3—the period of the Keswick-Grasmere intercourse. But the west country was Coleridge's own country; and in Cumberland the slate-grey of sky and lake and hills—and the slate-grey houses—bore heavily, it may be suspected, upon his health of mind and body; it was not for nothing that Jeffrey called the Lakists a 'school of hypochondriacs'—this slate-grey ate into their souls. During the three years that followed Coleridge was abroad—whether seeking or shunning health, it would be difficult to say. The influence of Wordsworth was withdrawn; and these were years of waste, and, to speak plainly, of ruin. Not until the beginning of 1807 do we get again from Coleridge any note of the old greatness; and then it is evoked by Wordsworth—by Wordsworth's recitation of the *Prelude*. To the year 1809 belongs the poem entitled *A Tombless Epitaph*: here Coleridge recaptures for a moment his height of power, in

[1] See especially lines 202–71.

writing about a great subject which he alone understood,
himself. Even so, when he wrote this piece, he had just
resumed at Keswick the frayed threads of intimate com-
munion with Wordsworth. From a later date I can think
of but seven pieces of Coleridge which deserve to stand
with his best work. Of these seven, three—'A sunny
shaft . . .', *The Knight's Tomb*, and the sonnet *To Nature*—
belong to the period when he was at work upon the *Biographia Literaria*, when the greatness of Wordsworth
recreated itself to his mind. The other four pieces are the
flotsam and jetsam of the once exuberant tides of his
imagination—of three of them the titles are sufficiently
significant: *Youth and Age*, *Work without Hope*, *An Epitaph*; and of the fourth, oddly compounded of dreamy
youth and listless age, he tells us that it was written

> in one of those most weary hours,
> When life seems emptied of all genial powers.[1]

Character, rather than talent, determined this depen-
dence upon Wordsworth. Both men bore souls consciously
dedicated to poetry, hearts weaned from worldly interest.
But it was as hard for Wordsworth, one might fancy, to
be ever false, as for Coleridge to be consistently true, to
his dedication. It was as natural for Wordsworth, in his
life and in his poetry, to pursue a single plan, as it was for
Coleridge to conceive each day a new enterprise, and, of
things grandiosely conceived, to carry none to its fulfil-
ment. Circumstance, upon the whole, was not unkind to
him; indeed, in more than one crisis of his affairs, that
hard step-mother of genius showed to him a melting
countenance. If it were proper from the fate of genius to
draw any moral applicable to common life, we might suppose ourselves to learn from Coleridge that Circumstance
is mostly placable, Character invariably merciless. To
opinion, and to disappointment, Wordsworth opposed a
panoply of inalienable self-righteousness; but through the
garment of self-pity in which Coleridge involved himself

[1] *Garden of Boccaccio*, ll. 1–2.

the winds of the world pierced with cruel penetrancy.
Yet of humour, in which Wordsworth was deficient,
Coleridge was finely redundant: sometimes, indeed, inap-
positely redundant—in the dark period of his opium-
slavery he laughed over Cottle's letters of religious advice,
when something of Wordsworth's covenanting humour-
lessness would have served him better. If Wordsworth
was humourless—or because he was—he was truthful; it
was impossible for him to describe anything otherwise
than as he actually saw it. But 'All poets go to hell',
Coleridge had been told by the ghost of Gray, 'we are so
intolerably addicted to lying'; [1] and he had a fancy to
prove the thesis.

Perhaps indeed the grand failure of Coleridge was the
failure to be completely honest. He was completely honest
neither with himself nor with his work. Where he was
honest with his neighbours, it was not from principle, but
by a flair which he had for grandiose behaviour. If his
best work came from his connexion with Wordsworth, it
was because here he made contact with an astonishingly
matter-of-fact honesty; which he was able to recognize,
let it be added, not as an ornament, or attribute, but as
the essence of Wordsworth's power as a poet.

Thereby he became the first (as he remains the greatest)
of the Wordsworthians. Wordsworth, it should in fairness
be recalled, was, if not the first, at least (after Lamb)
the most faithful, of the Coleridgians—with a faithfulness
often hardly tried. He spoke of Coleridge, when he died,
as of 'the most wonderful man he had ever known'; and
truly the early years of their friendship had been years of
wonder. In the quality of wonder, indeed, Coleridge was
easily pre-eminent; and his great examples of the quality
—the *Ancient Mariner*, *Christabel*, *Kubla Khan*—are work
beyond Wordsworth's range. But it is perhaps more
interesting, and more important, to observe that, in a
different order of work, in a genre which both poets affect,
Coleridge achieved some of his finest successes; and that

[1] *Letters*, p. 35.

of the peculiar talent which makes the kind he had given
notable premonitions some years before Wordsworth essayed it. Upon one of the blank-verse pieces which he
contributed to the *Lyrical Ballads* Coleridge bestowed
the subsidiary title 'A Conversation Poem'. But he had
already employed the type four years earlier. The expression 'A Conversation Poem' recalls (as it was perhaps
meant to do) the Horatian 'Sermoni Propriora'—words
which stand at the head of the poem *Reflections on having
left a Place of Retirement* (1795); and which were also at
one time, as it would seem,[1] prefixed to the earlier lines
To a Young Ass (1794). Both the two last-named poems
deserve study; not so much upon their proper merit, as
from their importance in marking development. In both
Coleridge is already a Wordsworthian[2]—at a time when
Wordsworth himself was still a 'Darwinian', a disciple,
that is to say, of the author of the *Botanic Garden*. If the
verses *To a Young Ass* are, as some critics have found them
to be, not altogether free from absurdity, they are at least
absurd in a manner not possible to a mean talent; and in
such lines as

> And oft with gentle hand I give thee bread,
> And clap thy ragged coat, and pat thy head,

we have already passed, the Popian couplet notwithstanding (a form which Coleridge never managed well), out of
Pope into the very world of the *Lyrical Ballads*. Take,
again, such lines as these:

> Low was our pretty Cot: our tallest Rose
> Peep'd at the chamber-window. We could hear
> At silent noon, and eve, and early morn,
> The Sea's faint murmur. In the open air
> Our Myrtles blossom'd; and across the porch
> Thick Jasmines twin'd: the little landscape round
> Was green and woody, and refresh'd the eye.
> It was a spot which you might aptly call
> The Valley of Seclusion.[3]

---

[1] See *Biographia Literaria*, i, p. 17 (Shawcross).
[2] As in a different species, we have seen, in the *Destiny of Nations* (1796).
[3] *Reflections on having left a Place of Retirement*, ll. 1–9.

Already there Coleridge is doing with credit what later, but only later, only when Coleridge had taught him, Wordsworth did with genius. Coleridge himself, with a true critical instinct, singled out his 'shorter blank verse poems' as the best part of his early work; [1] and the same critical instinct enabled him to diagnose their defect: where they fail, it is because their simplicity is affected, it is a 'pretence of simplicity'.[1] They are work not as yet quite honest. That supreme poetical honesty which belongs to Wordsworth Coleridge perhaps never quite learned. He achieves it in patches; but even in this species (of which he may plausibly be accounted the inventor), even in the short reflective poem in blank verse,[2] in the *Conversation Poem*, he never quite hits Wordsworth's settled manner.

In this species, none the less, is to be sought his finest work, excepting always the magical triad, the *Ancient Mariner, Christabel, Kubla Khan*. The three great Odes notwithstanding, this may still be said; and indeed, the last and greatest of them, *Dejection*, confirms the thesis. If *Dejection* is to be called an Ode at all, we must call it a *Conversation Ode*; and its opening lines sufficiently announce its character:

> Well! If the Bard was weather-wise, who made
> The grand old ballad of Sir Patrick Spence . . .

Did ever *odist* prelude with this 'Well!'? The other two Odes are less easily appraised; but neither of them suffices to assure us that Coleridge in fact knew what an ode was. In the earlier of them, *To the Departing Year*, a true and appealing rhetoric is fitfully intermixed with the crudest pseudo-Pindarics, verse nobly sonorous jostles with rhodomontade. How much of true and false is in this piece almost absurdly commingled, any one may satisfy himself

[1] *Biographia Literaria*, i, pp. 16 sqq.
[2] Mostly, but not always, in blank verse: a notably successful example in 'heroics' is the *Garden of Boccaccio*. An early example in blank verse is the *Eolian Harp*.

who will be at pains to read, first the splendidly impressive exordium,

> Spirit who sweepest the wild harp of Time,

and then the idle jig and flaunt of such stuff as this, from the penultimate stanza:

> Abandoned of Heaven! mad Avarice thy guide,
> At cowardly distance, yet kindling with pride—
> Mid thy herds and thy cornfields secure thou hast stood,
> And joined the wild yelling of Famine and Blood.

Was ever such Red-Flag rubbish heard upon lips which the hallowed coals have kindled?

France: an Ode is freer (but not wholly free) of this falsity. It sustains over wide tracts a high bardic level; yet admonishing us, even so, not once nor twice only, that between the bardic and turgidity there is no luxury of interspace. Its indubitable grandeur perhaps culminates in the indignant challenge,

> Was this thy boast, Champion of human kind,
> To mix with Kings in the low lust of sway?

But even here it may be permitted to ask whether this is, after all, the proper grandeur of an Ode, and not that of inspired conversation.

Inspired conversation. Here was an art in which not even his enemies denied to Coleridge an unchallengeable pre-eminence. It is valuable, in an age credulous of heroes but oddly sceptical of gods, to emphasize that character of the life of poetry which consists in inspiration. More fully and consistently than poets of greater effectiveness, Coleridge hit this character. With the same ease with which other men are protractedly dull, Coleridge was without intermission inspired. Yet with an inspiration curiously self-indulgent. He yielded himself wholly to the momentary rapture, to the melting influences of his own temperament. It was not in him to save the transport for epic or Ode, for tragedy or for a sustained Lucretian flight. But in conversation, and in the Conversation Poem, he was

for ever pouring out magnanimously, or with a grandly
calculated carelessness spilling, the wine of a spirituality
limitlessly fecund. Add (and you have perhaps said all)
that thrice in his life he punctuated the else unintermitted
vocality of his inspiration by a pause of supernatural
silence; and was content to hear, and thereafter with
curious fidelity—as though he were an instrument purely
passive—to record those eerie voices of nature which speak
to us articulately in the 'magical triad'.

Coleridge's rank in the poetry of his country has been
variously assessed; and the waxing or waning of his repute
follows, perhaps, the greater or less demand at different
periods for efficiency in character and performance. Never
perhaps was a poet of equal gifts equally inefficient: inefficient in affairs, in friendship, in poetry. That is easily
said, and truly, and is necessary to say. And yet, while of
what may be called clean efficiency Coleridge had nothing,
there may perhaps be registered for him, and indeed
pressed, a claim to that kind of blurred efficiency which
consists in being uniformly interesting and never negli-
gible. To the regard of a world in which most men—
and especially eminent men—are dull, this is perhaps an
equitable and enduring title. Among the men of his day
who were interesting, hardly one interested either a wider
circle or one better worth attaching. He influenced profoundly, not only the common opinion of his time, but
the opinions and feelings of great men. In his poetry he
has left a body of work in which nearly everything is imperfect, but in which, when all is said and done, almost
nothing is uninteresting. The Anthologies—aiming to
present consummate work—do him small justice. He is
more profitably, and more justly, read in bulk; and yet can
only be so read by those who, patient of blurred effects,
bring to the study of him a considerable charity. Most
of his life, boy and man, he lived (if truth be told) upon
charity. And in the history of literature he will continue,
the inspired foundling of our poetry, to live upon that
charity which is neither properly nor prudently refused to

genius and lofty aims struggling with infirmity of the will.
After all, just as in life he had qualities which compel
sympathy (even where they do not always deserve it), a
temperament hovering between magnanimity and sentimentality, a liveliness of mind perpetually driven from the
ingenious to the true, and back again, an instinct for pity
ludicrously divided between himself and others; even so
in his poetry he discovers those qualities which melt hard-
ness. That 'echo of magnificence of mind' which is the
mystery of style, his verse renders to us, if uncertainly,
yet insistently. In that part of poetry in which the
distinction fails, which obtains elsewhere so obstinately,
between the invention of images and the discovery of
truth, his mind moves in a fashion ingeniously liberating.
And above all, whenever he is most himself, most a poet,
he has that power to quicken sensibility, to make the spirit
beautiful or pitiful, which poetry shares with dreams and
our most precious memories, and the stars and either
twilight.

Of Coleridge's work in prose I have said nothing; and
not merely because I wanted time, but because I feel that
his critical essays and lectures receive, commonly, more
praise than they deserve, his poems—not only the best of
them, but the second best, especially—a good deal less.
A great prose-writer he is not; but in prose, as everywhere
else, he is a great, and arresting, *talker*. There is one scrap
of his conversation—a conversation with himself—which
will outlive, I should fancy, all his more formal writing.
He dates it 10 July 1834; and on 25 July of that year
he died:

'I am dying, but without expectation of a speedy release. Is it
not strange that very recently bygone images and scenes of early
life have stolen into my mind, like breezes blown from the spice-
islands of Youth and Hope—those twin realities of this phantom
world! I do not add Love; for what is Love but Youth and Hope
embracing, and so seen as *one*? I say *realities*; for reality is a thing
of degrees, from the *Iliad* to a dream; καὶ γάρ τ' ὄναρ ἐκ Διός ἐστι.
Yet, in a strict sense, reality is not predicable at all of aught below

Heaven. "Es enim *in coelis*, Pater noster, qui tu vere *es!*" Hooker
wished to live to finish his *Ecclesiastical Polity*; so I own I wish life
and strength had been spared to me to complete my *Philosophy*.
For, as God hears me, the originating, continuing, and sustaining
wish and design in my heart were to exalt the glory of His name;
and, which is the same thing in other words, to promote the improvement of mankind. But *visum aliter Deo*, and His will be done.'

All of Coleridge's strength and weakness is packed into
that affecting paragraph. 'I wish life and strength had
been spared to me to complete my *Philosophy*.' In truth,
it was not in him to complete anything. Of innumerable
critical enterprises, he brought to completion only one—
the *Biographia Literaria*: if indeed that odd medley of
personal reminiscence, metaphysic, letters, political tirade,
and criticism of poetry can be called complete. From
such a temperament as he had, it would be idle, in any
case, to expect either a safe critical judgement or a connected method and style. But these qualities—which
prose demands—poetry, which sees, and reveals, by flashes,
and unpredictably, neither affects nor misses. It is, in the
nature of it, not finite; and of this in it Coleridge, who
finished nothing, took magnificent advantage.

He took magnificent advantage of it; and yet the
tragedy of this unfinishing magnificence must be the abid-
ing thought in connexion with all he did. The poetry of
Wordsworth, 'a temple, like a cloud slowly surmounting'
the 'invidious hill' of conventional opinion, has long since
'risen out of darkness' into the space and light proper to
immortal work. It stands out in clear and sure proportion,
with 'spire star-high' and 'towers of deep foundation'
and arches consciously safe against the winds of fashion.[1]
Beside it, if men were masters of their own will or of
circumstance, there should have stood a sister temple not
less aspiring in its outline, fashioned in a more glowing
material, richer in detail, embodying ideas of beauty more
intricate and fantastic, and yet not alien. In remains, of
which it might be doubted whether they were perfect

[1] See the Sonnet *Immortality*, Oxford Wordsworth, p. 282.

work undone by the power of time, or grandiose beginnings made frustrate by human infirmity, we can still
trace, of this sister temple, the magnanimous proportions,
and catch against the sunset its pageant of colour. Here
and there a spirit that felt, before all needs, the need for
confession, has perfected with curious workmanship, so
that nothing remains to add, some shrine or niche or cell.
But, for the rest, the aisles are roofless, arches stand which
carry no towers, the columns end in air. The façade bears
a melancholy legend: 'The Mighty One that persecuteth
me is on this side and on that; He pursueth my soul like
the wind, like the sand-blast he passeth through me; He
is around me even as the air.' [1]

And thereunder, the cryptogram [2]—pathetically delu-
sive—ECTHCE.

---

[1] *The Wanderings of Cain*, ii. 33.

[2] The use of this cryptogram is due to Coleridge's belief that the Greek
word ἔστησε means 'stands firm'—for which the correct Greek is, in fact,
ἔστηκε.

LET me say at once that I am going to keep her secret—
or Wordsworth's. Indeed, I must; for I do not know
it—I am the only person who does not. She ought to be
Annette, as M. Legouis says that she is. She ought to
be Mary Hutchinson; but that would make her too
respectable. If we are to be cut off from both of these
alternative vulgarizations, she ought at least to be somebody, and no longer to be allowed,

> A dancing Shape, an Image gay,
> To haunt, to startle, and waylay

our hearts, without being made to stand and deliver. I
met the other day an enthusiastic student (as I am myself)
of the poetry of Matthew Arnold; and I found him lost
in the pursuit of Marguerite. He had one good clue.
Matthew Arnold's Marguerite had

> Eyes too expressive to be blue,
> Too lovely to be grey.

I have never thought that the lines made her more poetical. But, no doubt, they make her more findable; and
I await with curious complacency the discovery of a really
dark chapter in the life of one of my predecessors in this
Chair. Even so, all these inquiries start from a premiss
which I have never felt at full liberty to accept. They
assume of the poet what I should hesitate to assume of
any man—that he can never be in love with the moon.

I have known great lovers who never loved anything
else; who cried for the moon, like children, and who died
for the moon, the martyrs of her far cold purity.

Of this kind of abstract devotion Wordsworth was, I
still think, easily capable; albeit his youth is now known
to have been less like somebody else's old age than many
people thought probable.

The first person to speculate about the identity of Lucy
was the person most likely to come near the truth—I mean

Coleridge. Some time towards the end of 1798, or the beginning of 1799, Wordsworth, from the German town of Goslar, sent to Coleridge in Göttingen a poem which Coleridge writes out, with the title *Epitaph*, and sends to Poole:

> A slumber did my spirit seal,
> I had no human fears;
> She seemed a thing that could not feel
> The touch of earthly years.
> No motion has she now, no force,
> She neither hears nor sees:
> Mov'd round in Earth's diurnal course
> With rocks, and stones, and trees.

Coleridge had just received the news of the death of his son Berkeley. There is no connexion between the *Epitaph* and his loss; save that the loss has put him in mind of the *Epitaph*—Wordsworth had sent it to him 'some months' ago. 'A most sublime epitaph', Coleridge calls it. 'Whether it had any reality', he goes on, 'I cannot say. Most probably, in some gloomier moment he had fancied the moment in which his sister might die.' The *Epitaph* does not name Lucy. But that it belongs to the Lucy series has been generally assumed, and the inference seems justified by the fact that, when it was first printed (in the *Lyrical Ballads* of 1800), Wordsworth placed it with two others of the Lucy poems; with 'Strange fits of passion ...' and 'She dwelt among th' untrodden ways . . .'. (The second of these two pieces he entitled, when it first appeared, 'A Song'—an unlikely title, I cannot but think, for the expression of an actual and personal sorrow.) Of the three pieces, 'Strange fits of passion . . .' is, in the *Lyrical Ballads*, placed first. The order may be dramatic; or it may be chronological. It may be both. I am inclined to think the poem the earliest in time of the three; and my reason for that is Coleridge—is Coleridge's remark upon the *Epitaph*. Why does Coleridge suggest that the *Epitaph* proceeded from some gloomy mood when Wordsworth 'had fancied the moment in which his sister might die'?

As a girl, Dorothy Wordsworth was not what I may call
of the dying kind; she was what Wordsworth calls her, in
lines addressed to her, 'healthy as a shepherd-boy'. If
Coleridge supposed Wordsworth, in the *Epitaph*, to have
'fancied the moment in which (she) might die', is not the
most likely explanation of that the poem 'Strange fits of
passion . . .'? The 'fit of passion' which that poem
describes, you will remember:

> What fond and wayward thoughts will slide
> Into a lover's head—
> 'O mercy!' to myself I cried,
> 'If Lucy should be dead.'

I cannot but think that Coleridge had already seen that
poem; that Wordsworth had explained to him its origin—
a sudden 'fit of passion' in which it had occurred to him,
approaching their dwelling, that he might find Dorothy
dead.

Already, you will say, I have identified Lucy, and yet
had vowed that nothing was more outside my thoughts
and my power. But I have not. Dorothy, I think, was
the occasion of 'Strange fits of passion . . .'. Yet it is a
lover's poem—

> When she I loved was strong and gay
> And like a rose in June . . .

and Wordsworth dares tell the story 'but in the lover's
ear alone'. This 'lyrical ballad' is, not a domestic lyric, but
a dramatic lyric. Dorothy has been dramatized away.

Between 'Strange fits of passion . . .' and the *Epitaph*
Wordsworth placed—when he arranged his poems in 1800
—the so-called *Song*, 'She dwelt among th' untrodden
ways . . .'. Did he locate these 'untrodden ways' as being
'beside the springs of Dove' for no reason at all, or for no
better reason than to find a rhyme for 'love'? I think not.
'His second summer vacation', says Mr. Harper, whose
biography traces, month by month and almost week by
week, every traceable movement of Wordsworth, 'His
second summer vacation, that of 1789, was spent in the

north again. He explored Dovedale in Derbyshire, and some of the valleys in western Yorkshire and hidden tracts of his own native region. Between these wanderings he was blest, he tells us, with a joy "that seemed another morn Risen on mid-noon", the presence of his sister.' This account is based on a well-known passage in the sixth book of the *Prelude* (190–251). Wordsworth and Dorothy, as Mr. Harper goes on to tell us, were joined in their wanderings by Mary Hutchinson. But if I understand the passage of the *Prelude* aright, that was not in Derbyshire, among the 'untrodden ways' of the Dove, but, somewhat later, in the Lake district, round and about Penrith. Dovedale and the Dove [1] belong to Dorothy; and in reading the 'Song' we ought to bear in mind the vivid romantic impressions left on Wordsworth's mind by this tour with his sister through Derbyshire. If we had been told that Lucy dwelt beside the Wye, above Tintern, should we have had any doubt who Lucy was? I fancy that the Dove, associated in Wordsworth's mind with 'a joy above all joys' (*Prelude*, vi. 196–7), was not far behind the Wye in its claim upon his affections, its wealth of passionate memories.

Once again, I know, hunting Lucy (or rather, trying not to), I seem driven on to Dorothy. But I will not allow it: and you must hear me out. The *Lyrical Ballads* of 1800 contains yet a fourth Lucy poem, the longest of all the Lucy poems, the only one which exhibits any elaboration of style or thought, 'Three years she grew . . .'.

Familiar as this piece is, let me confess that I have never fully understood it. I am not perplexed, it is true, by what has perplexed others—the opening words. The 'three years' during which Lucy grew 'in sun and shower' have never bothered me. Those three years of Lucy no more perplex me than the six years (which, in the first edition, were four years) of the 'six years' darling of a

---

[1] The Dove rises in the Derbyshire Hills a few miles south of Buxton and flows into the Trent at a point a few miles north-west of Burton-on-Trent.

pygmy size' whose philosophy is given in the 'Immortal
Ode'. Heaven knows, I am but an amateur of the nursery,
a stranger within the gates of childhood. But I suppose
Wordsworth to have fixed *three* years for Lucy as giving
the age at which a child may be thought to be, for the
first time, both beautiful and interesting. So soon as Lucy
had become both beautiful and interesting,

> Then Nature said, 'A lovelier flower
> On earth was never sown;
> This Child I to myself will take;
> She shall be mine, and I will make
> A Lady of my own.

There follow those four stanzas, unmatched in their music
of speech and idea, in which Wordsworth has drawn for
us the character of a Child of Nature; a being to whom
Nature is 'both law and impulse'; who moves light as the
fawn; who yet is sensible, in all her quickness of life, of

> the silence and the calm
> Of mute insensate things.

The cloud, the storm, the swaying willow, school her
motions; the stars of midnight are dear to her, and the
sound of streams and all murmuring beauty lends loveli-
ness to her looks; 'vital feelings of delight' add glory to
her stature, what time she and Nature 'together live'.

> Thus Nature spake—The work was done—
> How soon my Lucy's race was run!
> She died, and left to me
> This heath, this calm, and quiet scene;
> The memory of what has been,
> And never more will be.

It is this last stanza that I have never understood. 'Thus
Nature spake', making high promises; and 'The work was
done'—the glory of these promises, we must suppose, was
fulfilled. But to what end or meaning? Lucy's race
was run. She died. Was it *that* work which Nature
schemed to do? 'The work was done', and Lucy died?
Is that what Wordsworth means to say? Or does he mean

to say that 'the work was done', the perfect woman planned was made—*and yet* Lucy died? No adversative particle suggests that, between the 'work' that 'was done' and the death of Lucy, there is any opposition of idea or feeling. I had thought at one time that such an opposition was intended; but that Wordsworth had, in this last stanza, confused the issue towards which the preceding stanzas move so magnificently. Over six stanzas he has sustained his inspiration at a height above his common level of art. Do the wings of it, here, all at once flag unaccountably, so that he merely *tumbles* to his conclusion? I think not. There could not be that drop, that confusion of collapse, and then the recovered strength, the steady poise, of the four lines in which the poem ends. The truth is, as I believe, that between Lucy's perfection in Nature and her death there is, for Wordsworth, really no tragic antithesis at all. Lucy belongs to a world where the distinction between 'rocks and stones and trees' and our breathing human flesh, between 'mute insensate things' and the heart which has received into itself 'the silence and the calm' of them, has no place. Dying, she is gathered up into her own world.

The real difficulty, I have said elsewhere, of understanding Wordsworth proceeds from our finding it so hard to believe that he means what he says. Of what he says upon the subject of man's place in nature, we miss a large part by being sceptical from the beginning. The distinction between people and things seems so obvious, and is so obstinate, that, confronted with a poetry which is everywhere sedulous to annul it, we allow our attention to stray. Yet take the poetry of Wordsworth where it is most truly poetry, where it is most like himself; keep within the lines of his strong period, before his thinking had lost that speculative rebel quality which makes its greatness, while he was still not afraid either of paradox or (what needs a gayer courage) platitude; take his poetry *there*; run it over in the mind, and ask yourselves whether it has any *dead* rocks and stones and trees; and again, whether of the living persons whom it presents there are any, or many, that are truly distinguished from pieces of nature, any or many who, however simple and human they may seem on casual inspection, do not, under contemplation, seem to slip away into appearances of nature, spirits of hill and sky and what not.

The truth is that, when Wordsworth tells us that rocks and stones and trees are alive, we do not stop to attend; still less when he merely hints it. Of course, if among his own hills you have read the series of Poems on the Naming of Places, it is not strange to you that one or two great rocks should *live*—'the ancient Woman seated on Helm-crag', Hammer-scar, Silver-how, and the rest. But are you prepared, even then, to find the *paving-stones* live, to *see* them *feel*?

> To every natural form, rock, fruit or flower,
> Even the loose stones that cover the highway,
> I gave a moral life; I saw them feel,
> Or linked them to some feeling; the great mass
> Lay bedded in a quickening soul. (*Prel.* iii. 127–31.)

When Wordsworth says there that he *saw* the stones *feeling*—a phrase astonishing in its bare power—I believe him. I credit that sight to 'the poet's eye'—

> an eye
> Which from a tree, a stone, a withered leaf,
> To the broad ocean and the azure heavens
> Spangled with kindred multitudes of stars,
> Could find no surface where its power might sleep.
> (*Prel.* iii. 159–63.)

Leave stones and trees, and take Wordsworth's people. While he still knew no better, he wrote a drama, a tragedy; and when he ought to have known better he printed it. But the *dramatis personae* of the *Borderers* are not Wordsworth's people. The real people of Wordsworth are those at whom he looks so steadily that they can never fade into action, are never dramatizable. His real people are such beings as Lucy, as Ruth, as Lucy Gray; an order of beings who seem to have lapsed out of nature—the nature of woods and hills—into human connexions hardly strong enough to hold them. Perpetually they threaten to fall back into a kind of *things* or a kind of spirits. Lucy is a *thing*: she seemed, says Wordsworth,

> a *thing* that could not feel
> The touch of earthly years.

That the years should not touch her was the dream, it is true, of a spirit which 'slumber', want of imaginative power, had 'sealed' into a false security. Even so, while she lived, Lucy did in fact belong to the world of things. In 'Three years she grew . . .', what really is she, except what the things about her make her, or give to her—the floating cloud, the bending willow, the midnight stars, the waters whose sound has passed into the beauty of her face? What is she else? Or take Ruth, who seems more distinctively woman in that she has met man's unkindness. She comes to us from the greenwood, a creature hardly distinguishable from it, a spirit of the greenwood, piping and singing:

> And she had made a Pipe of straw,
> And from that oaten Pipe could draw
> All sounds of winds and floods,
> Had built a bower upon the green,
> As if she from her birth had been
> An infant of the woods.

An infant of the woods, a nymph, a dryad, she seems a creature that has stepped unwisely for a moment out of the world of forests and streams, only to shrink back wounded, and at once, to her proper environment. Three bare lines suffice to tell us her tragedy, and forthwith her poet dismisses her again to the world to which she really belongs, the rocks and pools who are a sort of unkind sisters:

> rocks and pools,
> And airs that gently stir
> The vernal leaves, she loved them still,
> *Nor ever taxed them with the ill*
> *Which had been done to her.*

Rock and pool and the winds in the leaves not only live, and not only have they ears, they have feelings which Ruth is unwilling to hurt by hard words! How wonderful it is; but not with the wonder of human tragedy.

Or take a humbler creature—so humble that once, like a good many other people, I used a little to despise her—take Lucy Gray. When I read the piece now, I am affected before all by the supernatural wintriness of it, as of some Elfland winter. There is just a frozen stillness, in which is momentarily descried, only to be lost at once, the figure, not of any human child, but of some glacial elf, some fairy or imp of frost and storm.

I have come a long way from 'Three years she grew . . .' and its Child of Nature; a long way, but a way, I think, not really unprofitable. To be 'Nature's Child' is to be made one with Nature; and between Lucy's dying and her living in Nature there is, in truth, no difference save the difference which another of the Lucy poems expresses, the difference to a human creature not yet tamed, not yet subdued to Nature's purposes:

> But she is in her grave, and O
> The difference to me!

Some of our speculations about Lucy have seemed to lead us towards Dorothy Wordsworth; and if any one cares to think of the Lucy of 'Three years she grew . . .' as Dorothy, I have no protest to make, if at the same time he is prepared to think of Dorothy as Wordsworth thought of her. Of course, he had towards her the ordinary human feeling; though with some genuinely lover-like quality superadded, I fancy, some touch of spiritual passion:

> And she who dwells with me, whom I have loved
> With such communion that no place on earth
> Can ever be a solitude to me

—that goes beyond any mere human brotherliness. Yet, as often as not, Wordsworth, I think, does not stop to separate Dorothy from the appearances of nature; he so blends the thought of her with the setting of 'mute insensate things' in which she moves that you might think of her, or suppose him to think of her, as of a tree (the bending willow of 'Three years she grew . . .'), of a spirit of storm, of a waterfall, of the breath of spring—

> thy breath,
> Dear sister! was a kind of gentler spring
> That went before my steps.

Or again, she seems some faun or nymph or divine huntress; never quite tied to a settled humanity or to her proper identity.

This way of looking at people was habitual with Wordsworth from earliest youth; this inability to separate them from those appearances of nature among which he found them. In a remarkable passage of the eighth book of the *Prelude* he traces his perception of the dignity of man (the 'main region of his song') to the circumstance that he had, from childhood, seen actual men only against a glorifying and transfiguring background of nature, seen them as not dissociable from the clouds and mountains and setting sun.

> A rambling schoolboy, thus
> I felt his presence[1] in his own domain,
> As of a lord and master, or a power,
> Or genius, under Nature, under God,
> Presiding; and severest solitude
> Had more commanding looks when he was there.
> When up the lonely brooks on rainy days
> Angling I went, or trod the trackless hills
> By mists bewildered, suddenly mine eyes
> Have glanced upon him distant a few steps,
> In size a giant, stalking through thick fog,
> His sheep like Greenland bears; or, as he stepped
> Beyond the boundary line of some hill-shadow,
> His form hath flashed upon me, glorified
> By the deep radiance of the setting sun:
> Or him have I descried in distant sky,
> A solitary object and sublime,
> Above all height! like an aerial cross
> Stationed alone upon a spiry rock
> Of the Chartreuse, for worship . . .

[1] Man's presence.

The shepherd, so seen, is seen as a supernatural, or spiritual, appearance; at the same time, not forfeiting his naturalness:

> Meanwhile this creature—spiritual almost
> As those of books, but more exalted far;
> Far more of an imaginative form
> Than the gay Corin of the groves, who lives
> For his own fancies, or to dance by the hour,
> In coronal, with Phyllis in the midst—
> Was, for the purposes of kind, a man
> With the most common.

'Three years she grew . . .' was known to Coleridge under the title 'Nature's Lady'; not, I think, a happy title—you have the horrid expectation that Lucy will be married presently to one of 'Nature's gentlemen'. But Nature's children were still spoken of, in those days, as 'young ladies'; and to a Young Lady (called, in the first edition, 'a Beautiful Young Lady', the epithet 'beautiful' later cancelled, in one of those fits of blood-curdling honesty by which Wordsworth was periodically shaken), to a Young Lady were addressed the delightful stanzas 'Dear child of Nature, let them rail . . .'. That the Young Lady was Dorothy was a fixed tradition in the Wordsworth family, a tradition which cannot, I think, be reasonably impugned. We know from Wordsworth's own authority that the poem was 'composed at the same time' as, and 'designed to make one piece' with, a much inferior poem, bearing the title *Louisa*.

> I met Louisa in the shade . . .

There are names that are absurd in themselves, and enough to ruin the best poem. There is, as everybody knows, a sonnet of Wordsworth which begins 'Jones'. Nobody gets any further; no anthologist of Wordsworth has ever had the courage to print it. Yet, save for *Jones*— save for that 'lonely word'—it is one of the best of the *Sonnets Dedicated to National Independence and Liberty*. *Louisa* is not, in any case, an inspired piece; though it

has shreds and patches of inspiration. But Louisa is, it is
difficult to doubt, Lucy; Louisa stands to Lucy as one of
'Nature's Ladies' to a 'Child of Nature'. The mystery
of the poem is why, in the last year of his life, Wordsworth
cancelled the best stanza in it, a stanza that had stood in
every edition down to 1843:

> And she hath smiles to earth unknown;
> Smiles, that with motion of their own
> Do spread, and sink, and rise;
> That come and go with endless play,
> And ever, as they pass away,
> Are hidden in her eyes.

The solution of the mystery was found, I fancy, by
Knight. In 1849 Dorothy was still living; but with reason
darkened irrecoverably. The lines that describe her old
play of countenance, the smiles that died from her cheeks,
to live still in her eyes, Wordsworth now found too painful
to let stand.

In the definitive edition of his Poetical Works Wordsworth placed *Louisa*, not with what we know was its companion piece, but with 'Strange fits of passion . . .', 'She
dwelt among the untrodden ways . . .', and 'I travelled
among unknown men . . .' (in that order, *Louisa* first).
The last of these three pieces I have not yet mentioned.
It is assumed to have been written shortly after Wordsworth's return from Germany in 1799. If it was, it is
strange that it did not find a place, with the other Lucy
poems of that year, in the *Lyrical Ballads* of 1800. Wordsworth says that he will not leave England 'a second time'.
His sojourn in Germany was, in fact, his *third* visit to the
continent of Europe. It would be pleasant if we could
bring back the composition of this poem to the date of
the first of these three visits. But so early a date (1790)
is plainly incredible. Plainly incredible also is the date of
Wordsworth's second visit to France (1792–3): nor would
it help us with 'a second time'—we must be content to
take that phrase as merely dramatic. 1792–3, of course,
would carry the search for Lucy towards Annette. Yet

this poem is, in every line of it, decisive against Annette; for the whole power and charm of it derive from the emphasis which it lays on the English-ness of Lucy and her environment.

> Among thy mountains did I feel
>   The joy of my desire;
> And she I cherished turned her wheel
>   Beside an English fire.
>
> Thy mornings showed, thy nights concealed,
>   The bowers where Lucy played;
> And thine too is the last green field
>   That Lucy's eyes surveyed.

A twelvemonth ago, I had been re-reading that poem when I chanced to take up Mr. Nichol Smith's delightful *Book of Eighteenth-Century Verse*. It is not a century that I am overmuch in love with—so far, I mean, as its verse goes. But here in Oxford we live by admiration of one another's books, and of this new book I turned the pages sedulously. I was rewarded by finding some stanzas which, if they are not new to you, were new to me, and which I may be allowed to give here:

> Mine be a cot beside the hill;
> A beehive's hum shall sooth my ear;
> A willowy brook, that turns a mill,
> With many a fall, shall linger near.
>
> The swallow, oft, beneath my thatch,
> Shall twitter from her clay-built nest;
> Oft shall the pilgrim lift the latch,
> And share my meal, a welcome guest.
>
> Around my ivy'd porch shall spring
> Each fragrant flower that drinks the dew;
> *And Lucy, at her wheel, shall sing,*
> In russet gown and apron blue.
>
> The village church, among the trees,
> Where first our marriage vows were giv'n,
> With merry peals shall swell the breeze,
> And point with taper spire to heav'n.

That is a poem of Samuel Rogers—he did not often, I fancy, do better, or as well. There are Lucys in poetry, of course, long before Rogers. There is Tickell's *Colin and Lucy*. There is the Lucy of Lyttelton's best-known poem. Lucy figures with Collin, again, in one of the pastoral songs of Lyttelton's protégé, Edward Moore; and Lucy and Strephon make *The Happy Pair* of Chatterton. Yet I cannot but think that Wordsworth's Lucy, turning her wheel beside an English fire, owes something besides her name to Rogers's Lucy. I do not suppose that the reminiscence is conscious, if reminiscence there be. These influences are subtle and unpredictable. Yet so, too, is the range and power of mere coincidence. If there is a connexion between the two pieces, two consequences flow from it. It will mean, first, that the earliest of the Lucy poems is 'I travelled among unknown men . . .'. It will mean, secondly, that Lucy, when she first takes life, has the life of a purely ideal creation.

Yet why this poem, if it be thus early, appears neither in the *Lyrical Ballads* of 1798 nor in that of 1800, it is difficult to conjecture. But there is almost equal difficulty, as I have noticed, if we place the composition of the poem in 1799, the date usually given. Why is it absent from the volume of 1800? I do not know that we solve the difficulty by pointing to a similar trouble in connexion with two other poems of the Lucy series, *Louisa* and 'Dear Child of Nature . . .'. Of these two poems Wordsworth has himself recorded that they were composed at one time and for one another. Yet elsewhere he has told us that the one belongs to the year 1803, the other to 1805; despite the fact that 'Dear Child of Nature . . .' was printed in the *Morning Post* of 11 February 1802. Mr. Harper believes that both pieces were written in 1794, and has given interesting and plausible reasons for his belief.

It is just 130[1] years since the first edition of the *Lyrical Ballads* was published. Nothing so important had happened in our poetry since Milton. It is easy to see, and

---

[1] The lecture was delivered in 1928.

say that, now. But the book met contumely and ridicule; not perhaps from the best judges, but from good and honest judges. 'I found in these poems', writes De Quincey, ' "the ray of a new morning", and an absolute revelation of untrodden worlds teeming with power and beauty as yet unsuspected amongst men.' Exceptional men were able to appraise truly this exceptional poetry. But to critics who could not fairly be called either uninstructed or incompetent it seemed to be hardly poetry at all. When I read the *Lyrical Ballads* and, with them, the contemporary criticism which they provoked, I take order with myself, and I feel the need of humility. One hundred and thirty years ago, what should I have said of them? on which side should I have been? Should I have known good from bad? Do I know good from bad now, in the new poetry all about me, a poetry new and numerous beyond all precedent? How *does* one, in poetry, know good from bad? It is perhaps late to raise so large a question. Nor should I do so, if I did not think the answer to it almost absurdly simple. We know good from bad in poetry by that faculty which we call taste. *Porro unum est necessarium*—a clean palate. What that means, and how it is maintained or impaired, we know well enough in respect of what I may call earthly foods. And in respect of that food of the soul which poetry is, the analogy holds. To a true taste in poetry there is requisite just clean feeding in poetry. In addition, of course, the organism must be healthy; there must be a health of the soul. I have always supposed that this must be in some degree a moral health. But that, I am told, is to confuse ethics and aesthetics. We are no longer allowed to speak of poetry as a criticism of life. May we be allowed to invert the proposition, and to speak of life as a criticism of poetry? May we suppose, I mean, that our judgements of poetry will be deep and true in proportion to the depth and truth of our lives?

THE PLACE OF HAZLITT IN ENGLISH CRITICISM[1]

MAY I, before I take up my subject, say that, while I appreciate very much the honour which Professor Campagnac has done me in inviting me here, I feel something of an impostor in accepting his invitation? I mean by that that it must necessarily seem bold, or even brazen, that I should come to the Department of Education in this University, and speak, not about education, but about literary criticism. Perhaps, in justification of myself, I may say this much: Though of the theory of education I know nothing, I have been mixed with the practice of it for a quarter of a century. Recently, I have escaped from teaching into a (more or less) liberal leisure. But from the business of trying to teach I have brought away two lessons: the one, that any education is imperfect that does not leave with a man the love of letters; and the second, that the love of letters profits less than might be thought unless it be directed by criticism. The second of these two lessons is one which especially, I think, needs emphasizing at the present; in a time when accepted standards are everywhere vigorously, even rudely, challenged, and when the very forms of literature seem to be changing daily before our eyes, changing and giving place to developments of which the issue is still uncertain.

The publication some six weeks ago of a volume of *New Writings*[2] by Hazlitt may perhaps be allowed to furnish any excuse which I need for speaking of a writer whose repute, though it increases with each year, is still, I think, below what it should be. I may perhaps recall also that it is just a hundred years since Hazlitt published that work of his which is certainly his masterpiece, *The Spirit of the*

[1] A lecture to the Department of Education in Liverpool University.

[2] *New Writings by William Hazlitt*: Collected by P. P. Howe: The lecture dates from May 1925.

Age. I should not be surprised if, a hundred years hence, when Criticism makes up her jewels, she accounted this book her brightest ornament. If I need an excuse for speaking of Hazlitt in Liverpool, I may find it in the fact that in Liverpool he passed a period of his childhood. It was in Liverpool that he first went to church; 'and I do not care', writes this nine-year-old rebel, 'if I never go into a church again.' It was in Liverpool that he first went to a theatre, in Liverpool that he wrote his first dramatic criticism. But in Liverpool, I am afraid, he learned some bad habits—which clung to him through life. The Rev. Joseph Hunt records of him 'that he was not made so much of there as he had been' in his own home. The lady with whom he lived 'went out visiting, leaving him at home by himself. . . . the child thought himself slighted: he became sullen: and this sullenness continued ever after. . . . He now showed his talent for satire, mimicry and caricature. By the time he was twelve or thirteen, he would not attend the devotions of (his) family. He would not go to chapel. . . . he used to scamper about the fields . . . like any wild thing.' All this, I am sorry to say, he learned in Liverpool. When he first went there he wrote home letters in which 'the piety displayed', says his father, a nonconformist minister, 'was a great refreshment to me'. But two can play at nonconformity; and by the time he left Liverpool, Hazlitt was a good deal more of a nonconformist than suited his family and friends. Boy and man, it was not in him to be anything else. Indeed, I very much doubt whether Liverpool, and the Liverpool lady who 'went visiting', and left him alone, had very much to do with it, but far rather, in Homeric phrase,

Zeus and Fate and the gloom-acquainted Fury.

In any case, I wish to concern myself here neither with the fractious childhood of Hazlitt nor with his equally fractious manhood; but, leaving biography to the biographers, to consider only to what issues of literature it was given to him to shape the sullen material of his genius.

When he lay dying, something moved him to say that he
had 'had a happy life'. So it pleased him strangely to sum
up a sullen childhood, a youth moody and passionate, a
manhood of which poverty, middle-aged erotics, and the
self-torment of a temperament suspicious and morose,
were the distinguishing characters. I think it likely
enough, even so, that he knew what he was saying. His
real life lay in literature, hidden there as in some passion
of religious faith. After enumerating some of his favourite
authors, 'To have lived', he writes, 'in the cultivation of
an intimacy with such works, and to have familiarly
relished such names, is not to have lived quite in vain.'
I never read him without feeling that literature meant
more to him than it means, not merely to common men,
but to the other great critics.

As I said, his father was a nonconformist minister; and
he destined his son for his own calling. But Hazlitt dis-
sented from Dissent, as from everything else; and by
nineteen he had had enough of being educated for that
ministry. From nineteen to twenty-four he indulged the
only educational experiment worth trying—self-educa-
tion. For five years he sat at home, reading, marking,
inwardly digesting—in the world's phrase, doing nothing.
The five years, however, contained the great event of his
life, his meeting with Coleridge. At five-and-twenty he
turned painter; and at nine-and-twenty dropped painting
for philosophy. Later he played with the theory of politics
and with political economy; and he was thirty-eight before he found his true direction—the criticism of men and
books. Yet I should not suppose his failures lost. If he
never qualified for the dissenting ministry, at least the
genius of dissent was with him through life. If he never
learned to paint—to paint, that is, beyond a standard
better than tolerable (and therefore, to so passionate a
temperament, not tolerable at all)[1]—he may yet be con-

---

[1] Yet his portrait of Lamb (in the National Portrait Gallery) is a notable
picture. He painted Wordsworth, but destroyed the portrait—there was
that in Wordsworth, he knew well, which—on canvas or in words—he

ceived to have learned from painting some of the most
characteristic effects of his writing. From his studies in
philosophy, certainly, he carried over to the criticism of
literature results which were vitalizing to his whole critical
method. His first book was a philosophical essay, modestly,
but cumbrously, entitled: *An Argument in favour of the
Natural Disinterestedness of the Human Mind.* Whether
the argument was a good one or not—philosophically—
does not much matter; nor am I able to judge. What
matters is that Hazlitt begins and ends in the conviction
that men are, in fact, disinterested, and not selfish; a conviction real to him in a way that it hardly can be to a
corrupt or venal temperament; a conviction which helped
him in the interpretation of literature, particularly, I
should suppose, in the interpretation of Shakespeare,
whose greatest tragedies, if man be in his ultimate nature
little, mean nothing. *The Characters of Shakespeare's
Plays*—Hazlitt's first essay in literary criticism—was published in 1817, when, as I said, Hazlitt was already thirty-
eight years of age. This has always been a popular book;
and it would not be Hazlitt if it did not abound in fine
thoughts finely expressed. None the less, of Hazlitt's
purely literary works—and outside these it is beside my
intention to stray—I conceive it to be the least satisfactory. All Shakespeare criticism is, in the nature of things,
disappointing; and so far as Hazlitt can disappoint, he
does so here. There is defect of knowledge, a thing which
neither surprises nor offends me; but there is some defect
also of courage. Hazlitt is doing what later he neither
could nor would—he is holding himself in. But he liked
the book himself, and, looking back on it, claimed that he
had done 'more than any one except Schlegel' to 'vindi-
cate the characters of Shakespeare's Plays from the stigma
of French criticism'. A far better book is the *Lectures on
the English Poets*, and better still—principally as being

could never quite hit. It would have been interesting to have his portrait
of his father—'cracked and gone', he says of it, but 'as fine an old Nonconformist head as one could hope to see in these degenerate times'.

more courageous—the *Lectures on the English Comic Writers*—these belong respectively to the years 1818 and 1819.[1] Two years later came the lectures on the *Dramatic Literature of the Age of Queen Elizabeth*; and in 1825 *The Spirit of the Age*, followed, in the next year, by *The Plain Speaker*.[2] This period, 1817–26, is Hazlitt's height of power. Within it fall, besides the books I have mentioned, *The Round Table* and *Table Talk*—essays on men and manners rather than upon books, but containing also much miscellaneous literary criticism—to the *Round Table* series, for example, belongs the admirable critique of Wordsworth's *Excursion*. *The Spirit of the Age*, published in 1825, had been begun, in fact, in December of 1823; and about half of it was finished in the first months of 1824. Dates are dull things; but these are worth remembering for the reason that this book, Hazlitt's best, is the product of the darkest period of his personal history. He had just been divorced from his wife; and he had just come through the sordid and unhappy love-affair of which he wrote, in *Liber Amoris*, an unashamed history. Add to this that his finances were desperate; and that his books, upon which he depended for his living, had been the subject of savage and unjust critical attack. They had been attacked, although, as a recent critic has remarked, taken together, they constitute a body of literary criticism more vital than anything since Dryden. But neither fortune nor the malice of men could tame Hazlitt; and precisely from the period of his worst affliction springs his best work. From the experience of the man his work has taken, it would seem, a deeper dye of poetry—indeed, some tinge of tragedy. If he is still morose, yet he has discovered

[1] In 1818 Hazlitt published *A View of the English Stage*: 'a collection of Theatrical Criticisms', written for various newspapers during the four years preceding. The book belongs rather to journalism than to literature; but contains much vigorous and characteristic writing. It is a good deal more like Hazlitt than the rather timid *Characters of Shakespeare's Plays*.

[2] *The Plain Speaker* is a miscellany; but the best parts of it (some of them in Hazlitt's noblest style) are those which touch literature.

what we might have thought did not exist—the sublime of morosity.

Whether Hazlitt is the greatest of the English literary critics must depend upon the view you take of what literary criticism is or should be. If it is the business of literary criticism to criticize itself, to be chastened before it chastens, Hazlitt has no pretension to do this. He has many prejudices, and few reserves; he is sometimes mean, more often generous, rarely or never merely just. If it is the duty of the critic to separate the accidents of a literary work from its permanent effects, to isolate it, in analysing, from all possible contamination with interests and passions not completely relevant, to work upon it with no instruments of judgement not properly sterilized,— this, and the like, lies outside Hazlitt's scope and care. Again, if the best criticism rests upon the best information, upon a wide acquaintance with literatures ancient and modern, upon scholarship and the comparative method, here too Hazlitt is defective—his reading is deep and not wide. Indeed, he is bold to affirm that 'our love for foreign literature is an acquired or rather an assumed taste . . . like a foreign religion adopted for the moment to answer a purpose or to please an idle humour'. If it is a part of criticism, once more, to formulate laws, to reach inductively general principles of literature, and to bring particular examples of prose or poetry before this court of principles, then the talent of Hazlitt is not more than a brilliant empiricism. Nor, where he can find no law, has he that instinct for adjournment which serves lesser men; he never wants to wait for posterity; of that higher court he entertains no apprehensions; he must get on with his business—a part of which is writing for his living and living by his writing. In a word, if the essential qualities of criticism are knowledge, patience, impartiality, analytic industry, stay of judgement—these are not Hazlitt's characteristic virtues; and in some of them he is more wanting than is proper either to genius or good sense. On the other hand, the defects which come from the excess of

some of them it is a principal merit in him that he escapes.
He is never, like Macaulay, a prig, nor a posterity-server.
He does not, as Matthew Arnold does, just miss being a
dandy of criticism; and he never, like Bagehot, commits
the fault of philosophizing beyond what he can carry—of
being deeper than he was dug.

His positive merits are numerous and palpable; indeed,
I know no writer of such open excellencies, of excellencies
so readily seizable and so delightfully handle-able. First
among them I should put, what seems not so much a
talent of literature, as an accidental grace of nature, his
abounding *memory*. That sounds nothing much; but it all
depends on what you remember, and how it is done. Of
Hazlitt's memory, the principle is, not mental accuracy,
but sentiment. No man ever quoted so much, and in no
writer, I am afraid, will you find the same quantity of
misquotation; as an advertisement for the Pelman Company, Hazlitt is no good at all. But it makes no difference
—none, that is, if you take a free spirit freely. Macaulay
draws upon a memory extraordinarily apt and accurate;
he draws upon it—very impressively and deliberately.
What is so delightful in Hazlitt is that he never *draws*
upon memory at all. It all gushes, the spontaneity of it
is never suspect; of themselves the springs of memory well
up in inexhaustible freshness. Very often, as I say, the
quotations are inaccurate; and very often they emerge,
less their inverted commas, their patent marks effaced—
just Hazlitt himself, the swift flash of his own prose. You
must have plenty of the pedant in you to mind this. But
it is easier to be a pedant than the unlearned believe; and
there are not wanting people to tell you that this element
in the style of Hazlitt bores them. Only bores are bored;
and the truth is that this is neither an artifice nor an
artlessness in Hazlitt's style, but the native resonance of
his temperament. The great phrases of the great masters
of speech were a part of his life, perhaps the part most
real and effective; it was as natural for him to express
himself in these as it is hard for other men to express

themselves in any other terms than the meagre symbols of their individual crafts.

From this genius of sentimental memory flow a number of interesting consequences. As he grew older, Hazlitt wrote more and more, and read less;[1] and he is not the first man upon whom the need of feeding the body has imposed the necessity of scanting the soul. The late Professor Ker has observed, what once it is noted nobody can miss, that in his best writing Hazlitt is living on the spiritual riches of his youth. Of one or two other English writers, the same is true. The charm of Goldsmith, for example, hangs upon the sentiment of his years of vagabondage, his country youth and poverty. That gives him his tenderness, his lovable quality. Yet another example is Lamb. Of the first books which Hazlitt read, 'let me', he cries, 'still recall them, that they may breathe fresh life into me, and that I may live that birthday of thought and romantic pleasure over again!' Hazlitt's best reading and thinking were done, not only when he was young, but when the new world-interests ushered in by the French Revolution were also young. Just as Goldsmith remains always a child, so Hazlitt remains always a young man. It is one thing to remember one's youth; another to keep it by doing so; and Hazlitt masters both accomplishments. His zest for greatness—revolutionary greatness above all— never leaves him; and to the end he retails fine actions, and still more great words, with unmatchable gusto. I do not mean that you will not find in him some at least of the qualities of middle years; in particular, the persuasion that men and things are not so good, or rather, not so great, as they were. With most of us that is what I call a conservative persuasion. But it takes Hazlitt differently: with him it is a devouring radicalism. If to be more radical at fifty, and with less excuse, than at twenty; to retain an unalterable conviction that the revolutionary dreams of

[1] 'Books have in a great measure lost their power over me; nor can I revive the same interest in them as formerly' (*On Reading Old Books, The Plain Speaker*, 1826).

youth are the only truths—if all that be conservatism, be
middle-agedness, then middle-aged Hazlitt is, and a very
Tory of the Tories. He is esteemed a rather sour writer;
and certainly he is, in expression, sometimes a degree tart.
He judges men and things by the standard of a too fretful
righteousness. The age of which, in *The Spirit of the Age*,
he essays to delineate the dominant characters, was an age,
truly enough, of great men; but of great men all a little
absurdly situated. For Hazlitt, they were all of them
renegades—or, what fretted him yet worse, the best of
them were renegades—in that *best* was the sting. They
were the apostates of that revolutionary freedom of which
he was the Abdiel,

> faithful found
> Among the faithless, faithful only he,
> Among innumerable false, unmoved,
> Unshaken, unseduced, unterrified.

The just conviction of a mind unseduced by worldly
interest makes him unjust to others. That Wordsworth
should be an honest man and a distributor of stamps, that
anything but the seduction of the world should have
effected in Coleridge the shift from *Conciones ad Populum*
to the *Lay Sermons*, in Southey that from *Wat Tyler* to
The Vision of Judgment—all this appeared to him plainly
incredible. Of Scott—who was at least consistent—he
writes that he 'should be heartily glad if the greatest
genius of the age should turn out to be an honest man'.
He could kneel to Scott, he told Patmore, but he could
not take his hand. Hunt comes within the same condemna-
tion as Wordsworth and Coleridge:

'While my friend Leigh Hunt was writing the *Descent of Liberty*,
and strewing the march of the Allied Sovereigns with flowers, I sat
by the waters of Babylon and hung my harp upon the willows . . .
while others bowed their heads to the image of the Beast, I spit
upon it and buffeted it and made mouths at it.'

To these great men, therefore (whose situation was, really,
not so much unintelligible as absurd), he is unjust. Yet

unjust only to a certain point, and unjust always, I think, in a rather great fashion. Hear him upon Coleridge:

'I may say of him here that he is the only person I ever knew who answered to the idea of a man of genius. He is the only person from whom I ever learned anything. There is only one thing[1] he could learn from me in return, but *that* he has not. He was the first poet I ever knew. His genius at that time had angelic wings, and fed on manna. He talked on for ever; and you wished him to talk on for ever. His thoughts did not seem to come with labour and effort; but as if borne on the gusts of genius, and as if the wings of his imagination lifted him from off his feet. His voice rolled on the air like a pealing organ, and its sound alone was the music of thought. His mind was clothed with wings; and raised on them, he lifted philosophy to heaven. In his descriptions, you then saw the progress of human happiness and liberty in bright and never-ending succession, like the steps of Jacob's ladder, with airy shapes ascending and descending, and with the voice of God at the top of the ladder. And shall I, who heard him then, listen to him now? Not I! . . . That spell is broke; that time is gone for ever; that voice is heard no more; but still the recollection comes rushing by, with thoughts of long-past years, and rings in my ear with never-dying sound.'

To miss the merit of that is hardly possible. I do not suppose that Coleridge liked it—Coleridge who, when Hazlitt died, wrote upon him a mean satirical epigram. But it is unjust in the grand manner; and that manner mean spirits never compass. And after all, it is unjust only to a part of Coleridge; and to a very real greatness in him splendidly just; while in its passionate faithfulness to a great memory there is characteristic pathos.

It is the same with Wordsworth. I do not think that Hazlitt was ever drawn towards Wordsworth in the same impelling fashion as towards Coleridge. Wordsworth's 'egotism', he says, 'is in some respects a madness. For he scorns even the admiration of himself, thinking it a presumption in anyone to suppose that he has taste or sense enough to understand him'. There is personal pique in that, I fancy; but neither personal pique nor political

[1] He means common honesty.

wrath affect seriously the substantial justice of Hazlitt's judgements upon Wordsworth's poetry. He girds, he carps, he jibes; but it never occurs to him to think of Wordsworth otherwise than as indisputably the first poet of his age, or to allow you to think that he thinks otherwise. Perhaps the only really bad critic is the critic who has learned, in Matthew Arnold's phrase, to 'praise what he despises and to disparage what he admires'. Never, or very rarely, I think, does Hazlitt do that. Spiteful and intemperate he often is; and that the minds and motives of men should be so cross-tracked and convoluted as they are irritated him. He had that conviction that all roads are straight which belongs to men who have never turned the corner of their youthful radicalism. But at least his judgement is never seduced by interest. It is no small thing in a critic that he should keep always this unbribed judgement. Upon this Hazlitt prided himself, in a fashion more fussy, perhaps, than there was need; but not without title. The consciousness of his own disinterestedness brought with it the temptation to be perverse in his rectitude, to hunt opinions just because they were not those of other people. In a lesser man this would matter more. But not the least of Hazlitt's virtues is one which I have still to mention. The temptation to eccentricity was controlled by a natural truth of judgement, which he possessed in a degree not often equalled in the criticism of literature. Keats, who, if admirations must be mutual, had no particular reason to like Hazlitt, reckons as one of the three precious and incontestable realities of the time 'Hazlitt's depth of taste'. It is easy to forget, when enumerating the qualities of a great writer, some of the more obvious ones; it is easy to fly off in the praise of things about him not essential, easy not to remember that, in the long run, he is to be valued *for the truth of his opinions*. About Keats's phrase, 'depth of taste', I feel (quite apart from the confusion of metaphor which it involves) some difficulty. I do not feel that Hazlitt is properly to be thought of as a deep, or profound, writer.

Yet upon the whole I conceive him to have a flair for truth in which no English critic rivals him; to have a quicker sense than any other for the difference between good and bad, between the genuine and tinsel. This he owes partly to the fact that his mind is *steeped* in good literature; and still more, I am inclined to think, to a fundamental genuineness in himself—a genuineness that all his faults are not enough to overlay. He really *is* disinterested—and not merely morally, but (what matters almost as much) intellectually—that is to say, he is unpedantic, for pedantry is only a want of intellectual disinterestedness, it is an interest in something other than the direct object of criticism. Hazlitt's flair for the truth is especially illustrated in his judgement of contemporaries. I know no critic who has placed so well the great writers of his own time. It is usually esteemed a difficult and delicate business; and perhaps Hazlitt is successful in it because he thought it neither. All his judgements are direct, unhesitating, unembarrassed; and most of them are right. At least they are right on the broad issues. Upon points of detail he is sometimes perverse; as when he prefers Byron's *Heaven and Earth*, of which the whole is rubbish, to *Don Juan*, of which the best is better than anything else in Byron. Yet he always knows who is who, even if he cannot always say unerringly what is what. He is better in genial outline than in minute study. I think better of Byron than better critics do; but even here I am not outraged by, I find a substantial truth in, the sharp phrase in which Hazlitt tries to sum Byron's merits and defects, the 'sublime and provoking coxcomb of poetry'— there were two classes whom Hazlitt always hated, coxcombs and pedants. Even in detail, his judgements upon Byron, though he greatly underestimates his power in satire, flash often with fine penetration. What could be better, for example, than this, upon *Childe Harold*? The poem contains, Hazlitt writes, 'a lofty and impassioned review of the great events of history, of the mighty objects left as wrecks of time; but he dwells chiefly on what is

familiar to the mind of every schoolboy; and has done no
more than justice to the reader's preconceptions by the
sustained force and brilliance of his style and imagery'.
The last clause explains truly at least one-half of the immense vogue of Byron's poetry: Byron found the rhetoric
for the romantic prejudices of his age; he is clothier and
haberdasher to other people's preconceptions. That is
only one side of him, of course; and he had affronted
Hazlitt, it should perhaps be remembered, by blowing hot
and cold about Napoleon. About Napoleon Hazlitt had
a permanent kink in judgement. But what he says about
Byron's 'preposterous liberalism' is not more, I think, than
fair comment. With Byron's 'preposterous liberalism' he
contrasts what he calls the 'gratuitous (i.e. unpaid, un-
bought) servility' of Scott—to the advantage of Scott,
and still with some instinct for fairness and plausibility.
The phrase 'gratuitous servility' is itself cleverly adjusted.
Scott's poetry, it was easy to judge truly—easy, I mean,
for Hazlitt, and he does not mind doing it. 'What is he
to Spenser,' he cries, 'Spenser, over whose immortal ever-
amiable verse beauty hovers and trembles?' There you
have a criticism, not profound, but extraordinarily characteristic—bringing Scott into just that contrast in which
he cannot live, and in just the words which diffuse the
sense of what he is not. This contrasting eye is one of
Hazlitt's great critical gifts. He uses it, not merely to put
to you the difference between one great man and another,
but, what is less easy, to illustrate how different this or
that individual great man may be from himself, how antithetically mixed is any human greatness. To Scott's
novels he is splendidly just—by no one are they better
praised. 'The Author of *Waverley*, who has five hundred
hearts beating in his bosom!'—that is fine amends for
many slaps at 'Sir Walter' ('I have no liking to *Sir Walter*').
   He may be accounted lucky in his time. For what a
gallery of telling personalities is *The Spirit of the Age*—
to keep still to that work of Hazlitt by which he is best
judged! He has hung there, it is true, one or two glaring

portraits of nobodies—a thing which happens to all artists. Occasionally a figure is wanting which we miss—Keats, for example, or Shelley. Of his opinion of both Keats and Shelley he has given us scattered indications elsewhere; but neither here nor elsewhere a full-length portrait. He felt himself no longer young enough to enjoy the *Eve of St. Agnes*: 'but I know how I should have felt at one time'. He called Shelley a 'sophist'. One doesn't like it, but one can see what it is in Shelley that the phrase hits. Yet most of the interesting men of the time are in this book, and they are still interesting. If that is a merit in them, it is a merit also in Hazlitt. Many of them were bookish men, but in Hazlitt they are men, and not books. He valued books above all as the expression of human freedom, and in each and all of the persons he writes about what interests him is the relation in which they stand to the cause of human freedom. Thus he secures for them permanent connexions; and indeed, it was not in his nature to think of books in abstraction from the social and political life of man. He tended, it is true, to like books better than men; yet in books he was never quite happy until he had got down to the man in his habit as he lived. Upon the poetry of Wordsworth, he has made many fine critical observations; but we are grateful when he rounds them off with such a paragraph as this:

'Mr. Wordsworth in his person is above the middle size, with marked features, and an air somewhat stately and Quixotic. He reminds one of some of Holbein's heads, grave, saturnine, with a slight indication of sly humour, kept under by the manners of the age or by the pretensions of the person. He has a peculiar sweetness in his smile; and great depth and manliness and a rugged harmony in the tones of his voice. His manner of reading his own poetry is particularly imposing; and in his favourite passages his eye beams with preternatural lustre, and the meaning labours slowly up from his swelling breast. No one who has seen him at these moments could go away with an impression that he was a "man of no mark or likelihood".'

These traits he likes to keep for us; partly, no doubt,

because he was himself a painter before he was a writer;
but still more, I think, because he was sensible that a book
is but a part of a man, and that one of the plagues of
literature, and of time, is that we lose the comment of
personality. He is for ever pretending, of course, that it
is not a plague but a blessing. But he does not convince
even himself; and because he does not, he is a good critic.
He never deals in ghosts or abstractions. He likes always
flesh and blood and social environment, some touch of
drama and its ironies. Indeed, he allows himself, I am
afraid, to be too much preoccupied by the ironies. While
it is his merit to see that a man and his book are a unity,
he is too often too irritably sensible of the imperfect
character of the unity; so that he comes to speak sometimes as though man and book were a kind of unworthy
quarrel, or, indeed, the man a mere interruption to the
book. He rounds upon and rails at the interruption. That
personality and the expression of it should not fit, affronts
him—and the more in proportion as circumstance had
made his nature irritable and suspicious.

No word have I said of Hazlitt's style; and I have left
myself time for very few words indeed. 'We are mighty
fine fellows,' said Stevenson, 'but we cannot write like
William Hazlitt.' The grand style Hazlitt has not; but
of the *telling* style he is the consummate master. The
method of his style is sweeping and hurried. He paints
in broad slashes, caring little for subtlety in detail or for
harmonization of effects. He is wrongly spoken of as an
impressionist. There is a definiteness in the effects of his
style, a certainty of outline, which is in no way impres-
sionistic. His style has no mysteries, no seclusions of
depth, no faint horizons: it never runs into distance. It is
written in paragraphs but thought in sentences. It holds
together, not by any natural unity of the thoughts, but
by the astonishing swiftness of their succession. Telling
stroke follows telling stroke so rapidly that there is no time
to ask questions. Between the individual deliverances there
is no bond of unity save that all are telling. I suppose

that he should be called an epigrammatic writer. I
suppose that it is an epigram when, for example, of the
Rev. Mr. Irving—who took advantage of being a big man
to pose as a great one—he says, 'Take a cubit from his
stature, and his whole manner resolves itself into an impertinence'; or when he says of Mr. Gifford that 'he is
admirably qualified for the situation which he has held for
some years by a happy combination of defects, natural and
acquired'; or even when he says of Sir Francis Burdett
that 'he could not have uttered what he often did (in the
House of Commons) if, besides his general respectability,
he had not been a very honest, a very good-tempered,
and a very good-looking, man'. For epigram, however, as
a study in perfect expression, or as the art of saying what
you think so concisely as to suggest that you do not think
it, Hazlitt has no real aptitude. He has no real aptitude
for it, firstly, because he is an honest man in a hurry; and
secondly, because, as I have said, more than most men he
hated coxcombry and pedantry.

Will you bear with me still if I try to sum in half a
dozen sentences some of the merits in critical writing
which I suppose myself to discover in Hazlitt? First, I
would say, it is a good thing *not to be a dull writer*; I care
little how it is managed, it is a good thing in itself.
Secondly, it is a good thing to write about books as though
they really meant something to you. It is a good thing,
again, if you write about books, to be somebody—not to
be somebody else, but to be individual, to make criticism
reflect personality. It is a good thing, once more, even if
you pay for it in prejudice, to know what you like and
don't like. It is a still better thing—though this, again,
is not a complete insurance against prejudice—to be disinterested. Best of all is it to have a natural flair for the
truth, an eye for what is vital and vivifying. The first
book to kindle Hazlitt's interest in literature was Burke's
Letter to a Noble Lord. There, said Hazlitt, you have 'a
man pouring out his mind on paper'. Just that praise is
Hazlitt's own everywhere. To that praise you may add

something further. For his writings as a whole Hazlitt
made in his last years the claim that, whatever their
general merits, at least he had 'written no commonplace,
and no line that licks the dust'. That is a high claim for
a man to make for himself who wrote always for his living.
But it is, I think, a just claim; and because it is so, I should
think Hazlitt, of all men who, in this kind, have written
for their living, the most likely to live long.

COWLEY, JOHNSON, AND THE 'METAPHYSICALS'

> Thus Reason's shadows we betray,
> By tropes and figures led astray
> From Nature, both her guide and way.

'WHO now reads Cowley?' asked Pope, so long ago as 1737; and already in 1700 Dryden, to whom Cowley's authority was 'almost sacred', had noted with concern his master's diminished vogue. Yet in his own day (which was the day also, be it remembered, of Milton), who did *not* read Cowley? He was born two years after Shakespeare died; but if fame may be assessed in folios, Shakespeare by comparison is poor indeed. Wordsworth recalled that, in 1790, 'the booksellers' stalls in London swarmed with the folios of Cowley'; and in fact the demand for him in Dryden's time created a supply which has sufficed almost to our own day—any one who wants can still have a folio Cowley for a matter of shillings. Milton, it is said, reckoned as the three greatest of our poets Spenser, Shakespeare, and Cowley. Add Chaucer and Milton himself—and you have a list of 'greatest poets' which would have been accepted by Dryden, and, it is likely, by Wordsworth and Coleridge. I do not know that any great critic, save Johnson, has ever been at pains to depreciate Cowley; nor can it escape the notice of any one that, if Johnson is unfair to him, it is with that kind of unfairness which he would not have thought it fair to use against inferior talent. Nor can the criticisms of Johnson much have affected Cowley's repute; for the same essay treats Donne with plain contempt[1]—Donne whom the taste of our own time has elevated to a station among the great lights of the poetical heaven. If Cowley stands

---

[1] Yet Johnson studied Donne with care. His *Dictionary*, for the letters P Q R alone, has, Mr. Nichol Smith tells me, fifty-four quotations from Donne.

below Donne, he owes it to something else than the
qualified malice of Johnson; who, after all, while he could
afford to omit from his *Lives of the Poets* Chaucer and
Spenser,[1] made Cowley the first, and, as Boswell thought,
the best—certainly one of the most effective—of his essays.
Johnson liked a poetry which was in diction 'poetic', in
versification smooth, in thought and sentiment just; and,
liking that, it was hardly possible for him to like Cowley.
The romantic criticism which affected, for a while, so
adversely the repute of Dryden and Pope, but which has
since become so romantically critical as to admit these to
the canon—the romantic criticism used Cowley kindly.
Wordsworth, it is true, on behalf of Shakespeare and Milton, resented the flattery which fortune had paid to a far
inferior poet; yet he has no wish, he says, to speak 'in
disparagement of that able writer and amiable man'. If
any one thinks the phrase not wholly friendly to a great
fame, he must remember that it was Wordsworth's
manner to sow praise with the hand, and not with the
sack, and that he is, in compliment, mostly gauche. Himself, clearly, he owes something to the 'metaphysicals';
and as a practitioner in the 'irregular ode', he could
scarcely be insensible to the importance of Cowley in the
history of English verse-forms. But both he and Coleridge
had better reasons for being kind to Cowley than are
furnished either by the pseudo-Platonics of that poet
or his pseudo-Pindarics. 'One great distinction', writes
Coleridge, 'I appeared to myself plainly to see between
even the characteristic faults of our older poets, and the
false beauty of the moderns. In the former, from Donne
to Cowley, we find the most fantastic out-of-the-way
thoughts, but in most pure and genuine mother-English;
in the latter the most obvious thoughts, in language the
most fantastic and arbitrary. Our faulty elder poets sacrificed the passion and passionate flow of poetry to the
subtleties of the intellect, and to the starts of wit . . . the

[1] His poets were, of course, in the main dictated to him by the booksellers.

one sacrificed the heart to the head; the other both heart and head to point and drapery.'[1]

That is good and just criticism; and perhaps of the metaphysicals generally, but certainly of Cowley, it emphasizes the grand merit. Whatever defects he has, he is the master always of a 'pure and genuine' English. For this merit, I am inclined to think, he has paid as heavily as for any of his faults. If he is no longer a living influence in our literature, if he is as dead as it is the fashion to think him, it is this, as much as anything else, that has killed him. Indeed, it has killed him twice over. Before Dryden, Johnson has said, we had no poetic diction. The poetic diction of Dryden (and in a less degree his smooth numbers)—this first killed Cowley. He was killed a second time by the romantics—by a talent for pure English, not, I think, better than his own, but perhaps as good; and triumphant over his by its alliances—by the circumstance, I mean, that these poets employ it for the expression of a more genuine emotion and a more natural fancy. The same conditions should, no doubt, in common fairness, have proved fatal to Donne. I think, indeed, that they did; but that the glorified body of Donne's poetry is the body of a resurrection. That he has thus risen, Donne owes, partly, I do not doubt, to qualities in him greater far than any which time will discover in Cowley—to his far deeper spirituality, and, at the same time, richer sensuosity; partly to these qualities, but partly also to accidents of our own time—accidents which have operated with that degree of paradox that he has become at one and the same time the spoilt child of Anglo-Catholicism and the pattern of poets who like their passion perverse.

I should be sorry to entertain the ambition of reclaiming for Cowley the great place which he once held in our poetry; or even to bring his merits into comparison with those of Donne. I will not even ask, whether he is better worth reading than Pope. There are enough persons in the world already who are prepared to sacrifice poetry for

[1] *Biographia Literaria*, i. 15, Shawcross.

their favourite form of it; and I should be sorry, in any case, to put Cowley upon my list of favourite poets. I am content to be able to read him with pleasure, and to think better of him than of poets better esteemed; and at the same time I suppose him to be too good for the neglect of a generation properly more tolerant than others of effects which fall short of the greatest. There is room still in the world, as I think, and in our studies (which cannot sustain unbroken moods of exaltation) for a poetry ingenious, provocative, fertile of whimsical imagery, often graceful and tender, almost never unamiable, never descending to finery of diction, and rising, upon occasion, to nobility.

Of the life and character of Cowley we have a contemporary account from the eloquent, but not very discerning, pen of Dr. Sprat. To the little that it tells us neither Dr. Johnson, nor the enthusiasm of 'research', has added very much. He was born in London, of parents 'of a virtuous life and sufficient estate'. If he did not, like Pope, lisp in numbers, he at least wrote poetry before most of us talk grammar (his *Constantia and Philetus* was penned when he was eight), and he had printed his first tragedy when most boys want their first trousers—a portrait of the author, aged thirteen, is prefixed to this volume of 'learned puerilities'. Dr. Sprat quotes Mr. Clifford as affirming that the *Davideis*—a rhymed epic still infinitely readable—was the work of his undergraduate youth in Cambridge; and in the same period he entertained, with his comedy *The Guardian*, a prince of the blood. In the Prologue to this piece,[1] We perish, he says, rather wittily,

> We perish if the roundheads be about;
> For now no ornament the head must wear,
> No bays, no mitre, not so much as hair.

The roundheads *were* about; and he had scarcely taken his master's degree when, ejected from Cambridge, he found a

[1] Though not in the first edition of it.

refuge in St. John's College, Oxford. In Oxford, he enjoyed the friendship of Falkland, and the favour of the
Queen. The Queen was housed in Merton; and a royal
rescript gave the wardenship of that college for a brief
term to Cowley's friend, the great Dr. Harvey. In Merton
there still hangs a portrait of Cowley;[1] and in the library
is a copy of Cowley's works presented by Almesius Cowley,
whom I suppose to have been some near relative of the
poet. From Oxford, Cowley followed the Queen into her
French exile; and in France, for some twelve years, conducted the correspondence of the exiled court. In 1656
he returned to England; and was, for no good reason, put
in prison, and, for not much better, released and made a
Doctor of Medicine in the University of Oxford. At the
Restoration, he was denied, what two kings had promised
him, the mastership of the Savoy. From these tragedies,
he took refuge in comedy, adapting *The Guardian*, that
success of his youth, to a stage failure which he called
Cutter of Coleman Street. 'It may truly be applied to
poets', he says, in the Preface to his Poems, 'which St. Paul
speaks of the first Christians, If their reward be in this
life, they are of all men most miserable.' Having medi-
tated retiring to the American plantations, he contented
himself with a poetical solitude in Surrey, and an income
obtained through the interest of Buckingham. In 1667 he
was buried in Westminster Abbey, between Chaucer and
the master of his poetical youth, Spenser; and a prince,
who had neglected him while he lived, was pleased to say
over his grave that 'he had not left a better man in
England'.

   The lacunae which chance has left in this narrative may
be measured by the variety of change which it records in
Cowley's circumstances, and by his constant nearness to
great affairs and what passed for great men. These vicissitudes, and this contact with the world's business, are
thus far important that they remind us of what Johnson

   [1] It was discovered, in the nineteenth century, hidden in the ceiling of
a cellar belonging to a set of rooms at present occupied by myself.

comes near to forgetting: Cowley's poetry, deeply rooted
as it is, as most of the metaphysical poetry is, in books and
thinking, is yet a poetry which has, in fact, stood in the
winds of life. Of English poets, only Chaucer and Milton
have been so nearly mixed with the political life of their
time. Exile, and war, and bonds, and the ingratitude of
kings—all these Cowley had known, and most of them he
seems to have borne in a spirit singularly philosophical.
To the casual student of life and poetry, they will seem
to have affected his writings hardly at all. To Johnson
his poetry seemed unreal and perverse; and both, from
bookishness. But is not that to give to circumstance less
consequence than there is warrant for? Is it books, or life,
that has conducted Cowley to a sense of life's unreality?
Did he live twelve years in the Paris of Louis Quatorze,
and leave it to Pindar to teach him that life was a 'dream
of a shadow'? Does this poetry of whimsical surprise,
of 'starts of wit', of preposterous juxtaposition of images,
fetch nothing from the social and political effects of the
time? Is it in complete independence of one another that
his verse and fortune are alike so tiresomely ingenious? It
is not the highest employment of poetry to make fantastic
patterns out of fragments of coloured glass; but life itself
might seem to furnish to Cowley both analogue and
excuse.

Of the metaphysical poets, Dr. Johnson derives the
manner from Marino, the author of the *Adone*. Wit lies
in point. If a good line, like a straight one, is the shortest
distance between any two points, even so this world-
without-end epic—it runs to 40,000 lines—may be
thought to travel slow; and for myself, I should be sorry
to begin it, and certain never to end it. But, as later
writers have properly observed, the metaphysical wit is,
in fact, a manner as wide as the world. 'It began to be
fashionable', says Dr. Courthope, 'in almost every European
country about the time of the Council of Trent.' Thus
to carry back its beginnings beyond the beginnings of our
modern poetry is perhaps to indulge the study of develop-

ment beyond what is really helpful—and, in Courthope, a
defect which makes the best of what he writes seem always
less good than it is. The truth is that paradox, hyperbole, and the riot of fantastic analogy we have always with
us; and instead of searching too widely into the laws by
which, at particular seasons, these come to dominate literature in a fashion almost exclusive, it is simpler to note
that, in our own poetry, the period of their dominance
lies between the top achievements of the romantic
imagination and the beginnings of the Age of Reason,
between Shakespeare and Dryden: an interim period, of
which, as of other middle ages, a marked character is the
emergence of an—often trivial—dialectic. A good deal of
mystery has been made over the 'metaphysical' poets; and
the number and nature of them alike seems still to elude
inquiry. Dr. Johnson finds eight of them (including, even
so, Ben Jonson and Milton).[1] Professor Grierson recog-
nizes, dispensing with Ben Jonson, as many as twenty;
Dr. Courthope brings them down to one—for him Donne
alone has 'metaphysical' wit; to the others he allows 'theological Wit' (a thing we had not thought possible) or
'court Wit', in the various species of each. I like best this
limited class-list, with one name only among the 'firsts'.

[1] Johnson, mentioning Milton among the 'metaphysicals', qualifies what
he says by the statement that he is metaphysical only in the lines on
Hobson. This can hardly pass. The lines on Hobson, playing as they do
with words rather than with thoughts, are less metaphysical than much
else in Milton's earlier pieces. Mr. Grierson, in his selection from the
metaphysical poets, has quite properly included, not only the Nativity
Ode, but the lines on Shakespeare. Where shall we find metaphysical verse
if we do not find it in

> Only with speeches fair
> She woo's the gentle Air
>   To hide her guilty front with innocent Snow,
> And on her naked shame,
> Pollute with sinfull blame,
>   The Saintly Vail of Maiden white to throw,
> Confounded, that her Makers eyes
> Should look so neer upon her foul deformities—

and again in the concluding verses of the lines on Shakespeare?

It was not the habit of Dr. Johnson to make mysteries; and the mystery of the metaphysical poets, though it is often enough put at his door, is, in fact, none of his making. He happened to be in fashion when Dryden was out of it; and in the Life of Cowley he gave to a chance phrase of Dryden a perpetuity to which, upon merits, it had, I think, not much title. Speaking of Donne, Dryden had said: 'He affects the metaphysics, not only in his satires, but in his amorous verses, where nature alone should reign; and perplexes the minds of the fair sex with nice speculations of philosophy, when he should engage their hearts, and entertain them with the softnesses of love. In this . . . Mr. Cowley has copied him to a fault.'[1] Now Donne may be called metaphyscial in almost any of the senses in which the word can be used. The ground-colour of his mind is scholastic—to a degree which makes intelligible the dictum that metaphysical 'wit' is 'Jesuitism in art'.[2] But when you come to Cowley, not only have you passed out of medievalism, but you are in the very world of Hobbes and the Royal Society. Donne, of course, engages himself to give everywhere to the expression of passion a dialectical form, and his favourite form of reasoning is the analogical—the more he reasons, the further he fetches his analogies. In this—and in diction—the other metaphysicals imitate him. But here and here only are they his disciples, and 'metaphysical' at all. Dryden is thinking, above all, of the dialectics of the amorous, or pretended amorous, temperament; and it is worth observing, in passing, how closely connected these are with the new diction. How much the love-poetry of the Elizabethans strains after merely verbal point, even Shakespeare may instruct us. For verbal point the 'metaphysicals' substitute what may be called intellectual point; they twist, not words, but thoughts. There they were doing

[1] *Original and Progress of Satire*, ed. Ker, ii, p. 19. Mr. Nichol Smith points out to me that, in 1734-6, Pope spoke of Cowley's ' metaphysical style ' (Spence, *Anecdotes*, p. 173, Singer, 1820).
[2] See Courthope, *Hist. of Eng. Poetry*, iii, p. 105 (1917).

better than they knew; and when we have tired of the paradoxes of their thinking, we catch them out being greater, perhaps, than they bargained for—and certainly in a different kind, in the plain kind. That not merely love-poetry, but poetry, should want its diction, Dr. Johnson could not bear; and that love-poetry should first want diction, and then have dialectic, seemed to Dryden a double offence. The degree to which 'the fair sex' desire to be entertained, in poetry, only 'with the softnesses of love', it is hard for mere men to gauge. To use upon them dialectic is, on the face of it, to presume in them an intellectual equality with men; but of a dialectic of which everywhere the principal instruments are paradox, hyperbole, and licentious analogy the motive easily becomes suspect. Does it speak to women's hearts through their heads, or, cynically, over them? To Donne, I fancy, this extravagance of dialectic was of the very nature of the love-passion—male and female, flesh and spirit, and all other antitheses, meet and mix in his seething cauldron of paradoxes, his witches' pot of hyperbolical experimentation.

Dr. Johnson's account of the metaphysical wit is at least spirited and characteristic. 'It was about the time of Cowley', he says, 'that wit, which had till then been used for intellection, took the meaning, whatever it be, which it now bears.' It is a meaning, he goes on to say, different from that which, in a later age, Pope gave to it, when he described it as 'that which has been often thought, but was never before so well expressed'. The poets of the school of Cowley 'endeavoured to be singular in their thoughts, and careless in their diction'. 'If,' he continues, 'if by a more noble and adequate conception, that be considered as wit which is at once natural and new, that which, though not obvious, is, upon its first production, acknowledged to be just; if it be that which he that never found it, wonders how he missed; to wit of this kind the metaphysical poets have seldom risen. Their thoughts are often new, but seldom natural; they are not obvious, but neither are they just; and the reader, far from wondering that he missed them, wonders more frequently by what perverseness of ingenuity they were ever found.' The wit of the metaphysicals Johnson finds to consist in the 'discovery of occult resemblances between things apparently unlike'. 'The most heterogeneous ideas', he says, 'are yoked by violence together; nature and art are ransacked for illustrations, comparisons, and allusions; their learning instructs, and their subtlety surprises; but the reader commonly thinks his improvement dearly bought; and though he sometimes admires, is seldom pleased.'

Jane Austen said that Johnson was never clever. Yet how clever is all this, and at the same time how Johnsonian! The limitations of it, however, are, or ought to be, obvious. I am not sure there is all that degree of distinction which Johnson supposes between Pope's idea of 'wit' and his own 'nobler and more adequate' conception of it. But I am sure that there are ranges of wit which neither description covers. Of the wit of the metaphysicals Johnson's analysis is acute, and the quiet malice of some of it yet leaves much of it true. Grant the whole of it true. Does it follow that there is no place in poetry for wit of this kind, and that, where we meet it, its surprising subtlety draws admiration without giving pleasure? Grant the whole of it true, of course, we cannot. The truth of it is impaired by the typical eighteenth-century dogma that it is the business of poetry to have just ideas; and further impaired by the error of referring too many of the ingenuities of the metaphysicals to the operation of the intellect, of the intellect working almost mechanically towards a result the opposite to what is expected, as though the mechanical mind might escape being a machine by putting its engine into reverse. At least of Cowley, it would be truer to conceive the poetry as obeying whim the most unpredictable—whim only so far predictable as it follows a temperament endlessly and amiably ingenious.

The fact is that poetry must be taken as it comes; and

when you have catalogued all its known qualities and relations, you are likely to be taken unawares by a poetry
which is innocent of any of them. Dr. Johnson liked the
poetry of plain sailing; and the metaphysicals do not sail
plain. They have no commerce upon the great trade
routes; but they catch at every breeze of whim; seeking
no harbour they carry a light curiosity into every cranny
of coast, with whatever intricacies cumbered; they delight
to be tossed by fancies the most perverse, and to moor, if
they moor, in pedantic surprise. If you want to get somewhere—and Johnson always did—you will ship by some
other line. But if you think that life is long enough and
fantastic enough, and that curiosity and the wilful have
a place in poetry, there is worse, and more tedious, company than that of the metaphysicals.

It is rather learned company, it is true; and the learning
is often perversely misapplied. This learned wilfulness, let
us agree, can find excuse only in some quality of heart;
and if the metaphysicals do in truth want that, then they
are wanting in almost everything. I am concerned here
only with Cowley—I should be sorry, for example, to
be concerned with Cleveland. Pope, whom Cowley's
'pointed wit', his epic, and his Pindarics, alike tired, yet
found in him 'the language of the heart'.

> If he pleases yet
> His moral pleases, not his pointed wit:
> Forgot his epic, nay Pindaric, art,
> But still I love the language of his heart.

What Pope loved was what Wordsworth liked in
Cowley—his essential amiability. Pope is not thinking
of Cowley's amatory verse. It would in any case be
absurd to suggest that the once so much admired *Mistress*
of Cowley has all, or most, of the qualities which may
be expected from a volume of amatory pieces; or that
Cowley is a poet who, upon a subject which has powerfully exercised poetry from all time, the passion of
love, speaks either with authority or with any very compelling power. His Venus, Dr. Sprat says, oddly but

truly, has 'the salt but not the froth of the sea'. Nor
do I suppose, leaving aside *The Mistress*, that the other
tragic, or grand, affections of our nature, nor the great
events of human history, nor the aspects, sweet or severe,
of the external world, have been delineated by him with
any singular force or convincing truth. He had a nature
neither passionate nor brave; though why, from poetry
alone of the professions, we demand so insistently heroic
quality, insisting that the poet should be either an arch-
angel or a fallen angel, it would perhaps be difficult to say.
But Cowley was, what we need not disparage even in poetry,
he was what Wordsworth, in all simplicity, calls him, an
amiable man; and I do not know where we shall easily find
another poet who mixes the same degree of amiability with
equal art—with so much ingenuity of ideas and so great
variety in the expression of them. Let us add Johnson's
rather grudging praise, I will not say of his originality,
but of his first-handness. 'No man', Johnson says truly,
'could be born a metaphysical poet, nor assume the dignity
of a writer, by descriptions copied from descriptions, by
traditional imagery, and hereditary similes'—all the arts,
that is, that Wordsworth alleges against Dryden and Pope.
—'It was at least necessary to read and think.' Denham
says of him, to much the same effect,

> To him no author was unknown,
> Yet what he wrote was all his own.

Johnson liked the thought of poetry to be just; and if
that is essential to it, certainly Cowley is not a poet. His
poetry owes much, truly, to reading and thinking; but its
thinking is the least just conceivable, and at least as
whimsical as poetry has ever title to be. I suppose indeed
that Cowley saw, what Johnson missed, that a poetry bred
of reading and thinking ceases, in the act of being just, to
be poetry; it becomes, what no poetry can be, dull. Such
a poetry has to save itself out of this, its proper peril; and
the most obvious means by which it can do so imports
a new peril. Ingenuity can save it out of dullness; but it

still runs the risk of being tiresome. Dull, let it be said, frankly, Cowley sometimes is; and more often he is tiresome. But that he is often neither, he owes, not merely to his art, but to nature, to his pervasive amiability, his gentleness and humanness. His cleverness is nearly always sympathetic, his ingenuity, however perverse, kindly; where he is most provocative, he retains his gentleness. In his more recondite figures, or in most of them, the cleverness is still, whatever Johnson may say, of a kind in which you may cry halves; he is not 'superior'.

That Cowley lacks passion, it wants neither judgement to see, nor words to emphasize. If any one seeks from *The Mistress* those deeper qualities which redeem from all their faults the 'Songs and Sonnets' of Donne, he must expect disappointment. Nor are the qualities which he will discover in this collection equally distributed over the whole of it. Of the pieces in it Dr. Johnson has said that 'they have all the same beauties and faults, and nearly in the same proportion', yet it would be almost as true to call Wordsworth a level writer as to ascribe to *The Mistress* a level excellence. If a man would do for Cowley the best service he could (and one which his merits deserve) he would first annul, from the eighty-eight pieces which compose this collection, a little less than three-quarters of them; the twenty to thirty which remained would at least explain to a world in which Cowley is no longer read why he was once read with eagerness. Even then, it would be well to return to the sixty-odd rejects, and save out of them the occasional perfect stanzas which diversify Cowley's duller parts— often the architectonic ambition of Cowley will not look beyond the stanza. *The Soul* is a poem which runs to three long stanzas, but it had better have ended with the first:

> If mine Eyes do e're declare
> They've seen a second thing that 's fair;
> Or Ears that they have Musick found,
> Besides thy voice, in any Sound;
> If my Tast do ever meet,

After thy Kiss, with ought that's sweet;
If my abused Touch allow
Ought to be smooth, or soft, but Thou;
If, what seasonable Springs,
Or the Eastern Summer brings,
Do my Smell persuade at all,
Ought Perfume, but thy Breath to call;
If my Senses Objects be
Not contracted into Thee,
And so through Thee more powerful pass,
As Beams do through a Burning-glass;
If all things that in Nature are
Either soft or sweet or fair,
Be not in Thee so Epitomized,
That nought material's there comprized,
May I as worthless seem to Thee
As all, but Thou, appears to me.

This may not be the greatest poetry; but it is at least pleasing and effective in a class which it is better to note than to number. Take, again, this, from *Resolved to Love*:

If learn'd in other things you be,
    And have in Love no skill,
For God's sake keep your Arts from me,
    For I'll be ignorant still.
Study or Action others may embrace;
My Love's my business, and my books her Face:

or this, from *Counsel*:

What new-found Rhetorick is thine?
    Ev'n thy dissuasions me persuade,
And thy great power does clearest shine
    When thy commands are disobeyed.
In vain thou bidst me to forbear;
Obedience were rebellion here.

Poets who give us this kind of verse among their failures hardly deserve that we should not attend to their successes. And, as in Wordsworth, so too in Cowley, I may add, very often, not a perfect stanza, but a perfect couplet startles us in a series of otherwise uninspired verses. Who, for example, ever said of the lover's pains anything more adequate than

> My pains resemble hell in this;
> The Divine Presence there too is—?   (*The Thief.*)

If Johnson's judgement upon *The Mistress* is not to be trusted, he is happier in the selection of those poems which he chooses for special praise from the *Miscellanies*. 'Such an assemblage of diversified excellence', he writes, 'no other poet has hitherto afforded. To choose the best among many good is one of the most hazardous attempts of criticism.' 'The ode on Wit', he goes on, 'is almost without a rival . . . the Chronicle is a composition un-rivalled and alone: such gaiety of fancy, such facility of expression, such varied similitude, such a succession of images, and such a dance of words, it is vain to expect except from Cowley.' This is generous praise, and in respect of these two pieces, I fancy, exaggerated. Even so Johnson must needs speak slightingly of what all the world besides has agreed to regard as Cowley's masterpiece, the verses *On the Death of Mr. William Harvey*. It is true that, in the essay upon Milton, he praises the poem, in comparison with *Lycidas*; but the amends are shabby, since, in *Lycidas*, as everybody knows, he was bold to affirm that there was 'no nature . . . no truth . . . no art . . . nothing new'. Elegy can, perhaps, come into being only by some sacrifice of nature to art; and a prudent criticism may content itself with saying, of Cowley's poem, that of the four great elegies in our language, this alone is free from pastoral and mythological convention; this alone seems to commemorate a purely human friendship. The best of it is given in almost any anthology of our poetry; but the whole of it in none that I know; yet it is suffi-ciently great that we can bear with its less perfect stanzas. Seven out of nineteen stanzas are excluded from the *Oxford Book of English Verse*, and eleven from the *Golden Treasury*. What quality in it has deprived it of a place in Mrs. Meynell's *The Flower of the Mind*, I do not

know. To Mrs. Meynell's book we may at least be grateful that it finds room for the lines *On the Death of
Mr. Crashaw*, though that there, even so, Mrs. Meynell
should excise, in particular, a passage which Pope thought
it worth his while to imitate, is one of those circumstances
which bring mockery on the art of the anthologist.

> His faith perhaps in some nice tenents might
> Be wrong; his life (I'm sure) was in the right,

says Cowley; and Pope's echo of it has passed into a
proverb:

> For modes of faith let graceless zealots fight;
> His can't be wrong whose life is in the right.

Perhaps grief should be less epigrammatic than Cowley
has, in this poem, managed to be; but he at least instructs
us that epigram can be more feeling than we had supposed.
Did ever either Dryden or Pope excel, or match, the
felicity of

> Whilst angels sing to thee their airs divine,
> And joy in an applause so great as thine,
> Equal society with them to hold,
> Thou needst not make new songs, but say the old—?

In this poem Dr. Johnson has justly said that 'there are
beauties which common authors may justly think not only
above their attainment, but above their ambition'. It was
from Cowley, we may note in passing, that Dryden and
later poets learned to variegate the heroic line with
Alexandrines; and it is perhaps not too much to say that
neither Dryden nor any one else introduces the variant
with better judgement. I would even go beyond this.
Though Johnson, with his inveterate prejudice against
'irregular' verses, has hazarded the conjecture that Cowley's versification 'seems to have had very little of his care',
I am disposed to think that in his 'irregular' odes Cowley
has disposed verses of varying length with a surer instinct
than most poets.

I do not mean, when I say this, to place Cowley's
Pindarique Odes upon that pinnacle of repute to which

contemporary opinion lifted them. To Johnson the best part of the *Pindarique Odes* was the learning of the prose notes which accompany them. Such criticism claims notice only for the greatness of its author; and has its counterpart, perhaps, only in the dictum of Matthew Arnold, that Shelley's letters were better literature than his poetry. That the Pindaric Odes are very much like Pindar, I take leave to doubt; and though Cowley said a great thing when he said that 'if a man should undertake to translate Pindar word for word, it would be thought that one madman had translated another'—though that is true and salutary, I do not persuade myself that Cowley understood the character either of Pindar's verse or of his genius. Had he done so, could he have opened his *Praise of Pindar* after this fashion:

> Pindar is imitable by none;
> The Phoenix Pindar is a vast species alone—?

Such an exordium is not redeemed even by the dignity which characterizes the third stanza of the poem:

> Whether at Pisa's race he please
> To carve in polisht verse the Conqueror's images,
> Whether the swift, the skilful or the strong,
> Be crowned in his nimble artful vigorous song:
> Whether some brave young man's untimely fate
> In words worth dying for he celebrate,
> Such mournful and such pleasing words
> As joy to his mother's and his mistress' grief affords:
> He bids him live and grow in fame,
> Among the stars he sticks his name:
> The grave can but the dross of him devour,
> So small is death's, so great the poet's power.

The stanza gathers greatness as it grows; but even so, it is not Pindar's greatness; and its finest effect it owes to the Saxon plainness of the line

> Among the stars he sticks his name.

Yet I can hear Johnson calling the diction there defective in 'elegance'.

Among the more readable Odes, I should be inclined to place *Life and Fame*. Built out of two memorable phrases of Pindar, it is yet not only not Pindaric, but of these very phrases it has annulled the Pindaric character. Here is the opening stanza:

> O Life, thou Nothing's younger brother,
> So like that one might take one for the other!
> What 's somebody or nobody?
> In all the cobwebs of the schoolmen's trade
> We no such nice distinctions woven see
> As 'tis To be and not To be.
> Dream of a shadow! a reflection made
> From the false glories of the gay reflected bow
> Is a more solid thing than Thou.
> Vain weak-built Isthmus which dost proudly rise
> Up betwixt two eternities;
> Yet canst nor wave nor wind sustain,
> But broken and o'erwhelmed, the endless oceans meet again.

'The gay reflected bow' is just 'poetic diction'. But the rest has, at least, the impressiveness of plain English. In another of the Odes, Cowley speaks of the angels as of beings

Who all the nonsense of our language see,
Who speak things, and our words, their ill-formed picture, scorn.

Whatever nonsense there is in the Odes—and there is a good deal—there is less of 'the nonsense of our language' in them than in any of the Odes that imitate them—that is, all Odes. For here, be it remembered, is a species which, historically considered,[1] has no other father than Cowley; nor could anything better illustrate the injustice of the neglect upon which he has fallen. This is not to call the Odes great, or, save in their repercussions upon later poetry, successful; nor even to deny that they mostly want, what Pindar never wants, nobility, and that they frequently have, what should perhaps never appear in this species, cleverness. Yet if there shall ever be an ode in 'plain English', it will derive its lineage from Cowley. Coleridge alone of our odists—and he with many divaga-

[1] By which I mean that the Ode in English poetry owes little to Jonson.

tions—has employed in the Ode the same approximation
to the diction of real life.

Only of the *Davideis*, among Cowley's poems, has Dr.
Johnson said, in general, no more, and no less, than what
is just. Some of his detailed criticism may fairly be can-
vassed. Of the stone with which Cain slew Abel, Cowley
says, in the first book of the *Davideis*:

> I saw him fling the stone, as if he meant
> At once his murder and his monument.

That is what I would call *good Popian*: it is at any rate an
effective conceit. To contrast it as Johnson does, unfavourably, with the lines of Vergil which describe the
stone hurled by Turnus at Aeneas, is to misunderstand
the business of criticism, which can never consist in comparing incomparables. Again, in the lines, from the same
book, which introduce the description of the underworld:

> Beneath the silent chambers of the earth,
> Where the sun's fruitful beams give metals birth,
> Where he the growth of fatal gold does see,
> Gold which alone more influence has than he,

the 'polluting conceit' of the last couplet offends not only
Johnson but any rules that we can conceive for epic. But
the conceit is, in itself, good enough, and arresting, and
entertaining. The *Davideis* is not epic, any more than the
Pindaric odes are Pindaric. But a wise criticism will take
its good things as they come; and if only for its digression
upon the power of 'numbers' (sects. 33–9), and its description of the college of the Prophets (sects. 46 sqq.), the
first book of the *Davideis* still repays reading. To what
species of composition it truly belongs, matters less than
that it is everywhere readable, and sometimes poetry. I
do not know how, if Pope himself had wished to depict
the prophet Gad teaching geometry and arithmetic, he
could have done it better than Cowley does:

> The prophet Gad in learned dust designs
> The immortal solid rules of fancied lines;
> Of numbers too the unnumbered wealth he shows,
> And with them far their endless journey goes.

Upon the whole, I am satisfied with Johnson, who, after enumerating the many faults of this youthful epic, concludes: 'Still, however, it is the work of Cowley, of a mind capacious by nature, and replenished by study.'

The weakest work of Cowley is to be found in that section of his poems to which he gave the title *Verses Written on Several Occasions*. Many of the occasions were not happy, that is to say, not inspiring. I should suppose it to have been as difficult in Cowley's day to write an Ode to the Royal Society as it would be in our own to write one to the British Association; and hardly more easy to explain in verse (as Cowley did) Harvey's theory of the circulation of the blood than to make poetry— or prose either—of the doctrine of Relativity. Upon the *King's Return to England* and the *Queen's Repairing to Somerset House* Cowley has just so much to say (and it is always too much) as might be expected of a poet who has one eye upon his art and the other upon the mastership of the Savoy. The best of these pieces are the Ode 'Sitting and Drinking in Drake's Chair' in the Bodleian, and the *Hymn to Light*; and of these the first will be thought, by an exacting criticism, a little forced in its jocundity, the second less free and perspicuous than is warranted by so liberating a theme.

I began by asking, with Pope, Who now reads Cowley? and I do not know that I have got much further than discovering that I am still able to do so myself with pleasure. I am not disposed to speak of him with proselytizing fervour. He is still a name rather greater than, from his fall from fashion, seems natural; a Peter Schlemihl of our poetry, a substantial reputation which has lost that shadow of greatness, a public. Something of what he has lost he may some day regain. But in respect of much that was best in him, he will have only a vicarious immortality. He is a great and early master of 'plain English'; yet he wanted perhaps that kind of greatness which can sanctify paradoxical canons, and he left it to Wordsworth to finish here with the insistency of genius what he himself essayed with somewhat indolent talent. What we call the Ode, again, is in the main Cowley's creation; yet both the eighteenth and the nineteenth century have carried what they learned from him (whether directly or indirectly) to perfections which he cannot match. Yet again, he more than any one else familiarized in our poetry that quality which we denote by the terms point, brilliance, wit, and the like. The best of our recent poets has not disdained, here and in other things, to learn from him.[1] Yet his technique has less energy, his thought less masculinity than Dryden's; nor does he attain the supernatural neatness and deftness of Pope. It may be none the less that his more genuine humanity will one day place him in a position not far below either of these two poets. Devoted enthusiasts he will never have—Dryden and Pope, somehow, have. He will never, like Donne, be the object of an esoteric cult. He will never again be—where Milton put him—third in our list of poets. It will perhaps suffice that he continue on the list at all.

[1] See the lecture upon Rupert Brooke, p. 169.

THE NIGHTINGALE IN POETRY

'No mere egg-snatcher has ever written poetry, nor is he ever likely to do so.'—E. W. HENDY, *The Lure of Bird Watching.*

THE days are past—or I suppose they are—when a poet might sit in his garden in London and listen, like Keats, to the Nightingale. Yet London, it may be assumed, contains to-day more poets to the square yard than ever before in its history. No doubt, it is easier for them than it was a hundred years ago to go afield for their nightingales; and in the poetry of some of them I have seemed to myself to notice a real love, and knowledge, of bird-life. Re-reading recently Keats's great Ode, I was led to reflect on the place of the Nightingale in poetry; in our own poetry especially; and to wonder what degree of first-hand knowledge, what results of loving observation, the poets generally brought to a bird of whom most of them have something to say. That some good poets have been bad naturalists I knew; and I was prepared not to think much the worse of them for that. Nearly fifty years ago Mr. Phil Robinson[1] took all the birds and all the poets—or at any rate, the commoner British birds and the commonly read British poets—and amused himself by being very learned about the former and rather spiteful about the latter. Some palpable hits he certainly makes. I was not much concerned, it is true, to be told that Wordsworth did not know that a sand-lark and a dotterel are one and the same. Certainly, he ought to have known; for the Lake District is one of the few parts of England where the dotterel breeds. Wordsworth, I am afraid, does certainly call the ringdove a stockdove.[2] Even so, he is to my mind hardly so absurd as Mr. Robinson, who, provoked by these and like lapses, tells us that 'if the doves could ever read English poetry, they would put their tongues in

[1] *The Poets' Birds*, by Phil Robinson; London, Chatto & Windus, 1883.
[2] On some other lapses in this great poet, see below, p. 158.

their cheeks and wink at each other, and the worse-conditioned of them would explode with laughter'. Sallies of wit so oddly laboured hardly assist either poetry or ornithology. Everybody knows, again, that the singing Nightingale is frequently conceived, in poetry, as a female bird. Given the mythology that she has—or *he* has—it would be odd if it were otherwise.[1] But nothing pleases Mr. Robinson; and when Mallet, a bad poet of the eighteenth century, whose principal merit is to have been a friend of Thomson, and his worst crime to have been suspected of writing the National Anthem—when Mallet does his best to please by speaking of 'Philomela's song—his evening lay', Mr. Robinson will have none of this hermaphrodite nightingale, but arraigns Mallet's 'excess of poetical audacity'.

A disposition to slap the faces of naughty poets may be noticed occasionally in a more recent and much more likable book, Mr. Massingham's *Poems about Birds*.[2] I do not know why this book is not better known. I could spare some of its notes. Of Shelley's *Skylark*, for example, Mr. Massingham writes that 'It is strange that this poem maintains so bright a fame. The silver cord of the lyric is loosened and the golden bowl is broken. . . . The poem only stays alive, in fact, by the matchless beauty of detached stanzas, which might be hitched on to any other poetic wagon, trundling after its star.' That kind of note seems to me unnecessarily provocative; and the book, a most delightful anthology of Bird Poems, perhaps hardly wanted notes at all. Mr. Massingham was afraid, he says, of making his book too long. He has not done that. But I miss some poems which I should have liked to find in it, and I should not have missed the notes.

Mr. Massingham's book takes in all birds. But his night-

[1] I say nothing of the fact that the ancient naturalists—both Aristotle and Pliny—make the female bird sing. Mr. Robinson ridicules Campbell for making a nightingale sing in an apple-tree: but without any justice, I think.

[2] *Poems about Birds*: Chosen and edited by H. J. Massingham, with a Preface by J. C. Squire. London, Fisher Unwin, 1922.

ingales hardly sing, or do not become individual in their
singing, before the age of Elizabeth; and I do not like to
think of that age as the Golden Age of the Nightingale.
In no period is he more vocal. But in no period so wailful.
Mr. Massingham himself, it should be said, is no friend
of the 'wailful' Nightingale. Speaking of it, he says, more
bluntly perhaps than there was need, that 'in such nature-
poetry there is no more poetry than nature; it is pro-
fessionalism, exploiting stale odds and ends to poetic copy,
and the product not of reality and imagination but of
false sentiment'. It is a pity, accordingly, that he could
not spare space to illustrate from medieval poetry the
'mery nightingale' who 'did her might' to 'singen blithe'
not merely in the Merry England of Chaucer, but as early
as the reign of King John. This 'merry' bird, no doubt,
flew to us from France. But she flew to a folk ready to
receive her for what she was, and not in the least disposed
to think of her as a wailing and 'waymenting' creature.
She stayed in England for long after Chaucer; and I suspect—what no reader of Mr. Massingham's book will
guess—that the fourteenth and fifteenth centuries were
the period of our poetry in which this bird, and others,
were best known and loved.

The Nightingale in poetry begins where poetry begins;
that is to say, with Homer. Penelope, in one of the later
books of the *Odyssey*, asks Ulysses to interpret a dream
for her. 'Yet one little thing, Stranger',[1] she says, 'will
I ask of you; for soon it will be the hour for pleasant
rest—for those, at least, to whom sweet sleep comes
despite their sorrows. But to me a god has given grief
unmeasurable. For in the days I have joy in lamentation
and mourning, looking blankly at my tasks and the tasks
of my women in the house. But when night comes, and
rest comes over all men, I lie on my bed, and carking cares
crowd about my troubled heart, and I mourn. Even as
when the daughter of Pandareus, the Nightingale that
loves the green woods, sings, when the spring is new-set,

[1] 'Stranger', because she does not know that she is speaking to her husband.

her lovely song, sitting among the countless leaves of the trees; with ever various note she pours forth her far-heard voice, wailing for Itylus, her son, whom she slew in ignorance, the son of King Zethus.'

Homer calls the Nightingale by a name which, in the Greek, is synonymous with poetry itself and the poet. The *aēdon* is the 'singer',[1] and once or twice in Greek poetry the songs which the poet sings are called, prettily, his 'nightingales'. Even those who have no Greek will know this use of 'nightingales' for 'songs' from Cory's translation of Callimachus's epitaph on Heraclitus:

They told me, Heraclitus, they told me you were dead,
They brought me bitter news to hear and bitter tears to shed.
I wept, as I remembered how often you and I
Had tired the sun with talking and sent him down the sky.

And now that thou art lying, my dear old Carian guest,
A handful of grey ashes, long long ago at rest,
Still are thy pleasant voices, *thy nightingales*, awake,
For death he taketh all away, but them he cannot take.

But this same word, *aēdon*, which means 'singer' and 'song', has an accidental likeness to some other Greek words, of quite different meaning and origin; words which convey the notion of 'joyless', 'pleasureless'; and as early as Homer, we may suppose, the Nightingale, or singer, had become confused with the 'joyless' creature; the *aēdon* with the *a-hedon*—with the creature void of all *hedon*istic aptitudes. As early as Homer, again, the Nightingale had forfeited the privileges of the male sex. Homer's singing Nightingale is, in defiance of natural history, female. To the later Greek poets her femininity was so pronounced that they found it necessary, as you know, to cut out her tongue.

There are those who will tell you that Homer, just as he knew neither the joyousness of the Nightingale's song, nor the sex of the singer, was also ignorant of the appear-

---

[1] Bacchylides speaks of himself—in contrast with Pindar, the Theban eagle—as 'the Cean nightingale'.

ance of the bird. When he speaks, as I think he does, of 'the nightingale that loves the green woods', they, taking differently one Greek word, make him speak of 'the green' (or 'green-throated') 'nightingale'. The ground for that is that another Greek poet, not so great as Homer, yet one of the great poets, Simonides, certainly does call the Nightingale 'green-throated'. He calls her, moreover— though on the subject of sex he does not commit himself —'full of chatter'. I may so far at least defend him as to urge that his 'green-throated' Nightingale is not more absurd than the 'tawny-throated' Nightingale of a modern poet of whom I had hoped better things.

> Hark! ah, the nightingale,
> The tawny-throated!

That is Matthew Arnold [1]; and when I say that I had hoped better things of him, perhaps I say too much: for (if Mr. Massingham is right) in one of the most beautiful stanzas of *Thyrsis*, he has shown himself oddly ignorant of the habits of a much humbler bird, committing himself to the belief that the Cuckoo migrates in June.

We must think twice before we pick holes in Homer; and I will not complain, therefore, that the first poet to speak of the Nightingale takes her out of nature into mythology. Homer could not know what was going to happen; he could not guess that his Nightingale mourning for Itylus was destined through nearly three thousand years of poetry to repeat herself so often as to forfeit sympathy. I say 'his Nightingale'; but I ought to add at once that the Itylus legend which Homer knows is a different legend from that with which we are most familiar. Homer's story comes to him from Asia Minor. Though he speaks of Itylus, he knows nothing of King Pandion, of Tereus, and Philomela and Procne. These personages, so familiar to us from the Elizabethans and their successors,

---

[1] Matthew Arnold was misled, I suppose, by Aristophanes, who in the *Birds* (212–14) speaks of the Nightingale pouring her complaint ἱεροῖς μέλεσιν γένυος ξουθῆς. But γένυς means there, not *throat*, but *bill*. Elsewhere in the same play (744) *all* the birds are credited with a γένυς ξουθή.

have, it is true, a respectable antiquity; for their story, or parts of it, must have been known to Hesiod and to Sappho. The legend as we know it best is a combination of several independent traditions, achieving its final form in Attica. It was the Attic story which Ovid versified in the *Metamorphoses*; and this Attic version the Elizabethans took from Ovid.

In the Choruses of Attic tragedy the Nightingale is the stock symbol of unassuaged grief; a symbol often beautiful and effective. But outside Attic tragedy[1] she hardly has a place in Greek literature. Especially do we miss her from contexts where she is very familiar in modern poetry. A fragment of Sappho speaks of 'the Nightingale, herald of the spring, whose voice is the voice of desire'. But save for what we may conjecture from the isolated beauty of this one line, I can recall no passage of Greek poetry where the Nightingale is associated with the hopes of lovers.[2] The swallow has her place among these associations; and the dove. But the whole body of verse that goes by the name of Anacreon yields, I fancy, no single mention of the Nightingale. Once again, though more than one poet makes the song of the Nightingale a type of the music of grief, yet I can think of only one who seems to have a pure personal delight in the Nightingale's singing—Aristophanes. It appears in more than one passage of that most delightful of his comedies, the *Birds*. Let me give you an example—in such English notes as I am capable of:

> Nightingale, awake,
> Bride of my soul, and shake
> Slumber off; and once more ringing
> The never-enough-rung dirge of Itys,
> Pour from lips whose grief delight is
> The unmatched magic of thy singing.

[1] The Philomela story was dramatized by Sophocles in the *Tereus*, a play which Aristophanes makes fun of in the *Birds*; and a later tragedian, Philocles, devoted to it a whole tetralogy (a quartette of plays).

[2] I cannot vouch for it that the Greek Anthology does not furnish something in this sort. But I have not had the heart to search; and at the moment I recall nothing.

> Hark! from those dim bowers of bryony
> Pure it issues: hark! on high, on high,
> Surging. Golden-haired Apollo
> Hears and starts and, fain to follow,
> Wakes on his ivory-pointed lyre
> Strains responsive; while the Choir
> Immortal rise; whose feet divine
> Move in music one with thine;
> And humbly heavenly lips prolong,
> Nightingale, *thy* diviner song!

As the invocation ends, a flute is heard, imitating the voice of the Nightingale. 'Dear God', says Euelpides,

> Dear God, what music hath a Nightingale,
> In sweetness wrapping round this shady vale!

Of course Aristophanes has to take the Nightingale as he finds her; he accepts her tragic encumbrances, Itylus and the rest of it. But though he calls her song a dirge, he never, I think, feels it as such. He feels the pure sweet strength of the Nightingale's song; and pretend as he will, he cannot conceal that it is a joyous strength. Hear him once more:

> Sweet bird of tawny bill,
> Of all birds that trill
> Sweetly their song, most sweet;
> Heart with my heart wont ever,
> Hymn with my hymn, to beat,
> Here's home to you; nought shall dissever
> Your song and the song of my feet.
> Your flute-like lay interweaving
> With all the soft sounds of the spring,
> O sweet beyond believing,
> Nightingale, once again, sing!

Well, that is Aristophanes: or at least what Aristophanes becomes when you dilute him with Swinburne-and-water!

I do not remember that, in Latin poetry, any one has said of the Nightingale anything worth saying. The only memorable birds are, if my memory serves me, caged ones

—Lesbia's caged Sparrow[1] in Catullus, Melior's caged
Parrot in Statius. The first still lives, and the second is
at least handsomely entombed. But this poetry of pets in
prison does not suffice to persuade me that the Romans
had much genuine feeling for birds. If somewhere some
one of the Latin poets has paid either tribute due, or a
passable tribute, to the song of the Nightingale; if in any
Latin poet the song of the Nightingale has set the seal on
some romantic occasion, I have forgotten it. Yet I have
not forgotten, when I say that, Virgil's comparison[2] of
Orpheus to a Nightingale robbed of her brood:

> So under poplar trees the Nightingale
> Mourns for her young; whom, nothing pitying,
> Some keen-eyed yokel snatched unfledged; her wail
> Night hears; and what she sings hears her re-sing;
> There sits she on one bough, there sings one song,
> Thence sets the valley ringing with her wrong.

I find those admired lines rather academic; nor—for what
it is worth—have I ever seen a nightingale sitting on the
branch of a poplar-tree.[3] Pliny has a whole book on birds;
but as a rule the last thing that he thinks of in connexion
with them is their song. Of the song of the Nightingale he
could hardly say nothing: and something he does say—
indeed a good deal—and says it ingeniously. Even so he
is hardly more impressed by the Nightingale's tunefulness
than by its expensiveness. I am reminded of Horace. The
sons of Arrius, Horace tells us, having more money than
they knew what to do with, *dined* on nightingales. Horace
laments, not the nightingales, but the extravagance.[4]

To the history of the Nightingale in poetry the sole

---

[1] Some think it a thrush; e.g. Sir Archibald Geikie, who cannot believe
that Lesbia made a pet of 'the most impudent and greedy and shrill-voiced
of all European birds'.

[2] *Georg.* iv. 511–15.

[3] But I have encountered one interpolated into Moschus in the translation of the *Lament for Bion* made by Thomas Warton the elder. (I am told
that Mr. Warde Fowler has, from his own observation, vindicated Vergil.)

[4] *Sat.* ii. 3. 245 seq.

contribution of Rome is Ovid's narrative of Procne and
Philomela: a narrative neat and ingenious, but nowhere
touched to the finer issues of its subject.

Near the close of the fourteenth century, Ovid's story
was freely rendered in English by the two chief poets of
the period. But before I speak of Chaucer and Gower,
I may be forgiven for saying a word about some earlier
Nightingales of our poetry.

The first English Nightingale that I know of—English,
though in a Latin dress—occurs, towards the end of the
seventh century, among the *Enigmas* of Aldhelm. If Aldhelm's Nightingale is not the 'merry' bird of the fourteenth and fifteenth centuries, yet, for all that Aldhelm
is a scholar, she is not the Philomela whom we know best,
and may be forgiven for liking least—of that dreary Philomela the advent falls in the reign of Elizabeth. Aldhelm's
Nightingale, in fact, follows a rather private tradition.
Her song is approximated in its symbolism to that of the
swan. It is mantic and dirge-like, the dirge of her own
foreboded dying. Even so, it is a dirge of which the
prevailing note is a note of triumph. A Christianized
Nightingale, she symbolizes by her winter migration, and
her return in spring, the Christian dying and re-rising:

> Foreknowing death, not yet my singing dies;
> The winter kills me, but with spring I rise.[1]

Two centuries later, another great English Churchman,
Alcuin of York, wrote some Latin verses on the death of
a favourite Nightingale. Though he borrows his best line
from Aldhelm, calling the Nightingale

> Plain in her plumage, in her song not plain,[2]

and though he endeavours to draw from the song of the
Nightingale a moral lesson, yet his bird is not the dirge-
singing bird of Aldhelm, but a creature of joy and light—
of any sorrow in its song there is no hint. The same is
true of what may be called the first English Nightingale

---

[1] *Aenigmata* xxii; cf. *Aen.* lxviii.
[2] Alcuin, *Carm.* lxi: 'Spreta colore, tamen fueras non spreta canendo.'

of the vernacular. She comes to us, like Aldhelm's bird, in a riddle—an Anglo-Saxon riddle, which I will render as best I may:

> Wise are my lips, to sweet variety
> Not without art shaping my far-heard song:
> Still upon sweet notes, hark, the sweet notes throng.
> Ancient of nights, earth's oldest poet, I
> Bear gladness to the dwellers upon earth,
> Ringing the flexuous changes of my lay:
> They in their houses sit to catch my mirth,
> With forward-thrusting faces, all ears.
>   Say,
> What am I called that so divinely sing,
> That voice for men the heart's wild mirth, that bring,
> Each year, so great a gospel of the spring? [1]

'What am I called?' What else but the *merry* Nightingale? Whatever my lame version omits or adds, the gay note is in the original, and I have not attempted to intensify—I may have dulled—its purity. This Nightingale is, so far as I know, solitary in Anglo-Saxon poetry; of which most of the birds—the mythical Phoenix excepted—are unlovely or joyless.

Aldhelm's Nightingale follows, as I say, a somewhat private tradition—a tradition according to which the song of the Nightingale is prophetic of death and resurrection. This tradition reappears—infinitely elaborated—in two Latin poems [2] of the thirteenth century, which would not be worth mentioning save that both are (it is believed) written by Englishmen, and one or other of them was the source of two fifteenth-century poems on the Nightingale which are attributed to Lydgate. Lydgate's pieces have

---

[1] *Exeter Book, Anglo-Saxon Riddles*, 8. The Anglo-Saxon Riddles were at one time attributed to Cynewulf. I should add that many scholars think that, not the Nightingale, but some other bird, is the answer to this particular riddle.

[2] Both poems bear the title *Philomela*. One of them is believed to have been written by Archbishop Peckham, the other by John Hoveden. See the account of these two persons in *D. N. B.*, and see Glauning's edition of Lydgate's Minor Poems, *E. E. T. S.* lxxxiv, p. xxxviii.

no great claim to be thought poetry; but I mention here both them and their Latin originals for the reason that, in the Latin pieces, Aldhelm's Nightingale has already suffered the metamorphosis into Philomela. Chaucer and Gower, therefore, were not the first to bring the Philomela story within the range of our literature; and it is likely enough that Chaucer, like his pupil Lydgate, knew the Latin poems which I mention.

But in fact Chaucer, though he first made the Philomela story familiar, in its Ovidian form, neither cared much for it, nor was able to interest his contemporaries. His story, like all the other stories of the *Legend of Good Women*, is told in a fashion plainly perfunctory. If Ovid's narrative had no poetry, it had some life. Rendered by Chaucer it has little of either. Gower, working independently of Chaucer, uses his material rather more happily. Not only does he tell his story with more life, but he diversifies it with digressions which are still readable. Before he has finished with her, his 'Philomene' is what she nowhere is in Ovid's story, or in Chaucer's, a song-bird. It is not his fault, I think, that he is made to say that the Nightingale arrives in England

Betwen Averil and March and Maii.

That is the fault of his scribes and editors. Gower wrote, I suggest, better verse and sense—

Betwen*en* Averil and Maii

—but I do not find that a March Nightingale excites any suspicion in the mind of Gower's principal commentator.[1] Whether Gower is right in making his Nightingale a shy bird, and in giving her red cheeks, I do not know—both attributions hang with the story, they are the symbols of Philomene's shame. But Gower will not be so tied to his story as to rest satisfied in the belief that the song of the Nightingale is a sad one. His is in fact one of those natures that like having things both ways.

[1] Or that the order April–March–May worries any one. (I am afraid that my *betwenen* is too archaizing to be convincing).

And ek thei seide hou in hir song
Sche makth great joie and merthe among,
And seith, 'Ha, nou I am a brid,
Ha, nou my facë mai ben hid:
Thogh I have lost mi maidenhede,
Schal noman se my chekës rede.'
Thus medleth sche with joië wo
And with her sorwë merthe also,
So that of lovë's maladie
Sche makth diversë melodie,
And seith love is a woful blisse,
A wisdom which can noman wisse,
A lusti fievere, a woundë softe:
This notë sche reherceth ofte
To hem which understonde hir tale.[1]

Gower, I may notice, is free of the delusion, shared (as Mr. Robinson points out) by so many of our poets[2] (Shakespeare among them), that the Nightingale sings only after dark. 'Sche singeth day and night', he says plumply.

For the dullness of his story of Philomene Chaucer makes some amends elsewhere. When I say that, I am thinking, as you will guess, of the Nightingale in *Troilus and Criseyde*; of the passage where Criseyde, first playing with the idea of being in love with Troilus, for a while lies on her bed without sleep; but presently falls asleep listening to the song of a nightingale in the garden.

A nightingale, upon a cedre grene,
Under the chambre-wal there as she lay,
Ful loudë sang ayein the monë shene,
Paraunter, in his briddës wyse, a lay
Of love, that made her hertë fresh and gay.
That herkened she so longe in good intente
Til at the last the dedë sleep hir hente.

Philomela notwithstanding, the Nightingale is, to the men of Chaucer's time, always, I think, a happy bird—'most musical, *least* melancholy'—and of good omen to the

---

[1] *Conf. Am.* v. 5983–97.
[2] I find it as late as Stevenson, to whom 'to list at noon for nightingales' is to expect what you will not find (*Et tu in Arcadia vixisti*, 47).

lover. In the *Parliament of Foules* she comes in company
with the sparrow, the son of Venus:

> The sparrow, Venus sone; the nightingale,
> That clepeth forth the freshë levës newe.

In the Prologue to the *Canterbury Tales*, the 'yong Squyer',

> A lovyere and a lusty bacheler,

is like the Nightingale, not because he is love-lorn—a
malady of which he bears no trace—but for the fire of
his passion:

> So hote he lovede that by nightertale
> He sleep namore than dooth a nightingale.

The Tale of Sir Thopas, again, is 'merier than the nightingale'; and the gay Absolon, in the Miller's Tale 'singeth
brokkinge as a nightingale'.

With the Nightingale as a happy bird, as the bird of
lovers and the May, Chaucer had, of course, made acquaintance when he was translating the Romaunt of the Rose:

> Then doth the Nightingale her might
> To makë noise and singen blythe.

Even so, of this happy Nightingale he hardly needed to
fetch the character from France. He might have gone
to a native source; to a poem written somewhere towards
the close of the twelfth century,[1] the Middle English
'squabble poem', the *Owl and the Nightingale*. Already
there, two hundred years before Chaucer, the Nightingale's
song is clearly recognized as a song both of love and of joy.
Already there the Nightingale discharges precisely the role
which Chaucer assigns to her in *Troilus and Criseyde*:

> Ah! sooth it is I sing and call
> Where ladies are and fair maids all,
> And of love make my madrigal.[2]

What the poem may owe to French influences, and what
other English poetry of a like kind may have been available

---

[1] It should have been mentioned earlier, if I had thought that its
interest (which is considerable) was the interest of poetry.

[2]   Ah soth hit is ich singe ond grede
          thar lauedies beoth and faire maide,
          ond soth hit is of luue ich singe (1337-9).

to Chaucer, I am not able to say. But here already the
connexions of the Nightingale with joyous love are fixed;
and they were not broken until, with the classical Renaissance, the mythological Philomela drove out nature.
When Chaucer and Gower told the story of Philomela
they in fact told it to very little purpose, convincing
neither themselves nor their contemporaries.

We are not allowed to believe, as Keats believed, that
Chaucer wrote *The Flower and the Leaf.* Yet of the poetry
consecrated to bird-life and bird-song there is no passage
more delicate and beautiful than that which, in this poem,
describes the 'herber' where the two factions of Ladies
assemble; and where, till their coming, the writer listens
to, and looks at, the birds. A gold-finch,

> leping pretily
> From bough to bough,

and eating 'as him list' 'of buddes and floures sweet',
presently begins to sing. From a 'laurer-tree' near by,
a Nightingale answers him:

> The nightingalë with so mery a note
> Answered him, that al the wodë rang.

Keats, I fancy, in his Ode to the Nightingale, in the
passage where, among the 'sweets' that he guesses in the
'embalmed darkness', he mentions the 'pastoral eglantine',
may have remembered the 'laurer-tree' of this poem

> That gave so passing a delicious smell
> According to the eglantere ful wel.

He perhaps remembered more than that. He conceives
himself, as he listens to the Nightingale, carried with its
flight to the heaven of heavens, where the moon sits throned
with her clustering fays about her. Similarly, but with
less elaboration, the Chaucerian poet is 'ravished into
Paradise' by the 'mery' song of *his* Nightingale:

> Wherof I had so inly greet plesýr
> That, as me thought, I surely ravished was
> Into Paradysë, where my desýr
> Was for to be and no ferther to passe.

I say so much because the poem—of which I would
have liked space to quote more—is as well worth reading
to-day as it was when Keats read it; and because the
'merry' Nightingale of the Chaucerians has, I think, so
much more of truth and nature in it than the melancholy
bird of later, and more conventional, poetry.

Of another poem once credited to Chaucer, *The Cuckoo
and the Nightingale*, I think less favourably. In form it
recalls the old medieval *certamen* or *tenson* or 'squabble
song';[1] and has something, consequently, of the tiresome
quality of the earlier *Owl and Nightingale*. But it has its
pleasant places; and just as *The Flower and the Leaf* provoked a sonnet of Keats, so to this poem we owe a sonnet
of Milton—the only poem, among his English poems, in
which Milton appears in the character of a lover. To hear
the Nightingale before the Cuckoo meant luck in love.
In what land the superstition had its origin I do not know;
for in this country—where lovers may be presumed to be
not more unlucky than elsewhere—the Cuckoo is commonly heard first. Nor do I know what to think about
those victims of love who live outside what is called
the 'Nightingale Line'. You will hear the Cuckoo in
Northumberland,[2] and you will hear him in Devon and
in Cornwall. But, be you never so much in love, you will
wait long before you hear, in any of those counties, the
voice of the Nightingale. But the superstition furnishes the
motif both of the Chaucerian poem and of Milton's sonnet.

> And then I thoghte, anon as it was day,
> I woldë go som whider to assay
> If that I might a nightingalë here,
> For yet had I non herd of al this yere,
> And it was tho the thriddë night of May.

The third of May, it is worth remembering, fell earlier

---

[1] If these 'squabble-songs' were not so tiresome, I might be tempted to
try and enshrine in one an hour-long *certamen* between a Nightingale and
a sheep which I listened to last summer not three miles out of Oxford.

[2] Albeit only in transit. A map showing the 'Nightingale Line' may
be seen in W. H. Wintringham's *Birds of Wordsworth*.

in those times than in ours by twelve days; and that is
why the advent of Nightingale is commonly associated, in
the poetry of the period, not with April, but with May.

I cannot leave this period without mentioning one other
poet of the Nightingale, who belongs to the generation
following Chaucer: King James I of Scotland. Of all
Nightingales, the Nightingale of the *Kingis Quair* may
be accounted certainly the most *romantic*. The story of
James's captivity—a love-story which is like a leaf from
Chaucer's *Knight's Tale*—is too well known to repeat.
But over the love of this captive prince it was the
Nightingale of the *Kingis Quair* that kept watch—

> The little sweetë nightingale, and sung
> So loud and clear the hymnis consecrate
> Of Lovë's use; now soft, now loud among,
> That all the gardens and the wallis rung. . . .
>
> O worship, ye that lovers been, this May,
> For of your bliss the Kalends are begun;
> And sing with us 'Away, Winter, away!
> Come, Summer, come, the sweet seasón and sun!
> Awake for shame, that have your heavens won,
> And amorously lift up your headis all:
> Thank Love, that list you to his mercy call!' . . .
>
> And to the notis of the Philomene,
> Quhilkis she sang, the ditty there I made
> Direct to her that was my heartis queen,
> Withouten whom no songis may me glad. . . .

James's Nightingale, it will be noticed, is called 'Philomene'; and James, who knew the Chaucerian-Ovidian
story, refers, in addressing her, to her unhappy past. But
he expects her to be, none the less, and she is, a bird
of mirth.

James, for all he was a Scot, from a land unvisited by
the Nightingale, had plenty of opportunity in his exile to
hear the bird's song. Another Scot, a later and a better
poet, had less opportunity, but used well what he had.
I mean Dunbar. No history of the Nightingale would be
complete which omitted to mention Dunbar's dialogue

of the Nightingale and the Merle 'singing of love among the levis small'. I will give you here if it be only a few lines of it; of which I will, so far as I can and dare, accommodate the dialect to our jejuner southern speech:

In May as that Aurora did upspring,
With chrystal eyn chasing the cloudis sable,
I heard a merle with merry notis sing
A song of love, with voice right comfortable,
Againe the orient beamis amiable,
Upon a blissful branch of laurer green;
This was her sentence sweet and delectable:
'A lusty life in Love's service been'.

Under this branch ran down a river bright
Of balmy liquor chrystalline of hue,
Againe the heavenly azure skyis light;
Where did upon the other side pursue
A Nightingale, with sugared notis new,
Whose angel feathers as the peacock shone;
This was her song, and of a sentence true:
'All love is lost but upon God alone'.

With notis glad and glorious harmony
This joyful merle saluted so the day
Till rung the woodis of her melody,
Saying 'Awake, ye lovers, O, this May.
Lo, freshe Flora has flourished every spray,
As Nature has her taught, the noble queen;
The field been clothit in a new array;
A lusty life in Love's service been.'

Ne'er sweeter noise was heard with living man
Than made this merry gentle Nightingale;
Her sound went with the river as it ran,
Out through the fresh and flowery lusty vale. . . .

—and so like a river in its running runs on Dunbar's charming poem; not the poem of a naturalist, or he would not have made this plain-coloured bird as bright as a peacock. Its form follows that of the old 'squabble poem'. Yet of all the 'squabble poems' this alone is all poetry. Its 'merry gentle Nightingale' and its 'joyful merle' sing both in the service of love, respectively the heavenly love and the demotic. Nor is this the only poem of Dunbar in which the Nightingale appears in a religious connexion. Elsewhere he identifies the Nightingale with the Virgin Mary:

> Hail, plight, but sight. Hail, mickle of might!
> Hail, glorious Virgin, hail!
> Ave Maria, gratia plena!
> Hail, gentle Nightingale!

If any one finds this identification mysterious, he may turn to a Nightingale poem a century older, the *Thrush and Nightingale*. That poem owes something to the *Owl and Nightingale*, which I have already mentioned. Its opening lines are pretty enough to be quoted:

> Summer is come, with Love, to town,
> With blossom and with birdies' soun';
> The nut of the hazel springeth;
> The dewës dankeneth the dale;
> For longing of the Nightingale
> The fowlës merry singeth.

One or two words I have modernized.[1] The lines are interesting, for the reason that two of them recur—and the whole stanza is imitated—in a fourteenth-century poem, preserved in one of the Harley MSS. of the British Museum.[2] But the concluding lines are even more interesting; for in them the Nightingale celebrates the praises of the Virgin Mary. The reason is, perhaps, not far to seek. The Nightingale is essentially the bird of

---

[1] The original runs:

> Somer is comen with loue to toune,
> With blostme and with brides soune;
> The note of hasel springeth
> The dewes darkneth the dale;
> For longing of the niʒttegale
> The foweles murrie singeth.

In the fourth line *darkneth* seems to be a scribe's blunder: *donketh* = dankeneth conj. Holthausen.

[2] MS. Harley 2253: printed in Sisam, *Fourteenth-Century Verse and Prose*, p. 164; Boeddicker, *Altengl. Dicht.*, p. 164.

May; and 'Marie, mother and mai'—mother and virgin—
'of alle floures feirest', was easily and early identified with
both the season and the flower of the May.

But it was not on Scots tongues only that the Nightingale in this period was still alive. In the south a not much
esteemed poet, Skelton, besides writing the spirited Philip
Sparrow poem, which is perhaps, of all his poems, the
best and best known, was able, on the subject of the
Nightingale, to be as charming as this:

> Ennewed your colówre
> Is like the daisie flowre
> After the April showre.
>   Star of the morrow gray,
> The blossom on the spray,
> The freshest flowre of May,
> Maidenly demure,
> Of womanhood the lure;
> Wherefore I make you sure,
> It were an heavenly health,
> It were an endless wealth,
> A life for God himself,
> To hear this Nightingale
> Among the birdis smale
> Warbeling in the vale,
> Dug, dug, jug, jug,
> Good yere and good luck,
> With chuck, chuck, chuck, chuck.

To the same period, or to a period just a little later,
belongs, it is believed, a poem which, until the philo-
logians touched it, was attributed to Chaucer—*The Court
of Love*. Of its very charming conclusion, I may be allowed
to give you the first stanza:

> On May-day, when the lark began to rise,
> To mattins went the lusty Nightingale
> Within a temple shapen hawthorn-wise;
> He might not sleep in all the nightertale,
> But 'Domine labia' gan he cry and gale,
> 'My lippes open, Lord of Love, I cry,
> And let my mouth thy praising now bewrye'.

Once again, the religious connexions are noteworthy. But this Nightingale is still the 'lusty' and cheerful bird of the old tradition. Of that tradition, however, these are perhaps the last notes; and it is not a little melancholy to pass from the happy Nightingale of the first spring-time of our poetry to the ever-complaining Philomela of the second spring. The patrons of this mournful Nightingale, a good many of them, I may notice, studied Ronsard. They might well have taken to heart a paradox of that poet, who, in his poem *The Lark*, says that the Nightingale's real complaint is a complaint against the poets themselves:

> Larks, not to you alone the tongue
> Of lying poets doth great wrong.
> For this alone the Nightingale
> In covert green lifts high her wail—
> Hating to be a poet's tale.

The resuscitation of Philomela must be laid, I think, at the door of George Gascoigne—not a poet of high consideration, yet, after Wyat and Surrey, the most considerable name in our poetry between the Chaucerian and Shakespearian periods. Gascoigne told Ovid's story over again, with many additions of his own, some of them more curious than need was. He is not, I should think, a good natural historian; for he seems to assign to the Nightingale an exclusive diet of seeds. But it was he who first, so far as I know, isolated from among the notes of the Nightingale the *Tereu* which later poets have made so tiresome to us. This he combines, as the later poets do, with the *jug jug* which is found already in Skelton. Other notes that he detects are *fy fy fy*—to which he was guided by the old French poets—and *Nemesis*. The *fy fy fy* and *Nemesis* notes I have not observed to recur in later poets, though the *tis tis* of Brathwaite[1]—a very minor Elizabethan—is perhaps the same as Gascoigne's *Nemesis*.

If the Nightingale, in the Elizabethan period, makes a rather shabby re-entry with Gascoigne, she gathers about

[1] *The Nightingale: Natures Embassy*, 1619.

her, only a few years later, some melancholy splendours
of sound in a poem of Sidney, which is worth quoting
in full.[1] It is a degree formal; but its cadences have
more of music in them than is likely if there were no
true feeling behind them:

> The Nightingale as soon as April bringeth
>   Unto her rested sense, a perfect waking;
> While late bare earth, proud of new clothing, springeth—
>   Sings out her woes, a thorn her song book making—
>   And mournfully bewailing,
>   Her throat in tunes expresseth
>   What grief her breast oppresseth
> For Thereus' force, on her chaste will prevailing.
>
> O Philomela fair! O take some gladness!
> That here is juster cause of plaintful sadness.
>   Thine earth now springs! mine fadeth;
> Thy thorn without! my thorn my heart invadeth.
>
> Alas, she hath no other cause of anguish
>   But Thereus' love; on her by strong hand wroken;
> Wherein she suffering, all her spirits languish,
>   Full woman-like, complains her will was broken.
>   But I—who, daily craving,
>   Cannot have to content me—
>   Have more cause to lament me:
> Since wanting is more woe than too much having.
>
> O Philomela fair! O take some gladness!
> That here is juster cause of plaintful sadness.
>   Thine earth now springs! mine fadeth;
> Thy thorn without! my thorn my heart invadeth.

Who first figured the Nightingale as singing with her
breast against a thorn, I do not know. She is so figured
already in Gascoigne. But in the use that they make of
her thorn some at least of the Elizabethans may well be

[1] With the refrain of it may be compared the *Nightingale* Ode of J. B.
Rousseau:

> Hélas! que mes tristes pensées
> M'offrent des maux bien plus cuisants!
> Vous pleurez des peines passées,
> Je pleure des ennuis présents . . .

thought to carry too far the love of point! The rich and
various music of the Nightingale deserved perhaps that it
should be distinguished from plain-song. But when in
allusion to the thorn Lyly speaks of the bird's 'brave prick-
song', and Barnabe Barnes, elaborating this, writes

> I'll sing my Plain Song with the turtle dove;
> And Prick Song with the nightingale rehearse;

—the cleverness offends. And in general very little of the
poetry of this period which is dedicated to the Nightingale
rises out of the region of the clever or pretty. Barnfield's
'As it fell upon a day . . .' is pretty enough to have been
claimed for Shakespeare. Even prettier is Dekker's
Nightingale and Cuckoo; and since it is prettier and less
known, it perhaps deserves quoting:

> O the month of May, the merry month of May,
> So frolic, so gay, and so green, and so green!
> O, and then did I unto my true love say,
> 'Sweet Peg, thou shalt be my Summer's Queen.
>
> Now the nightingale, the pretty nightingale,
> The sweetest singer in all the forest's quire,
> Entreats thee, sweet Peggy, to hear thy true love's tale:
> Lo, yonder she sitteth, her breast against a brier.
>
> But O, I spy the cuckoo, the cuckoo, the cuckoo;
> See where she sitteth; come away, my joy:
> Come away, I prithee, I do not like the cuckoo
> Should sing where my Peggy and I kiss and toy.
>
> O the month of May, the merry month of May,
> So frolic, so gay, and so green, and so green!
> O, and then did I unto my true love say,
> 'Sweet Peg, thou shalt be my Summer's Queen.'

Yet perhaps the prettiest of all the Elizabethan
Nightingales are two which belong, not to lyric, but to
dramatic verse. One of them is Shakespeare's:

> *Juliet.* Wilt thou be gone? it is not yet near day;
> It was the nightingale, and not the lark,
> That pierced the fearful hollow of thine ear—
> Nightly she sings on yon pomegranate tree:
> Believe me, love, it was the nightingale.

Romeo. It was the lark, the herald of the morn,
No nightingale: look, love, what envious streaks
Do lace the severing clouds in yonder east.
Night's candles are burnt out, and jocund day
Stands tiptoe on the misty mountain-tops.
I must be gone and live, or stay and die.
Juliet. Yon light is not daylight, I know it, I:
It is some meteor that the sun exhales,
To be to thee this night a torchbearer
And light thee on thy way to Mantua.
Therefore, stay yet, thou need'st not to be gone.
Romeo. Let me be ta'en, let me be put to death,
I am content, so thou wilt have it so.
I'll say yon grey is not the morning's eye;
'Tis but the pale reflex of Cynthia's brow;
Nor that is not the lark whose notes do beat
The vaulty heaven so high above our heads.
I have more care to stay than will to go.
Come, death, and welcome, Juliet wills it so.
Juliet. It is, it is. Hie hence, begone, away!
It is the lark that sings so out of tune,
Straining harsh discords and unpleasant sharps.
Some say the lark makes sweet division.
This doth not she, for she divideth us.
Some say the lark and loathed toad change eyes—
O now I would they had changed voices too,
Since arm from arm that voice doth us affray,
Hunting thee hence with hunt-ups to the days.
O now begone, more light and light it grows.
Romeo. More light and light; more dark and dark our woes.

There is a freshness and feeling about that which is
wanting to the lyrics innumerable which celebrate 'Philomela fair'; and whether Nightingales may be found sitting
on pomegranates or not matters nothing. Less familiar,
but even more charming in their freshness, are some lines
from Ben Jonson's *Sad Shepherd*:

Amie. O Karol! he is fair and sweet.
Maud. What then?
Are there not flowers as sweet and fair as men?
The lily is fair, and rose is sweet.

Amie. Ay, so.
        Let all the lilies and the roses go:
        Karol is only fair to me.
Mar. And why?
Amie. Alas, for Karol, Marian, I could die!
        Karol, he singeth sweetly too.
Maud. What then?
        Are there not birds sing sweeter far than men?
Amie. I grant the linnet, lark, and bullfinch sing,
        But best the dear good angel of the spring,
        The nightingale!

This, and much else of the time, is delicate and charming; and certainly the best Elizabethan nightingales are those which, like these of Shakespeare and Jonson, are not too heavily premeditated; and those, again, which are, not a theme in themselves, but the illustration of one. Sir Henry Wotton's Nightingale, if a little learned, yet falls in well with the stars and violets, to figure the beauty of Elizabeth, princess of Bohemia:

> You curious chanters of the wood,
>   That warble forth Dame Nature's lays,
> Thinking your passions understood
>   By your weak accents; what 's your praise
>   When Philomel her voice shall raise?

Rather later, Carew recalls this poem of Wotton,[1] and this Nightingale of Wotton, to even happier effect:

> Ask me no more whither doth haste
>   The Nightingale when May is past;
> For in your sweet dividing throat
>   She winters and keeps warm her note.

In general the Nightingale poetry of the Elizabethans sticks in triviality and convention. The poets of the time took the parables of bird-life in a superficial spirit. It would hardly have crossed the imagination, I think, of the greatest of them that there could be drawn from the song of the Nightingale poetry of the order of Keats's great

[1] The two poems should be read together, to bring out what the one owes, in suggestion, to the other.

Ode. Drummond of Hawthornden—who spent, however, most of his life far north of the 'Nightingale Line'—endeavoured, in one of two sonnets which he gave to the Nightingale, to draw from her song a religious lesson. But the sonnet remains chiefly notable for the chance that one of its lines may have lingered in Keats's memory. By the Nightingale's song, he says, the soul is led

> *Quite to forget* earth's turmoils spights and wrongs.

Yet the resemblance which this bears to Keats's

> Fade far away, dissolve and *quite forget*
> What thou among the leaves hast never known,
> The weariness, the fever and the fret . . .

is, I think, only accidental; and a resemblance equally close might be traced in Gascoigne, who speaks of himself as listening to the same bird's song, and

> *quite forgetting* all the *wearie* woe
> Which I myself felt in my fantasie.

To the poetry of the period immediately following the Shakespearian belong two notable Nightingale poems: the one Milton's sonnet, which I have already mentioned and of which, since it is so well known, I need say no more; the other, Crashaw's *Music's Duel*. Of Crashaw's poem the ingenious elaboration is everything; it is too long to cite whole, and the effectiveness is gone if less than all of it is given. I do not know that there is much of nature in it; its full sensuosity suggests some intensive care of cultivation. But in the kind to which it belongs it deserves a high place. Of the heroic metre, so called, the variety of power is nowhere so well illustrated. This was the kind of poem which Keats, in his early period, was for ever trying to write: you might read large tracts of it and credit them to Keats—to Keats, and to no one else. It is not a poem of the order of Keats's Ode. But if Keats had not written the Ode, and if ingenuity were truth, and truth beauty, this would be our best Nightingale poem.

Between Crashaw and Coleridge, the Nightingale hardly has a history in our poetry. For I cannot call poetry—or natural history either—Cowper's *Nightingale* or his *Nightingale and Glowworm*; and of the other eighteenth-century poets only one was capable of writing well and truthfully about birds—Burns.[1] But Burns, living north of the 'Nightingale Line', wrote, as we might expect of him, only about that which he knew.[2] The Muse of Blake, 'half angel and half bird', and with the birds and the angels commingling mystically stars and flowers and all else that flashes and fades, is too indeterminate for the effects we seek. His 'painted birds', as he calls them, are not well seen; and the fashion of their singing is too dimly ecstatic.

To Coleridge we owe the re-establishment in our literature of 'the merry Nightingale':

> In Nature there is nothing melancholy,
> But some night-wandering man whose heart was pierced
> With the remembrance of a grievous wrong
> Or slow distemper, or neglected love,
> And so, poor wretch, filled all things with himself,
> And made all gentle sounds tell back the tale
> Of his own sorrow, he, and such as he,
> First named these notes a melancholy strain.

Not only Keats, but, I think, Shelley also took to heart Coleridge's poem—though it failed to convince Hartley Coleridge. To both of them the song of the Nightingale is essentially a song of joy. With Shelley it is perhaps a little difficult to be patient. He liked birds, I fancy, better than he knew them. Some one has reported a remark of Wordsworth to much that effect with regard to the Ode to a Skylark. That Ode offers little to a naturalist. It is not the poem of an observer. Yet it is what it is; and time will hardly touch it. But 'the voluptuous nightingales' of the *Prometheus* are more clearly defined than was wise. At least in one particular, they

---

[1] Yet there is something to be said for Thomson's *Spring*, lines 590–613.
[2] As, e.g., in his *Address to a Woodlark* (i.e. a tree pipit).

THE NIGHTINGALE IN POETRY

are more like larks than they should be. Like larks, or one species of larks, and like no nightingales that ever I heard of, they soar as they sing:

> there is heard through the dim air
> The rush of wings, and rising there
> Like many a lake-surrounded flute,
> Sounds overflow the listener's brain,
> So sweet that joy is almost pain

—and so absurd as to make you sorry. Other poets of the same period, no doubt, have said of the Nightingale things more absurd.

Of Keats's great Ode I have spoken elsewhere. But I have not said, what I had not then noticed,—my attention was called to it by Lord Grey of Fallodon—that in the final stanza of his Ode Keats forgets that the Nightingale sings always in her own domain. When he hears her 'plaintive anthem' fade

> Past the near meadows, over the still stream,
> Up the hill-side; and now 'tis buried deep
> In the next valley glades

—when he hears, or thinks to hear, all that, and asks, 'Do I wake or sleep?' the answer is that, like Homer, he nods. Nor is it the only place where the naturalist may catch him nodding over nightingales. 'The nightingale up-perched high' of his *Endymion*[1] has no place in Nature; though she has a place, let it be whispered, in as good a poet as Marvell, and, again, in Cowper.[2]

But these are idle criticisms; and I have said already how little store I set by them. I will add here that the critic who makes them is criticized already, long since, in Aristotle. It is not so important, in any case, that poets

---

[1] When he wrote *Endymion*, I may notice here, Keats still lingered in the tradition of the 'melancholy' Nightingale. *Sorrow* borrows 'mellow ditties from a mourning tongue', 'To give at evening pale Unto the nightingale' (*Endymion*, iv. 160 sqq.).

[2] Of Cowper W. H. Hudson writes: 'He was as bad a naturalist as any singer before or after him, and *as any true poet has a perfect right to be*. As bad, let us say, as Shakespeare and Wordsworth and Tennyson.' *Birds and Man* (New Readers' Library, 1927, p. 70).

should be naturalists as that naturalists should have in them something of poetry. Some of them have; those especially, I think, who have been lovers of birds. When I say that, I have in mind above all W. H. Hudson, a naturalist who was too good a poet to care to scold the poets for not being naturalists. He notes that Wordsworth; 'confounds the sparrow and the hedge-sparrow'[1] but he does not allow it to trouble him. Wordsworth, save in his brief sojourn in the north of Somerset, lived where the Nightingale is not heard. He finds the note of the Nightingale more 'tumultuary and fierce' than suits a temperament wedded to 'steady bliss' and the life of contemplation. He likes better the stock-dove's plain-song. 'This was the song, the song for me!' The poem was written, not in Grasmere—where the Nightingale never comes, but at Coleorton. It is less interesting that the stock-dove should have been a ring-dove.

I have mentioned already in passing Matthew Arnold's beautiful *Philomela*. Its 'tawny-throated' Nightingale still jars on me; and I am sorry that this great poet brought the Nightingale back into her mythological connexions. These regrets apart, the poem has, if not the grand manner, yet an individual elegance of melancholy. A celebrated composition, more or less contemporary with this, is Mr. Swinburne's *Itylus*—in its triumphs of sound the finest of ears will yet miss one sound, the beating of any kind of human heart. I suppose its author to have had a special liking for that line of it which he repeats oftenest. Yet, with whatever small variant it recurs, that iterated

Swallow, my sister, O sister swallow,

has never convinced me; and I can only save it for myself

---

[1] I do not know the grounds for this. (The sparrow of 'Behold! within the leafy shade ' is a hedge-sparrow; for it has blue eggs.) Mr. Hendy, I notice, has no better opinion of Wordsworth's bird-lore than Hudson. 'Wordsworth', he says, 'was not a good field-naturalist: there were not many in his day' (*The Lure of Bird Watching*, p. 233). My lecture was made before Mr. Hendy's chapter on 'Birds and Poets' appeared.

out of absurdity by a strong effort of the will. I set my
teeth, and from the horrid suspicion that these everlasting
'swallows' may be, not vocatives, but imperatives, I pray
to Mercury and Philologia, and whatever gods there be
that preside over just interpretation, to keep me pure.

The best that has been said since of Nightingales has
been said by the best of our living poets. I may well end
with Mr. Bridges' poem; and wonder when again we shall
hear, in the same connexions, notes so full and rich:

> Beautiful must be the mountains whence ye come,
>   And bright in the fruitful valleys the streams, wherefrom
>   Ye learn your song:
> Where are those starry woods? O might I wander there,
>   Among the flowers, which in that heavenly air
>   Bloom the year long!
>
> Nay, barren are those mountains and spent the streams:
>   Our song is the voice of desire, that haunts our dreams,
>   A throe of the heart,
> Whose pining visions dim, forbidden hopes profound,
>   No dying cadence nor long sigh can sound,
>   For all our art.
>
> Alone, aloud in the raptured ear of men
>   We pour our dark nocturnal secret; and then,
>   As night is withdrawn
> From those sweet-springing meads and bursting boughs of May,
>   Dream, while the innumerable choir of day
>   Welcome the dawn.

RUPERT BROOKE

NOT long since, speaking of Keats,[1] I was guilty of an act of innocence. I was so innocent as to indicate the kind of poetry which I liked best. It was my intention, I said, for so long a period as I held the Chair of Poetry, to lecture upon good poets rather than upon bad ones. I did not know how ill-considered the remark was, how wide the class which might be hurt by it. I know now what it conveyed. It meant that, as dons do, I preferred the dead to the living, the distant to the near, tradition to experiment. One of my critics, accordingly—whom I suspected of being one of somebody else's poets—reproached me with lecturing upon Keats because he was safe and easy and pre-war; while of the poets of the war and after, of all that surging life, of that unexampled stirring of new forces, I was content to say nothing, or nothing that was gracious. Certainly, that Keats was safe and easy it had not, until then, occurred to me to think. Safe, in a sense, he is—safe as Shakespeare; safe from me, and from criticism good or bad; safe from time itself. That he is safe *for* me, it does not, I think, follow. Far safer for me would be far more modern poets; about whom I might say much that was not true, and never be found out hereafter. If Keats is easy, he was not so to me; and in this, in the circumstance that he was not easy, he resembled, I had supposed, all great poets. Pre-war he is; yet the poet, he too, of the period of a great war; and, as I tried to show, not so entirely unmoved by the political interests and passions of his time as we have been used to suppose.

In truth, if I am to say what I think, the newer poets who have been commended to me seem to me to be, in many ways, safer poets, easier poets, and even more pre-war than the poets whom they have superseded. When I say 'more pre-war', I mean that, in reading them, what

[1] In a lecture reprinted in my *Keats* (Clarendon Press, 1926).

has perplexed me most is to feel how many of the lessons
of the war some of them seem to have missed. I reflect
especially, how personal, how individual, much of this
poetry is, how egoistic—I am sorry to use a term of dis-
praise, for I am not, in fact, insensible of the power, the
obscure striving, of this new poetry. Yet I cannot but feel
it strange, how this poetry, born of the war, comes back
so much upon self—of which the war was so grandly for-
getful; and how often it wants just that without which
no war is won, discipline.

However, it is beside my intention to essay here any
studied characterization of this poetry. Yet I would
hazard, in general terms, the conjecture that the best and
safest parts of it are not those which distinguish it from
the best poetry of other periods. To say that is, once
again, as I know, to be academic. But, then, I do not
know why a man comes to an academy at all unless it be
to say and hear academic things. I except, of course, the
poets who come here—and the poetesses. Yet, after all,
even they come here, I suppose, for criticism—at least
they find it. That a college is, upon the whole, the best
place for a poet, I am far from suggesting. Often, indeed,
it is the last place where a poet is either safe or easy. So
much is this true that I am afraid of what I am going to
say next. I was speaking generally of the poetry of the
war period. By a queer paradox, it happens that the three
poets of whom I think most often in connexion with the
war, and with the least reserve in my appreciation, are
three Fellows of Colleges. One of them is still living, a
deserter, it is true, from Oxford to Cambridge, but a very
real poet, and the father, for good and ill, of a considerable
school of poets, Mr. Housman. Perhaps no short occasional poem was ever so direct in its effectiveness as the
Epitaph on a Mercenary Army. Very different in character, of larger compass, more intricately laboured—indeed, too curious in its craftsmanship—but yet a great
poem, was Mr. Phillimore's poem upon the death of
Charles Fisher. When it first appeared, a critic who did

not give his name—but I may, I think, give it now—
Professor George Gordon, spoke of it in *The Times* as the
noblest poem which the war had produced. The poem is
still not so well known as it should be; and the same is true
of other poems of Mr. Phillimore. It is a fault of the
time—not enough people take trouble enough to distinguish, in poetry, good from bad. Mr. Phillimore's death,
three weeks ago,[1] was a very real loss to English letters;
and a very real loss to Oxford. ἀγαθός ποιητὴς καὶ
ποθεινὸς τοῖς φίλοις. Though he had been gone from Oxford
five-and-twenty years, many of us here knew him well—
the man, and the poetry that was in him. Perhaps he was
not easy to know well; just as his poetry is not, I think,
easy to read. Both as a man and as a literary artist he was
reserved. His character and his craftsmanship alike (he
was essentially a craftsman) had a quality of reserve akin
to the antique. But both invited and rewarded affec-
tionate study. At least the poem I have mentioned will
not easily be let die. Certainly not in Oxford, of which
it distils subtly the finer spirit:

> Dear and familiar stones and greens, when once more peace
> Lies large on summer nights in Wolsey's moonlit Quad,
> When ebb comes home to flood, in the hour when eyes release
> The arrested tear, in the hour of the reblossoming rod,—
> Let not the stature of his renown admit decrease.

Like Mr. Housman, and like Mr. Phillimore, Rupert
Brooke was a Fellow of a College. You may live well,
even in a palace, said Marcus Aurelius; and perhaps the
rather drab luxury of Common Rooms is not necessarily
fatal to poetry. I dare say that Rupert Brooke would have
been a better poet if he had never gone to Cambridge;
and certainly, it was when he got away from Cambridge,
as I think, that he began to be a great poet. For a great
poet I do account him, great and safe. I say safe, because,
despite the critic I have mentioned, I do not, in fact,
experience, in respect of the writers near my own time,

[1] The lecture was delivered on 7 December 1926.

that sense of insecurity which assails some people when
they attempt to assess contemporary greatness. With the
general habit of mind which remits to posterity the judgement of all great causes and all considerable reputations
I feel, in fact, no sympathy at all. I hate it for its timidity;
and I suspect that, in the complex of its motives, may
be discovered, often enough, jealousy and disappointed
vanity. There are two characters of criticism without
which I account it dead. First, it must have a gay
courage; and this comes to it only with the sense of living
multitude. He who has his eye always upon posterity can
no more criticize than he can create. And secondly, all
good criticism is magnanimous. It has noble partialities,
and it takes generous risks. After all, the end of criticism
is, not to be right, but to do right by whatever seems
great or like to greatness. Put more simply, the end of
criticism is, not one's own reputation, but some one else's.
I submit, in any case, that that cannot be a healthy criticism of which the children are always overdue, and their
very conception haunted by the doubt, whether we can
afford to have them. I will not even admit that it is
hazardous to judge contemporary greatness. In fact I
believe it to be, like tiger-shooting, one of the safest pur-
suits under the sun—provided always that it be practised
by persons who understand greatness, or are used to tigers.
And when I say 'understand greatness', I do not demand
much. Shakespeare, Wordsworth, Dickens, Scott—Scott
in the Novels—just these four, I have sometimes thought,
these four so oddly unlike, are enough. Steep your critic
in the greatness of these four, and I will chance his judgement upon any greatness in literature.

Rupert Brooke suggests yet another, and rather different, trouble. He was a poet; as I think, a great poet;
in any case an interesting one. But he was not only an
interesting poet. He was also, beyond question, an interesting and rarely attractive young man, crowning vivid
days with a death enviably romantic. It is not for nothing
that Henry James, when he writes of him, becomes at once

wholly sentimental—and partially intelligible. There are
people who do not like this; who dislike mixing up the
poet and his poetry; who chafe at the intrusion of what
they call the personal judgement. These, perhaps, beyond
all others, beyond even those toadies of posterity of whom
I have just spoken, are the pedants of criticism. No doubt,
theirs is a very plausible pedantry. The standards of art,
they mean, are absolute; we no longer judge artistically
when we relate the object of our judgement to something
outside it. That a poet died young, that he was unhappy,
that he was personally beautiful—these and other like
characters of his life, interesting and affecting in themselves, and perhaps proper for our study, must not be
allowed to colour our judgement of his poetry. We may,
doubtless, use any or all of these circumstances to explain
why his poetry is what it is, and not something else, why
it creates in us just those emotions which it does, and not
other, perhaps deeper and fuller, emotions. But we have
no right to use these circumstances in order to educe from
his poetry what would otherwise not be there, or in order
to make patent what would otherwise be merely latent.

In answer to all this—which expresses a view at once
fashionable and plausible, a view which has the advantage
that it seems to lift the criticism of poetry into an ideal
region uninfected by the infirmities of the personal judgement—in answer to all this, though I could say a great
deal, I prefer to say here only that I like a criticism which
is a degree more human. A man's poetry is, after all, only
one part of his greatness; and indeed, only one part of his
poetry. I have always liked Aeschylus the better for his
epitaph—with its touch of human vanity, its appeal from
the poet to the man. Aeschylus wrote many great dramas.
But when he had written his last drama, he felt that there
was something in him still craving expression and explanation. And he wrote an elegiac couplet to tell the ages
unborn that he had fought at Marathon. Only then did
he feel that he had explained himself.[1]

[1] I may notice that the poet Collins, in his *Ode to Fear*, lets his praises

I should be sorry, then, to rob Rupert Brooke of any
of the adventitious circumstances of his glory, the luck of
his death, or the beauty of his person; to exclude from
the estimate of him either the soldier who 'found himself', or the 'young Apollo golden-haired' of the sentimental poem—the young Apollo who looked at one time
very like *never* finding himself. Just because I should be
sorry to do that, I should put in the forefront of his
Poems the second of the War Sonnets of 1914:

> Dear, of all happy in the hour, most blest
> He who has found our hid security,
> Assured in the dark tides of the world at rest,
> And heard our word, 'Who is so safe as we?'[1]
> We have found safety with all things undying,
> The winds, and morning, tears of men and mirth,
> The deep night, and birds singing, and clouds flying,
> And sleep, and freedom, and the autumnal earth.
> We have built a house that is not for Time's throwing.
> We have gained a peace unshaken by pain for ever.
> War knows no power. Safe shall be my going,
> Secretly armed against all death's endeavour;
> Safe though all safety's lost; safe where men fall;
> And if these poor limbs die, safest of all.

There is a soldier's poem, written in the conviction of
a soldier's end. I confess that I have no wish to separate
from it—far rather, I wish to take up into its splendid
effectiveness—any of those advantages of fortune, of temperament, of person, which accident allows us to snatch.
I am greedy to know that the writer did in fact die as he
anticipated; that he died in the flower of youth; that the
'hid security' which he attained was born in him after
some faltering; that, speaking thus strangely of peace, he
had something of the temperament of what is called
pacifism; that the 'poor limbs', again, of which he speaks

of Aeschylus culminate in the reflection that he was one of the Μαρα-
θωνομάχαι.

[1] *Who is so safe as we?* where none can do
Treason to us, except one of us two.
Donne, *The Anniversarie.*

were of faultless Greek beauty; that no one ever met him
without being sensible that he belonged to the company
of the gods. Says Sir Ian Hamilton of him: 'I have seen
famous men and brilliant figures in my day. But never
one so thrilling, so vital. Like a prince he would enter
a room . . . and put a spell upon every one around him.'
With the kind of criticism which would isolate this poem
from all contact with these adventitious circumstances,
fencing it from all possible infection of the sentimental,
I feel little sympathy. I cannot grudge the poem the
benefits of the man; rather than do so, I would risk the
fall into sentimentality.

I have spent all these words, because I find the argu-
ments which I have noticed a good deal in use recently
whenever the poetry of Rupert Brooke is spoken of. The
reaction was, no doubt, to be expected. Rupert Brooke
was scarcely dead when the manuscripts of his poems
were deposited, some of them among the treasures of
the nation, in the British Museum, some of them in the
Fitzwilliam Museum among the treasures of Cambridge
University. Inspired officials are not common. But so
things happened. Presently, the critics began. There was
a feeling that Brooke had been made a spoiled child. It
began to be whispered that a man was not necessarily a
good poet because he was nice-looking and died for his
country. Rupert Brooke had been carried into fame on six
good sonnets—the sonnets of 1914—and a romantic death.

I will not disguise a liking that I have for spoiled
children; and certainly, while he lived Brooke was absurdly spoiled. I have heard it whispered of the sister
university—I know not with how much of truth—that
gods and heroes are made there too easily, and that the
cult of them is sometimes intensive to the verge of the
sloppy. Here, perhaps, we believe in one another too
little. Be that as it may, there was in Cambridge a cult
of Rupert Brooke; and I suspect that it was overdone.
I can sum what I take to have been the worst evil of it
by saying that it very nearly, I think, made Rupert Brooke

vulgar; and vulgar in that most dreary order of vulgarity, the Georgian. Of the work of Brooke's Cambridge period, a great deal is, I think, merely poor. But parts of it are tiresomely vulgar. A fair portion of it, again, blends genius and vulgarity. As a tolerable specimen of the blend I may take the two sonnets, *Menelaus and Helen.*

I

Hot through Troy's ruin Menelaus broke
To Priam's palace, sword in hand, to sate
On that adulterous whore a ten years' hate
And a king's honour. Through red death, and smoke,
And cries, and then by quieter ways he strode,
Till the still innermost chamber fronted him.
He swung his sword, and crashed into the dim
Luxurious bower, flaming like a god.

High sat white Helen, lonely and serene.
He had not remembered that she was so fair,
And that her neck curved down in such a way;
And he felt tired. He flung the sword away,
And kissed her feet, and knelt before her there,
The perfect Knight before the perfect Queen.

II

So far the poet. How should he behold
That journey home, the long connubial years?
He does not tell you how white Helen bears
Child on legitimate child, becomes a scold,
Haggard with virtue. Menelaus bold
Waxed garrulous, and sacked a thousand Troys
'Twixt noon and supper. And her golden voice
Got shrill as he grew deafer. And both were old.

Often he wonders why on earth he went
Troyward, or why poor Paris ever came.
Oft she weeps, gummy-eyed and impotent;
Her dry shanks twitch at Paris' mumbled name.
So Menelaus nagged; and Helen cried;
And Paris slept on by Scamander side.

Very young, you will think some of this—'white Helen'

and the rest of it. I seem to myself to find here, even so, both real genius and quite genuine vulgarity. Any one who knows what is what will easily perceive which is which. Of *more* vulgarity in this early period, I will spare you examples; remarking only that Brooke is never so vulgar as when he is quite unconscious of it. Of a poem like *Wagner* the humourless vulgarity is irritating, but conscious. No ray of self-suspicion illumines the wholly depressing vulgarity of such pieces as those entitled *Success* and *Lust*. It is pleasanter, and more important, to recall that, in the poems of the Cambridge period, there are perhaps seven pieces neither vulgar nor ineffective. Let me take the best of them first.

> When the white flame in us is gone,
>   And we that lost the world's delight
> Stiffen in darkness, left alone
>   To crumble in our separate night;
>
> When your swift hair is quiet in death,
>   And through the lips corruption thrust
> Has stilled the labour of my breath—
>   When we are dust, when we are dust!—
>
> Not dead, not undesirous yet,
>   Still sentient, still unsatisfied,
> We'll ride the air, and shine, and flit,
>   Around the places where we died,
>
> And dance as dust before the sun,
>   And light of foot, and unconfined,
> Hurry from road to road, and run
>   About the errands of the wind.
>
> And every mote, on earth and air,
>   Will speed and gleam, down later days,
> And like a secret pilgrim fare
>   By eager and invisible ways,
>
> Nor ever rest, nor ever lie,
>   Till, beyond thinking, out of view,
> One mote of all the dust that's I
>   Shall meet one atom that was you.

Then in some garden hushed from wind,
　　Warm in a sunset's afterglow,
The lovers in the flowers will find
　　A sweet and strange unquiet grow

Upon the peace; and, past desiring,
　　So high a beauty in the air,
And such a light, and such a quiring,
　　And such a radiant ecstasy there,

They'll know not if it 's fire, or dew,
　　Or out of earth, or in the height,
Singing, or flame, or scent, or hue,
　　Or two that pass, in light, to light,

Out of the garden, higher, higher . . .
　　But in that instant they shall learn
The shattering ecstasy of our fire,
　　And the weak passionless hearts will burn

And faint in that amazing glow,
　　Until the darkness close above;
And they will know—poor fools, they'll know!—
　　One moment, what it is to love.

Whatever else may be said of that, it is certainly as
ingenious as any poem in the language; and the verse has
a rush and fire that sorts with its subject. With the silli-
ness of the expression 'your swift hair' in the second
stanza, it would be silly to make too heavy a quarrel. Nor
do I wish to take anything from the praise of this poem
when I call attention to the fact that the main idea of it
is elaborated from Cowley's *All-over Love*.[1] Let me give
you an example, from another species, of the best of
Brooke's early manner—the sonnet entitled *Victory*:

All night the ways of heaven were desolate,
Long roads across a gleaming empty sky.
Outcast and doomed and driven, you and I,
Alone, serene beyond all love or hate,
Terror or triumph, were content to wait,
We, silent and all-knowing. Suddenly
Swept through the heaven low-crouching from on high,
One horseman, downward to the earth's low gate.

[1] 1678 ed. *The Mistress*, p. 25.

Oh, perfect from the ultimate height of living,
Lightly we turned, through wet woods blossom-hung,
Into the open. Down the supernal roads,
With plumes a-tossing, purple flags far flung,
Rank upon rank, unbridled, unforgiving,
Thundered the black battalions of the Gods.

I am not sure that I quite know what it all means. But
it is at least individually conceived, and in its sonorous
phrasing I seem to hear a kind of preluding mutter of
greatness. Side by side with this I would put two other
early sonnets, 'Oh, death will find me . . .' and *The Hill*.
The other pieces that make up my seven are the experimental Choriambics, the poem *Ante Aram*, and *The Fish*.
The sources of inspiration are obvious. But even when
you see where it all comes from, can you neglect this kind
of thing?—

Before thy shrine I kneel, an unknown worshipper,
Chanting strange hymns to thee and sorrowful litanies,
Incense of dirges, prayers that are as holy myrrh.

Ah! goddess, on thy throne of tears and faint low sighs,
Weary at last to theeward come the feet that err,
And empty hearts grown tired of the world's vanities.

How fair this cool deep silence to a wanderer
Deaf with the roar of winds along the open skies!
Sweet, after sting and bitter kiss of sea-water,

The pale Lethean wine within thy chalices! . . .
I come before thee, I, too tired wanderer
To heed the horror of the shrine, the distant cries,

And evil whispers in the gloom, or the swift whirr
Of terrible wings—I, least of all thy votaries,
With a faint hope to see the scented darkness stir,

And, parting, frame within its quiet mysteries
One face, with lips than autumn-lilies tenderer,
And voice more sweet than the far plaint of viols is,

Or the soft moan of any grey-eyed lute-player.

Well, there are these seven poems out of fifty of the

Cambridge period. I suspect that Brooke wrote them
by running away one day from the people who admired.
him—by getting clear of Cambridge. And in fact, I
know that this happened; for except for these seven
poems nothing which Brooke wrote in Cambridge is equal
to almost anything that he wrote out of it. Far out of it,
perhaps. He first began to write really well in Munich—
it was there that he wrote *Grantchester*. There for the
first time in his poetry you discover humour, there for
the first time that engaging naturalism without which no
poetry, except the greatest, is really good. There, for
good and all, *exit* Swinburne. There dies finally the
charlatanism which characterizes the first puberty of all
poets worth talking of. In the place of Swinburne sits
now, one may judge, Stevenson—a man in my opinion
who only needed not to be a Scotsman in order to be one
of the purest sources of truth in our literature since
Wordsworth. The influence of Stevenson—Stevenson the
poet—upon the poetry of the twentieth century has not,
I fancy, been sufficiently observed. I can trace it plainly,
I think, in Mr. Housman, and in the epigoni of Mr. Housman. I remember Mr. Phillimore telling me that he once
showed the *Shropshire Lad* to Andrew Lang, but could
not interest him. This was the sort of thing, said Lang,
that Stevenson could write; and the connexions are real,
I think; and are not merely *verse*-connexions, but touch
thought and temper. Stevenson might have guessed that,
in the hands of the first poet of genius who imitated him,
his sham optimism would issue as sham pessimism.[1]

Whether the influence of Stevenson had anything to do
with drawing Brooke to the South Seas, I do not know.
But undoubtedly from those southern airs which kept
Stevenson alive Brooke drew his finest and subtlest inspiration. There he wrote *The Great Lover*—perhaps a little
overrated—there three among the finest of English sonnets, there the two Mamua poems, there the pretty

[1] In the lectures on Stevenson and Mr. Housman (pp. 179 ff., 211 ff.)
I have qualified these too sharply pointed expressions.

agnostic fancy called *Heaven*. Let me give you the first
of the two Mamua poems, and the end of the second.
Mamua purports to be some Samoan mistress—and I
wonder what she made of Brooke's Platonics:

> Mamua, when our laughter ends,
> And hearts and bodies, brown as white,
> Are dust about the doors of friends,
> Or scent a-blowing down the night,
> Then, oh! then, the wise agree,
> Comes our immortality.
> Mamua, there waits a land
> Hard for us to understand.
> Out of time, beyond the sun,
> All are one in Paradise,
> You and Pupure are one,
> And Taü, and the ungainly wise.
> There the Eternals are, and there
> The Good, the Lovely, and the True,
> And Types, whose earthly copies were
> The foolish broken things we knew;
> There is the Face, whose ghosts we are;
> The real, the never-setting Star;
> And the Flower, of which we love
> Faint and fading shadows here;
> Never a tear, but only Grief;
> Dance, but not the limbs that move;
> Songs in Song shall disappear;
> Instead of lovers, Love shall be;
> For hearts, Immutability;
> And there, on the Ideal Reef,
> Thunders the Everlasting Sea!

> And my laughter, and my pain,
> Shall home to the Eternal Brain.
> And all lovely things, they say,
> Meet in Loveliness again;
> Miri's laugh, Teïpo's feet,
> And the hands of Matua,
> Stars and sunlight there shall meet,
> Coral's hues and rainbows there,
> And Teüra's braided hair;

And with the starred *tiare's* white,
And white birds in the dark ravine,
And *flamboyants* ablaze at night,
And jewels, and evening's after-green,
And dawns of pearl and gold and red,
Mamua, your lovelier head!
And there'll no more be one who dreams
Under the ferns, of crumbling stuff,
Eyes of illusion, mouth that seems,
All time-entangled human love.
And you'll no longer swing and sway
Divinely down the scented shade,
Where feet to Ambulation fade,
And moons are lost in endless Day.
How shall we wind those wreaths of ours,
Where there are neither heads nor flowers?
Oh, Heaven's Heaven!—but we'll be missing
The palms, and sunlight, and the south;
And there's an end, I think, of kissing,
When our mouths are one with Mouth!
    Tau here, Mamua,
Crown the hair, and come away!
Hear the calling of the moon,
And the whispering scents that stray
About the idle warm lagoon.
Hasten, hand in human hand,
Down the dark, the flowered way,
Along the whiteness of the sand,
And in the water's soft caress,
Wash the mind of foolishness,
Mamua, until the day.
Spend the glittering moonlight there
Pursuing down the soundless deep
Limbs that gleam and shadowy hair,
Or floating lazy, half-asleep.
Dive and double and follow after,
Snare in flowers, and kiss, and call,
With lips that fade, and human laughter
And faces individual,
Well this side of Paradise! . . .
There's little comfort in the wise.

It may be that Mamua has no more substantive existence than the other ingenious images figured in this luxuriously conceited piece. Yet the companion-poem comes back to her, ending on a mood that seems deeper and more serious:

> O haven without wave or tide!
> Silence, in which all songs have died!
> Holy book, where hearts are still!
> And home at length under the hill!
> O mother-quiet, breasts of peace,
> Where love itself would faint and cease!
> O infinite deep I never knew,
> I would come back, come back to you,
> Find you as a pool unstirred,
> Kneel down by you, and never a word,
> Lay my head, and nothing said,
> In your hands, ungarlanded;
> And a long watch you would keep;
> And I should sleep, and I should sleep!

There are two poems which, plainly, I do not know how to praise enough. If you agree with me, you will perhaps bear also with a piece of somewhat different character—the poem entitled *Heaven*. If it is religious satire, it yet satirizes a smug comfortableness which there still is in parts of our best beliefs:

> Fish (fly-replete, in depth of June,
> Dawdling away their wat'ry noon)
> Ponder deep wisdom, dark or clear,
> Each secret fishy hope or fear.
> Fish say, they have their Stream and Pond;
> But is there anything Beyond?
> This life cannot be All, they swear,
> For how unpleasant, if it were!
> One may not doubt that, somehow, Good
> Shall come of Water and of Mud;
> And, sure, the reverent eye must see
> A Purpose in Liquidity.
> We darkly know, by Faith we cry,
> The future is not Wholly Dry.

> Mud unto mud!—Death eddies near—
> Not here the appointed End, not here!
> But somewhere, beyond Space and Time,
> Is wetter water, slimier slime!
> And there (they trust) there swimmeth One
> Who swam ere rivers were begun,
> Immense, of fishy form and mind,
> Squamous, omnipotent, and kind;
> And under that Almighty Fin,
> The littlest fish may enter in.
> Oh! never fly conceals a hook,
> Fish say, in the Eternal Brook,
> And more than mundane woods are there,
> And mud, celestially fair;
> Fat caterpillars drift around,
> And Paradisal grubs are found;
> Unfading moths, immortal flies,
> And the worm that never dies.
> And in that Heaven of all their wish,
> There shall be no more land, say fish.

To-day, people tell you that Brooke was too good too
soon; that he died only just in time; that they can find
in him no promise of a procession from strength to
strength. Never believe it. If you see a man becoming,
as he grows older, daily more solemn and self-conscious,
the tides of humour ebbing, and the waste spaces, where
no childhood plays, stretching wider—there you have a
man who perhaps may grow into a prophet, but into
a poet never. But with Brooke, it is all the other way.
Look at the poems *Lust* and *Success*, with their humourless
and almost senile vulgarity. Compare with them *Mamua*
or *Heaven*, or this from Fiji—it shall be my last extract,
mixing prose and verse:

'It 's twenty years since they (the Fijians) have eaten anybody,
and far more since they've done what I particularly and unreason-
ably detest—fastened the victim down, cut pieces off him one by
one, and cooked and eaten them before his eyes. To witness one's
own transubstantiation into a naked black man, that seems the last
indignity. Consideration of the last thoughts that pour through

the mind of the ever-diminishing remnant of a man, as it sees its late limbs cooking, moves me deeply. I have been meditating a sonnet, as I sit here, surrounded by dusky faces and gleaming eyes:—

> Dear, they have poached the eyes you loved so well—

. . . I don't know how it would go on. The fourth line would have to be

> And all my turbulent lips are *maître-d'hôtel* . . .

The idea comes out in a slighter thing:—

> The limbs that erstwhile charmed your sight
> Are now a savage's delight;
> The ear that heard your whispered vow
> Is one of many entrées now;
> Broiled are the arms in which you clung,
> And devilled is the angelic tongue: . . .
> And oh! my anguish as I see
> A Black Man gnaw your favourite knee!
> Of the two eyes that were your ruin,
> One now observes the other stewing.
> My lips (the inconstancy of man!)
> Are yours no more. The legs that ran
> Each dewy morn their love to wake,
> Are now a steak, are now a steak! . . .

Oh, dear! I suppose it ought to end on the Higher Note, the Wider Outlook. . . . So must I soar:

> O love, O loveliest and best,
> Natives this *body* may digest;
> Whole, and still yours, my *soul* shall dwell,
> Uneaten, safe, incoctible. . . .

It's too dull, I shall go out and wander. . . .'

All that is at least finely irresponsible, and grimly ingenious. I have put it last among my extracts; because—absurd as it is—yet it hints two out of the three characters of Brooke's poetry which I conceive, upon an impartial review of it, to be the most valuable. First, as soon as the clever people let him alone, he goes forward as one of the most delightfully natural of poets. In his own phrase, 'God catches his youth', and, 'with hand made sure, clear eye and sharpened power', he leaps into cleanness and

humour—worlds away from the prigs and the decadents
and the

> half-men with their dirty songs and dreary.

Secondly, he has in his most characteristic poetry an
ingenuity unbeaten outside Marvell. It comes to him, of
course, from the metaphysical poets, to whom—and to
Donne among them especially—he became more and more
bound as his art developed. Yet the gift is not taught,
but caught. Thirdly, even in his early period, but still
more in the six sonnets of 1914, he has a large Elizabethan
utterance—some of his effects in this kind I cannot easily
match in the last three hundred years. Yet perhaps what
I like most about him is due to the sense I have that in
his best work he is not a 'half-man'. Neither the cleverness of others, nor his own wilfulness, nor success, were
ever going to make him, or leave him, really Georgian.
He breaks away. 'I want to walk a thousand miles', he
writes, 'and write a thousand plays, and sing a thousand
poems, and drink a thousand pots of beer, and kiss a
thousand girls—and oh! a million things.' That way lies
salvation.

I am afraid I have in fact done little more than declaim
Brooke to you. I had meant to say something about the
man; and I had meant to try and place him among the
English poets. But, to be honest, when I read him, and
still more when I turn the pages of Mr. Marsh's delightfully frank Memoir, I feel a curious unconcern about the
fate of reputations; and I no more care what a hundred
years hence will say of Rupert Brooke than I care what it
will say of the light and air and glow of some phenomenal
dawn. I dare say Keats, or Marlowe, did finer work at
like years. Even so, I feel Brooke to be somehow an
unmatched effect in our literature. As a poet he is in the
first class, let us say, some five-and-twenty times in all.
But as an effect in literature, as a piece of the *life* of
poetry, as a kind of flesh and blood carelessly incarnating
what other poetry only ailingly conceives, he seizes and

holds a romantic pre-eminence. And at least in these days of distracted effort and uncoordinated achievement, we cannot afford to be cold to the romantic sum of him—to a unique fullness of life, to a most rare conjunction of genius with bodily accomplishment, to a certain luck of social temperament and environment, to the appeal of a nature prodigal of gifts and of life. After all, what an ailing crowd, or what a dull crowd, are most poets! Rupert Brooke has left us, I suggested, five-and-twenty poems of the first rate. Yet the man himself is a fine addition to the five-and-twenty poems and to the sum of the world's effects. To meet, you might have supposed him a very typical product of an English public school and university—charming, good-looking, not a little spoilt, but taking spoiling, upon the whole, well, ultimately boyish and unaffected, and the more so as the boy passed into the man. Yet with all, the five-and-twenty poems! Did there ever before in our literature blow five-and-twenty prodigal blossoms of Elizabethan genius upon a tree whose roots stand in what I may call the tradition of the *average nice man*?

And as for reputation—Brooke has passed to where Glory gathers to her early her spoiled children, while they are still lovable. I should be surprised if Time dealt with him less tenderly than with some others, the 'inheritors of unfulfilled renown'. He has something which they have not. They are some of them a little anaemic, others of them not a little pretentious. Brooke, I think, keeps blood and nature among those shades. One sees him,

> a broad-browed and smiling dream,
> Pass, light as ever, through the lightless host,
> Quietly ponder, start, and sway and gleam—
> Most individual and bewildering ghost,
> And turn, and toss his brown delightful head
> Amusedly, among the ancient dead.

THE POETRY OF R. L. STEVENSON

A GOOD many persons (perhaps most) would be inclined to find Stevenson's best poetry in his prose.
That is where the best poetry of most of us is found—and
we have all of us some. The best poetry of Scott is in the
Scotch novels. The dunderheads who compared him with
Homer were not thinking of the Scotch novels. Yet there,
and not where they looked for it, lives what there is in
Scott of the truly Homeric. I am not going to lift Stevenson to the level of Scott—I feel him to be, essentially, of
a lower stature. Yet I think him a better poet; narrow
as is his range, I think him more genuinely and intimately
a poet. Save to put them decisively below Scott, I would
not depress the fame of his novels. And I would so far
qualify what I say of Scott's decisive superiority as a
novelist that I rank the first five chapters of *Weir of
Hermiston* above anything that Scott achieved—in that
fragment Stevenson, I think, touches the top of English
fiction. Scott, again, is plainly deficient in art; and that
is true whether we compare him with Stevenson or with
artists a good deal inferior to Stevenson. There is, of
course, too much of the artist in Stevenson. But he was
getting away from it—this too much of the artist was
dropping from him. That balance of art and nature which
alone deserves to be called art Stevenson would quicker
have found than Scott would have found art, art in mere
sufficiency. Where he falls below Scott is in vital and
breathing quality—that quality which makes the world of
Shakespeare and of Dickens and, in a less degree, of Scott
himself a kind of second reality. The kings of the earth,
and the great of the earth, and the odd of the earth, gather
and go by together in Shakespeare, in Dickens, in Scott,
a pageant as convincing as life itself. There is no such
Stevenson world that we can set up against our own world
or Scott's world. Of the greater breadth of Scott's

humanity I need say nothing; nor of the pervasive manliness and justice of his temper.

Even so, I rate Stevenson's novels high; and not, I think, below their proper value his essays. There may seem, therefore, to be something of perversity in directing attention from a great novelist and essayist to a minor poet. A great novelist I think Stevenson was; and if there were anywhere in the world minor poets, I suppose he would be among them. But there are, in fact, *no* minor poets. A decree has gone out against them, the decree of three powers conjunctly irresistible—the three powers named by Horace, 'the gods, men, and the booksellers':

> mediocribus esse poetis
> non di, non homines, non concessere columnae.

Sometimes, when I survey the waste of modern talent, I thank God for 'the gods, men, and the booksellers'— who so swiftly pass down into silence the poets who were not worth listening to; so swiftly, indeed, that of the idols of my youth, few have influenced yours. I wonder sometimes how many of the poets who are a religion to-day will retain twenty years hence so much as the dignity of a superstition. There is a good sense in time which is always fatal to minor poetry.

Still, Stevenson wrote little; and there is, of course, something in magnitude. When we say that 'quality is everything', it must yet be the quality of something. That is no more than good metaphysics. But, like bad metaphysics, it could perhaps be put more simply. The single-poem poet is not impossible; but he happens only very rarely. It needs a great and single soul to pack itself into a single poem. I should suppose that Emily Brontë had done it, in her *Last Lines*, in that 'too bold dying song' which 'stirr'd like a clarion-blast the soul' of Matthew Arnold. I should suppose that, were it not that in one other perfect poem she has enshrined another soul of her —I am thinking of the lines 'Cold in the earth—and the deep snow piled above thee . . .'—lines of which the melancholy cadences haunt the mind like a fire. I do not think that you can point in Stevenson to any single poem as decisive as either of these. With all his art he is nowhere quite so much a poet as, without any art at all, Emily Brontë is in these two pieces. On the other hand, he shows the power of a poet far more often. The quality of his poetry is diffused, not widely indeed, but sufficiently. There is enough of it, I mean, to make it sensibly felt— in its gentle diffusion, it cannot be mistaken for some effect less pure than poetry.

I do not mean, of course, that the pure quality of which I speak is equally diffused over the whole body of Stevenson's verse. He wrote a great deal of verse which is not poetry at all; how much we have only recently learned. I know nothing of the Bibliophile Society of Boston. But I think it did a bad day's work when it published the *New Poems* of Stevenson. If it had published six of them, I could have borne it—or twelve, or even eighteen. But two hundred and eighteen did it see fit to publish; and if there had been more than two hundred and eighteen, it would, we may suppose, have published more. Stevenson's step-son, I know, says that we owe the Bibliophile Society of Boston 'a debt of gratitude'. From the fact that Stevenson 'preserved these poems through all the vicissitudes of his wandering life', he infers that he 'valued them dearly', and that he meant that they should one day be published. I do not say that that is impossible. There is about the office of a father always some element of blind fanaticism; along every street there are pushed brats who would not have been preserved save that some one begat them. That for these two hundred and eighteen children, begotten under grudging stars, Stevenson did not mean to make some provision, I cannot certainly affirm. That he concealed them, I know. That he did not destroy them will surprise nobody who, in an age when we are all so happy as to be poets, searches his heart and looks into his cupboards. But that a poet who published so little while he lived should wish to publish so much when he was dead; that an artist who, in life, cared so much for the decencies of craftsmanship should be willing, in dying, to expose the disorder of his workshop, his stop-gaps and subterfuges; that this cautious earth-keeping genius should hope to reach heaven by stacking his lumber—all this I find it hard to believe. I find it hard to believe; and I find it hard not to hate the Bibliophile Society of Boston. Of course, the *New Poems* were bound to be interesting. Many of them are intimate and personal; and I should be sorry if we might not express unblamed the curiosity which we properly feel about that best part of a book, the writer of it. Many of them are interesting, again, for the manner in which they illustrate the influences under which Stevenson's poetical talent developed itself. I am not sure that I knew before—though I might have guessed from his Letters—how much Stevenson's verse owes to Latin verse and to French verse. I had not before marked so plainly the influence of Matthew Arnold. I had not suspected the degree to which Stevenson was interested in metrical experiment. Some of the best pieces of the *New Poems* are experiments in classical metres. Yet again, one or two of the poems give, or hint, the first version of something done better at a later date. There is a first version, for example, of the famous *Requiem*—'Under the wide and starry sky'; yet a version so much inferior to that which we know that I could wish it away, interesting as it is.

However, there the *New Poems* are; and if a man comes to them only when he has been won to Stevenson's poetry by the best of it, they will do less harm than they should. One important lesson they do, I think, teach. Most of us write bad poetry because we cannot help it. From the *New Poems* I learned, what I had long suspected from the old ones, that Stevenson wrote bad poetry on purpose. And not only that. It was because he did so that his best poetry is as good as it is. I speak darkly; and it is time to be obliged to lighten my darkness. But in fact what makes the poetry of Stevenson interesting, what makes the best of it as good as it is, proceeds from his unremitting effort to escape from art into nature. I spoke just now of that balance of art and nature which alone deserves—I said— to be called art. That balance, that inspired adjustment, Stevenson never quite finds in his prose—in his essays he comes nowhere near it; he comes near to it in his later novels. Whether he brought to verse less conscience, or more, I am never quite certain. There were moods of poetizing when, in his own phrase, he did not think 'a day too long to make One line or letter bright'; when he set his heart on the jewelled finish of Horace, of Martial, of de Banville. He speaks of himself, in one of the *New Poems*, as planing and bevelling his verse 'like Banville's rhyming devotees'. But he was a Scotsman. You may open the heart of an Englishman, and find engraved on it almost anything—Italy, Calais, Soviet Russia. But open the heart of a Scotsman, and it is always the same story: graved inside of it you find always 'Burns'. It was not in Stevenson to write like Burns; and he knew it. It is not in any man to write like nature; the art of it ended with Burns. But it is not in any man who has been baptized into Burns not to try it. No sooner has Stevenson managed one of his half-successes in the manner of Martial or de Banville than conscience gets him.

> Sing clearlier, Muse, or evermore be still,
> Sing truer, or no longer sing!
> No more the voice of melancholy Jacques
> To wake a weeping echo in the hill;
> But as the boy, the pirate of the spring,
> From the green elm[1] a living linnet takes,
> One natural verse recapture—then be still.

It is this effort to recapture natural notes that so often makes him write the kind of verse of which all his books contain some and the *New Poems* a great deal: verse in which the studied avoidance of art conducts, not to nature, but to prose. We shall be just to this kind of verse if we conceive it as written, not to exercise Stevenson in an art, but to exercise him out of it. He is bullying

[1] But does the linnet nest in elm-trees?

himself out of that too much art which was, in fact, a disease of the mind with him—so much a disease of the mind that, if you read his Prayers, you discover that he can only *pray artistically*. That even in his best poetry he is successful in recapturing natural notes, I should not like to say. Indeed, I should not like to say that it can be done. Art is so far like nature that you can expel her with a pitchfork, but she comes running back. Like nature, she knows better; she knows that the poet cannot do without her. But it is, I think, true that into the best of his poetry Stevenson has put enough of nature to serve for holdfast.

A good many people, I know, are offended, in his poetry, by nothing so much as by what they feel to be its *pretended* naturalness. I think them stupid; but I so far follow them that I recognize the degree to which a particular kind of make-believe colours all Stevenson's poetry. I am not thinking merely of the *Child's Garden of Verses*. No doubt, a Child's Garden of Verses would be best made by children, if children could make as good verses as grown-up people. But they cannot; and the pretended naturalness of the *Child's Garden* has no greater element of pretence than accompanies any other attempt at communication between grown-ups and children. This genre Stevenson created; whether a valid and enduring one, I am not sure. At least he is as successful in it as his imitators. The *Child's Garden of Verses* was his first book of verse; and here at least his genius for make-believe exercises itself without offence. But I have the suspicion that the book could have been written only by some one who had first learned to be a child late in life; that in it Stevenson is, in fact, trying to recapture a nature from which circumstance had excluded him. He was an ailing child; and from an ailing childhood he passed to an ailing boyhood, youth, and manhood. For children, boys, young men, pirates, soldiers, and sailors, for all naturally healthy life, Stevenson had an affection the more real because, in each successive stage of his own development, the body plucked him back from the desire of the mind. When he dramatizes these characters, or some of them, in his novels, he does well with them. But in his poetry, which is rarely impersonal, his preoccupation with this kind of life takes, often, a strained expression. Loving it intensely, he can recapture it only by indulging the same kind of make-believe speech and sentiment as he employs to recapture childhood in the *Child's Garden*. The world of all his poetry becomes something of a garden-world, accordingly, and is to that extent, and in that sense, a sham world. Lecturing last term, I spoke in passing of Stevenson's 'sham optimism'. His sham optimism was the subject of some letters which passed between him and his friend William Archer; and all Stevenson's skill hardly avails, I think, to clear his character. A sham optimist he was; and it is only one of a number of shams. He shammed happy; he shammed well; he shammed young and piratical; he shammed the natural man. But it is all the shamming of a heroical invalidism; and as such gains, perhaps, in poetry, as much as it loses, by being found out. In all this pretended naturalness there is more of nature than in some of the robuster sincerities with which it contrasts. I prefer, for example, Stevenson's sham optimism to the boisterous pessimism of Henley.

> O to be up and doing, O
> Unfearing and unshamed to go
> In all the uproar and the press
> About my human business!
> My undissuaded heart I hear
> Whisper courage in my ear.
> With voiceless calls, the ancient earth
> Summons me to a daily birth.
> Thou, O my love, ye, O my friends—
> The gist of life, the end of ends—
> To laugh, to love, to live, to die,
> Ye call me by the ear and eye.

Half the poetry of Stevenson, be it remembered, is sick-bed poetry.

Among his shams was the sham of not being a poet.

'I do not set up to be a poet', he writes to Symonds; 'only an all-round literary man; a man who talks, not sings. . . . I don't like to come before people who have a note of song, and let it be supposed that I do not know the difference.' He affects surprise at the success of *Underwoods*; and attributes it to the 'prose merits' of the book. It followed the *Child's Garden* at an interval of two years. Of the poems 'in Scots' I do not pretend to be able to assess the quality; and of the thirty-nine English pieces I could spare perhaps one-half. When Stevenson says that the book pleased by its 'prose merits', he knows better, of course. And yet he knows what he is saying. It is not his best book of verse; that was to come; his best book of verse is, beyond doubt, the *Songs of Travel*. But the characteristic notes of the later and better book are heard already in *Underwoods*. Perhaps the fourth poem of *Underwoods* better illustrates them than anything else:

> It is the season now to go
> About the country high and low,
> Among the lilacs hand in hand,
> And two by two in fairyland.
>
> The brooding boy, the sighing maid,
> Wholly fain and half afraid,
> Now meet along the hazel'd brook
> To pass and linger, pause and look.
>
> A year ago, and blithely paired
> Their rough-and-tumble play they shared;
> They kissed and quarrelled, laughed and cried,
> A year ago at Eastertide.
>
> With bursting heart and fiery face,
> She strove against him in the race;
> He unabashed her garter saw,
> That now would touch her skirts with awe.
>
> Now by the stile ablaze she stops,
> And his demurer eye he drops;
> Now they exchange averted sighs,
> Or stand and marry silent eyes.

And he to her a hero is
And sweeter she than primroses;
Their common silence dearer far
Than nightingale and mavis are.

Now when they sever wedded hands,
Joy trembles in their bosom-strands,
And lovely laughter leaps and falls
Upon their lips in madrigals.

That has, no doubt, its 'prose merits'. But I am more impressed, on the whole, by its lyrical tenderness, by the natural sweetness of it; or, it may be, by the way in which these qualities wed themselves with the 'prose merits'. Familiar lyric of this kind Stevenson wrote when Victorianism was still at the height of its pretension; and as much as any other man, I am inclined to think, he found both the notes and the words for the poets who since have done so much to put us out of love with Victorian standards. Something of this I hinted last term, when I was speaking of Rupert Brooke; and something more I will say about it presently, if time allows. Here, I would like to illustrate from *Underwoods* Stevenson's power in a different order of verse. I have always thought that in blank verse—in the short poem in blank verse, in what may be called, perhaps, blank verse lyric—Stevenson achieved, at least occasionally, work of a quality which places him with the great masters in this kind. As an example of his power here let me give you first some lines from the poem entitled *Et tu in Arcadia*. They describe a common case—the bewilderment of a man who has lived with good poetry and finds himself thrown into a world of bad poetry or none:

Now things there are that upon him who sees
A strong vocation lay; and strains there are
That whoso hears shall hear for evermore.
For evermore thou hear'st immortal Pan
And those melodious godheads, ever young
And ever quiring, on the mountains old.
What was this earth, child of the gods, to thee?

Forth from thy dreamland thou, a dreamer, cam'st,
And in thine ears the olden music rang,
And in thy mind the doings of the dead,
And those heroic ages long forgot.
To a so fallen earth, alas! too late,
Alas! in evil days thy steps return,
To list at noon for nightingales, to grow
A dweller on the beach till Argo come
That came long since, a lingerer by the pool
Where that desired angel bathes no more.

I have chosen that because the movement of it owes
something, I fancy, to Matthew Arnold; and I have mentioned already this influence. I am going to ask you to
bear with me while I read to you a piece of which the
manner is somewhat more individual and the theme more
personal; a piece which expresses a characteristic ethical
bias. The ethical bias was strong in Stevenson; and it is
in what I call his blank-verse lyrics that it finds its most
sincere and effective expression. The poem has no title;
but it embodies the reflections of an invalid on the duty
of not dying:

Not yet, my soul, these friendly fields desert,
Where thou with grass, and rivers, and the breeze,
And the bright face of day, thy dalliance had'st;
Where to thine ear first sang the enraptured birds;
Where love and thou that lasting bargain made.
The ship rides trimmed, and from the eternal shore
Thou hearest airy voices; but not yet
Depart, my soul, not yet a while depart.

Freedom is far, rest far. Thou art with life
Too closely woven, nerve with nerve entwined;
Service still craving service, love for love,
Love for dear love, still suppliant with tears.
Alas, not yet thy human task is done!
A bond at birth is forged; a debt doth lie
Immortal on mortality. It grows—
By vast rebound it grows, unceasing growth,
Gift upon gift, alms upon alms, upreared,
From man, from God, from nature, till the soul
At that so huge indulgence stands amazed.

Leave not, my soul, the unfoughten field, nor leave
Thy debts dishonoured, nor thy place desert
Without due service rendered. For thy life,
Up, spirit, and defend that fort of clay,
Thy body, now beleaguered; whether soon
Or late she fall; whether to-day thy friends
Bewail thee dead, or, after years, a man
Grown old in honour and the friend of peace.
Contend, my soul, for moments and for hours;
Each is with service pregnant; each reclaimed
Is as a kingdom conquered, where to reign.

As when a captain rallies to the fight
His scattered legions, and beats ruin back,
He, on the field, encamps, well pleased in mind.
Yet surely him shall fortune overtake,
Him smite in turn, headlong his ensigns drive;
And that dear land, now safe, to-morrow fall.
But he, unthinking, in the present good
Solely delights, and all the camps rejoice.

Four years after *Underwoods* Stevenson published his volume of *Ballads*. Of the *Ballads* I will not say more than that, firstly, you cannot keep a Scot from this kind; secondly, that, without being especially readable, they can be read, and that, in *Rahero*, the talk between Rahero and Tamatea has character; but thirdly, that two lyric quatrains of it are worth all the rest of the book—the one Rahero's song:

House of mine, in your walls, strong sounds the sea,
Of all sounds on earth dearest sound to me.
I have heard the applause of men, I have heard it arise and die:
Sweeter now in my house I hear the trade-wind cry.

There is nothing in it; but the ring of it stays; and of Rua's song in the *Feast of Famine* the same is true:

Night, night it is, night upon the palms,
Night, night it is, the land-wind has blown.
Starry, starry night, over deep and height;
Love, love in the valley, love all alone.

At the same time that he was writing the *Ballads* Stevenson wrote most of the *Songs of Travel*—and this is, as I have said, far and away his best book of verse. I do not know that, in comparison with *Underwoods*, it brings anything new in kind. As far as kind goes, it repeats the successes of *Underwoods*. But the percentage of failures is far smaller—there are not many pieces which you could reasonably wish away, and of the best there is enough, I think, taken with the best of *Underwoods*, to make it proper to think of Stevenson as more certainly a poet than any writer whose fame was founded in the same period or in a later period. In both the kinds in which he is successful in *Underwoods*, the late Victorian lyric preluding the Georgian, and the blank verse lyric, he shows, in *Songs of Travel*, both more power and more ease. The improved ease is most notable in the lyrics proper. There is more of music in them, more of that bright hurry of notes proper to lyric:

> The infinite shining heavens
>   Rose and I saw in the night
> Uncountable angel stars
>   Showering sorrow and light. . . .

Of this more song-like lyric some examples which I might take are familiar—the Skye poem, for example, and 'Bright is the ring of words'. Less known, and perhaps less deserving to be known, but yielding a good example of Stevenson's skill in domestic lyric, and at the same time illustrating the new music in him, are the lines on Mrs. Stevenson:

> To you let snow and roses
>   And golden locks belong:
> These are the world's enslavers,
>   Let these delight the throng.
> For her of duskier lustre,
>   Whose favour still I wear,
> The snow be in her kirtle,
>   The rose be in her hair.

> The hue of highland rivers
>   Careering, full and cool,
> From sable on to golden,
>   From rapid on to pool—
> The hue of heather honey,
>   The hue of honey bees,
> Shall tinge her golden shoulder,
>   Shall gild her tawny knees.

Even so, even in the *Songs of Travel*, it is in the graver
lyric, in those poems where he weds ethical reflection to
lyrical expression, that Stevenson attains his purest felicity. One or two pieces in this order, the lines, for
example, to S. R. Crockett, and the stanzas beginning 'In
the highlands, in the country places . . .' have found their
way into the anthologies. For myself, I like better, and
think more like Stevenson, a poem which I have not seen
in any anthology, the poem entitled 'Youth and Love':

> To the heart of youth the world is a highwayside.
>   Passing for ever he fares; and on either hand,
> Deep in the gardens golden pavilions hide,
>   Nestle in orchard bloom, and far on the level land
> Call him with lighted lamp in the eventide.
>
> Thick as the stars at night when the moon is down,
>   Pleasures assail him. He to his nobler fate
> Fares; and but waves a hand as he passes on,
>   Cries but a wayside word to her at the garden gate,
> Sings but a boyish stave, and his face is gone.

A dozen of other pieces I could mention where, in this
book, Stevenson achieves individual expression; some of
them executed in measures of a strangely haunting quality
—I am thinking, when I say that, especially of the
'Wandering Willie' verses, which I have not time to quote.
I do not know whether any one has made a 'Fifty Best
Poems of Stevenson'. I should like to see a book of just
that compass, disengaging from the too great weight of
inferior work the work of pure and noble quality.

There is much else that I wanted to say about the
poetry of Stevenson, and about its connexions; so much

else, indeed, that I have scarcely managed to hint the theme which I had primarily in mind when I engaged myself to lecture upon Stevenson. I had meant to take up one or two things that I had said, or half-said, about Stevenson when I lectured last term upon Rupert Brooke. I called attention then, in particular, to the degree in which the verse of Stevenson had influenced, as I thought, the verse of the two best poets who have come after him, Brooke and Mr. Housman; the degree in which it had influenced these two, and, either directly, or through these two indirectly, many of the younger poets. The poetry of Stevenson, both in its studied naturalism of sentiment, and in the pains which it shows to quicken diction from living sources of speech, has always seemed to me to build a bridge, as it were, between the de-colorated Victorianism into which some of us were born and the lush Georgianism in which most of us, perhaps, will be so unhappy as to die. I had wanted to say some-thing about this; and something, too, about the accident, or fate, by which we owe to poets who were primarily novelists the disintegration in poetry of Victorian stan-dards. For so I think it is. The poetry of Stevenson, Meredith, Mr. Hardy, has influenced the younger poets more deeply than better poetry. The best poet of the three I suppose to be Stevenson—I do not think that it was in Meredith, or in Mr. Hardy, to 'recapture natural notes', to sing clearly enough to be heard hereafter. For the greater Victorian poets Stevenson entertained an ad-miration so naive that he thought the *Ode on the Death of the Duke of Wellington* a poem unsurpassed 'in any tongue or time' (*Letters*, xxiii, p. 293). Yet he must share, I think, with Meredith and Mr. Hardy the responsibility for about half of the poetry called Georgian. I wish I had time to pursue the theme. But I will end with a con-fession of faith. For the Victorian age, I will say, frankly, I have never had that religious regard which is now, I am told, once again becoming fashionable. It was not fashion-able when I was young enough to follow fashion; and I

cannot change now. If I think less highly of the Victorian
poetry than I should, it is because it was just beginning
to be found out when I myself was just beginning to be
young and clever. Among youth's raptures, second only—
I should suppose—to first love is that zest of discovery
which consists in seeing through the things that have
taken in better men. Dull men had over-praised the
Victorian poetry; and they had done so because they
believed in it. To-day very clever ones are beginning to
over-praise it again; but whether because they believe in
it or because they are clever, I am too dull to discover.
No doubt, it is good fun to find again the poetry that has
been found out; but whether there is enough sense in it
to excuse the bright talents which it requires, I am not
sure. For myself, I believe in knowing good from bad;
and I began so early that I doubt whether the Victorian
poetry will *ever* seem to me better than it is. The Victorian novel does. If two hundred years hence I were to
wake up, in somebody else's lecture, and hear it said that
the Victorian age had only two things to its credit—the
Victorian novel and the *Origin of Species*—I might perhaps be irritated, but I do not know that I should be
surprised. That is why it interests me to observe the dis-
integrating influence exercised upon Victorian poetry by
the later Victorian novelists. Yet, as I say, I like to know
good from bad; and in Victorian poetry I find both. I will
even go further. Living with, and lulled by, the new
poetry, sensitive, as I think I am, to the pervasive enchantments of the 'Georgian' age, I none the less have my
hours of weakness, when I ask myself whether the last
enchantments of the Victorian age were not at once more
lively and better for me.

MR. HUMBERT WOLFE

I HAVE been reproached (I have said before) with preferring the dead to the living; and certainly, for a critic, they have the advantage that they cannot answer back. I might urge that, as between the living and the dead, it is not always easy, in poetry, to know which is which. But I might very well be told that just that is my business (if I have one); and indeed, for something like this I conceive myself to be paid. I am paid, not perhaps to know, but to divine. My divinations, I will say frankly, have sometimes been badly out; not, however, because I felt that I did not know, but because I was sure that I did. I remember a time when I refused to interest myself in Rupert Brooke. Yet to-day I confess gladly that I think he brought to poetry a richness of nature for the like of which we must go back to Keats.

Mr. Humbert Wolfe is not yet dead, though he was born in 1884 and educated at Bradford. I give you the date, because you will not find it in *Who's Who*. Mr. Wolfe has in this matter something of the sensitiveness of celebrated actresses, and would wish it believed that he was made and not born. However, he was, in fact, born forty-three years ago—where I know not; but he was, as I say, educated at Bradford. Being possessed of an essentially climbing disposition, he passed from Bradford to Wadham College. The golden age of Wadham poetry he just missed; he was just too late, that is, to know Lord Birkenhead, Mr. C. B. Fry, Sir John Simon. But unlike any Oxford poet I know, he took a first in Greats. Before I call him a living poet, I should like to see a little more of him. If any one thinks that he is not a poet at all, and that I ought not to be lecturing on him, I might perhaps defend myself after the fashion of Jules Lemaître, who, reviewing *Serge Panine*, said that he proposed to vary the monotony of talking about literature by talking about

M. Ohnet. But in fact Mr. Wolfe, whether or not he be a living poet, is beyond doubt a very lively one. My temperament dislikes caution; and I am prepared accordingly to call him a *considerable* poet. I use the word as it should be used. I mean that his recent work entitles him to be thought about; and, after all, it is much better for him that he should be thought about than talked about. Very likely, it has not happened to him before. Talked about he certainly has been. For it will not be contested, I think, that his *Requiem* has been the most successful poem of recent years. Rupert Brooke published nothing which had so notable a vogue. Perhaps not even Mr. Masefield's *Everlasting Mercy* was discussed with so much interest. I am too young (absurd as it may seem) to remember the sensation created by Swinburne's *Poems and Ballads*. But forget *Poems and Ballads*, and for a vogue equal to that of *Requiem* you will perhaps be driven back to that morning of February 1812 when Byron 'awoke and found himself famous' . Whether Mr. Wolfe is as good a poet as Byron, or a better poet than Byron, or a worse, or no poet at all, does not—for the moment— matter. I am merely comparing one success with another; and by a success I mean, here, a publishing and reviewing success. Poetical success, success *in* poetry as distinct from success *with* it, is another matter. Mr. Wolfe has quick enough wits to know that; and sufficient tenacity, I will hope, of mind and character not to forget it. Many things helped Byron which have not been at Mr. Wolfe's service. Byron was a nobleman, at a time when it counted. He was wicked, before wickedness had shed its Gothic romance. He had just returned from a tour of Europe, which invested him with a glamour only to be won to-day by flying the Atlantic. Having once discovered what the public wanted, he was base enough to go on supplying it.

Mr. Wolfe has none of these advantages. He is by birth, I believe, partly Austrian, partly Italian. There is a strain of Semitic blood in him; and he has had to contend, not only with the temptations which these origins set him, but with the prejudices which they create. He plies a profession commonly accounted humdrum. Like a better poet, Matthew Arnold, he is a civil servant; and his merits as such, like those of Arnold, have not, I am inclined to think, had entirely adequate recognition. At one time I worked under him in a Government office; and I thought his abilities (albeit they seemed sometimes more like prestidigitation than intellection) the most extraordinary that I had encountered. But he has to contend with environment; and more able men have been killed by environment than by drink or wars or women. He is not in a position to fly the Atlantic; and though he has made, I believe, as representative of the Ministry of Labour at the League of Nations one or two half-hearted attempts to set fire to the Lake of Geneva, he is likely, in the end, to owe such distinction as he wins to his writing. In the past twelve months [1] he has achieved by his writing a success which was, if anything, a little overdue. I say that because, in respect of these publishing and reviewing successes, there is ground sometimes for suspicion. But recognition came to Mr. Wolfe somewhat late; and I hope the more sweetly as from men who gave it grudgingly.

I said that Byron, having once discovered what the public wanted, was base enough to go on supplying it. He did that partly because he despised men, and partly because he had no belief in his own poetry. By this time Mr. Wolfe knows what the public likes. I do not think that he despises men; but he has, I fancy, a too-particular regard for one class of men, namely, clever men; and this may well lead him to forget that the proper subject of poetry is human nature; human nature as it is essentially; and not those perversions and vagaries of it the study of which so much attracts men who are just clever. Unlike Byron, Mr. Wolfe quite certainly believes in his own poetry. That he believes in a better poetry than his own I am not so sure. But I feel that only by doing so, only

[1] The lecture was delivered in November 1927.

by believing in a better poetry than his own, will he make
his own poetry better.

Aristotle counted it a merit in himself that he 'preferred
truth to his friends'. He did not add that, while it is
always virtuous to do so, it is sometimes also very good
fun. It was the exhilaration of the exercise which kept
Hazlitt alive; when he could no longer prefer truth to
Coleridge and Wordsworth, all the power of him wilted.
I am going to take the privilege of friendship and prefer
truth to Mr. Humbert Wolfe; and I shall not disguise a
certain mild enjoyment that I feel in telling Mr. Wolfe
what I think of him. If I did not think a good deal of
him, I should not speak of him at all; nor should I have
invited him to come here next week and lecture upon
The Craft of Verse. He could not, I fancy, have a better
subject; for I will say freely and at once that I think him,
in his own verse, save in one or two particulars which I
shall note presently, a singularly accomplished craftsman.
Indeed, that the master of so much craft should not one
day rise out of it, shake off the excess of artifice and put
on truth and nature, I find it difficult to believe.

You will infer that I do not think all Mr. Wolfe's poetry
equally good. It isn't. Nor is all the poetry of Wordsworth equally good. Wordsworth was really good when
he was really young. If he had waited till he was Mr.
Wolfe's age, we should have had from him only those
parts of his poetry which nobody reads. Mr. Wolfe, when
he was young, did not write poetry which was really good.
He wrote poetry which was just young; and there is no
more to be said about it. I say nothing against him for
writing it; but I can remember a time when he used to
read it to me. It was usually about midnight; and from
this kind of midnight peril no one, I suppose, who asso-
ciates much with literary persons is ever wholly safe.
Some of this early poetry, if I may tell tales out of school,
was what I call smart; other parts of it, by contrast, were
elegantly languorous. Something of both qualities survives,
it may be, into Mr. Wolfe's later and better verse. One

or two of his books I do not know. I have not read *London
Sonnets*; for I hate sonnets and I hate London. Of *Shylock
Reasons with Mr. Chesterton* I thought sufficiently well to
lend it to a friend who confessed that he liked 'clever'
poetry; and I have not seen it since. Those two books
were, I think, the first poetry which Mr. Wolfe published.
Shylock was, unless my memory is at fault, a good enough
example of the craft of satire to deserve more attention
than it got. But it was followed by two volumes not
calculated, I fancy, to sustain the promise of it: *Kensington
Gardens* and *The Unknown Goddess*. One or two of the
pieces in *Kensington Gardens* are, in their over-modern
fashion, none the less delicate and charming:

> Who thought of the lilac?
> 'I', dew said,
> 'I made up the lilac
> out of my head.'
>
> 'She made up the lilac!
> Pooh!' thrilled a linnet,
> and each dew-note had a
> lilac in it.

That, and one or two pieces of similar kind, I like. But
I do not know that I like them very much. Of this book—
Kensington Gardens—I will confide to you a criticism
which I heard passed across the dinner-table—a criticism
pert and crude, and not even half-true, but perhaps about
one-quarter true. 'Mr. Wolfe had determined', it was
said, 'to write a book which should be too clever by half;
and he had proved not half-clever enough to write it.'
I hate malice; and I could not see that some of the things
in Mr. Wolfe's book were clever at all. I could not see,
for example, that it was clever to put all the commas in
the wrong place. Large numbers of Mr. Wolfe's lines
begin with a comma *before* the first word; it is the comma
which ought to stand after the last word of the line before. Mr. Wolfe believed that there was something in the
nature of poetry—or of *his* poetry—which compelled him

to this whimsical punctuation; and he even dared to say
that he felt that he 'could not change a comma without
troubling of a star!' That was in the Preface to *The
Unknown Goddess*; and when poets write prefaces, sometimes, I think, the devil gets them. *The Unknown Goddess*
is Mr. Wolfe's longest book. I am afraid I think it long
and dull. Mr. Wolfe is not often dull; but if a man *will*
write a Preface all about punctuation and false rhyme,
he must expect to suffer some deterioration of spiritual
quality. About false rhymes Mr. Wolfe has a theory; and
as it still affects his practice, I feel obliged to say something about it. The first poem in *The Unknown Goddess*
consists of forty lines; and contains only two rhymes that
are not false. For instance, the word 'false' itself Mr.
Wolfe rhymes with 'yours'; he rhymes 'Homer' with
'summer', 'Paris' with 'cherries', 'trouble' with 'pebble'.
Some of these rhymes might pass, if they were not thrown
at you as part of a theory. 'They are not', says Mr. Wolfe,
'due to an inability to make true rhymes, nor are they the
result of any deliberately innovating intention. They
happen to be the way in which the verse has come
through.' I admire there what I may call the pleasant
impudence of it. But the ultimate question in respect of
all verse is not whether it 'has come through' in this or
that way, but whether ('come through' as it may) it is
good verse or bad. There is something, none the less, in
what Mr. Wolfe says. Of some of his best verse the merit
is that it 'comes through' like verse that cannot wait. It
girds and carries Mr. Wolfe, I will not say whither he
would not, but to issues which make against small delays.
He cannot wait for a true rhyme, and he snatches at any
rhyme that comes. Yet if he were a better rhymist, he
would find better rhymes to snatch at. Where he is at his
best, where he is, as I think he often is, swung along by
a true lyric impulse, he can hide successfully—or even
parade as a success in itself—his defect of rhyming faculty.
But that is only when he is in luck. He is not in luck
consistently and always. Yet consistently and always he

prefers, what better poets prefer only occasionally, bad
rhymes to good. There is only one question about a bad
rhyme—can the verse carry it? Some of Mr. Wolfe's
verse can. Most of it can't. If I may speak plainly of
the poem which first brought him celebrity, his *News of
the Devil*, the defect, to my mind, of that Satire—which
has some qualities of good satire—the most serious defect
of it is that, by the persistent use of false rhymes, Mr.
Wolfe has obliterated, often, the distinction which there
is between the verse of satire and that of comic opera.
Now and again, no one is going to cavil at such rhymes
as 'purpose' and 'warp us', 'feature' and 'preacher',
'thicket' and 'pluck it'. But Mr. Wolfe will not be done
with it; and very often his rhymes are weak without excuse
—he rhymes 'had' with 'God', 'dust' with both 'rest' and
'ghost', the syllable -ness (as in 'busi*ness*') with 'brass' and
'face' and 'this', 'been' with 'men', 'sense' with 'advance'
—and I know not what else; with endless tiresomeness,
and often with grievous loss of effect. The finest paragraph of his Satire—the fifty lines which begin

> Each of us has the God that he deserves

are ruined, just as they seemed to be culminating greatly,
by a final false-rhyming couplet. Of *Humoresque* also and
of *Requiem* some of the best pieces are spoilt by bad and
ineffective rhyming.

I must not, however, leave *News of the Devil* without
praising its Epilogue. It ends with an Epilogue which
might indeed be the epilogue to anything else in the
world, but which certainly illustrates Mr. Wolfe's lyrical
gift at its best:

> I have sung of love. I am feign of
>   love that I cannot sing,
> love that is cleansed from the stain of
>   the heart's imagining;
>
> Not the love of living and being
>   not my own love to me,
> but the quiet over-seeing
>   of man by eternity.

There is a silence folded
    within the heart of peace,
and there our time is moulded
    into the curve of these.

There is no need for anger,
    there is no cause for pain,
and love's enchanting danger
    bewitches there in vain.

And the music, we had made of
    a whisper and a guess,
will there be unafraid of
    its own full loveliness.

No more as here encumbered
    between the heart and wit,
between the thought remembered,
    and song that failed of it,

between the beauty waiting
    on eyes that dared not see,
and vision hesitating
    on immortality,

But one with what love sings of,
    and one with love that sings,
the soul will touch the strings of
    the harp of which the strings

are chords of light revealing
    the vision absolute,
where love surpasses feeling,
    and song fulfilled is mute.

I do not know that I like that the less either for knowing where some of it comes from or for not knowing what much of it means. Of the last stanza but one, I see the perils—

But one with what love sings of,
    and one with love that sings,
the soul will touch the strings of
    the harp of which the strings . . .

There, as in parts of *Requiem*, I catch the notes of what
I call Mr. Wolfe's 'Black Aceldama' manner:

> O to be wafted away
>   from this Black Aceldama of sorrow
> Where the dust of an earthy to-day
>   is the earth of a dusty to-morrow.

However, even Mr. Wolfe's 'Black Aceldama' manner
has its proper magic; and the verses I have read to you
have enough of melodious quality to make a quarrel with
them ungracious. No doubt you will have been sensitive,
as I read them, to one or two bad rhymes; and in the
stanza that I have condemned you will have found out
one of the artifices by which Mr. Wolfe tries to hide his
defect of the rhyming faculty—'sings of', 'sings', 'strings
of', 'strings', these are just one rhyme masquerading as
two, by the aid of an 'of'; and when Mr. Wolfe writes
a Preface to show that he is perfectly well able to find
rhymes when he wants them, the answer is, not merely
that he fails to do so, but that he would not write the
Preface if he *could* find the rhymes. Still, the poem I speak
of is good enough; at least it is good enough for the effects
at which Mr. Wolfe aims. I am not sure that, as yet, he
aims high enough; I think him too much content everywhere to make an impression, rather than to touch the
heart or the mind.

I have taken *News of the Devil* out of its proper place.
It immediately preceded *Requiem*; but it was preceded by
Humoresque. Parts of *Humoresque* are not much better,
perhaps, than a good deal of *The Unknown Goddess*. Some
of the poems are ingenious with a rather tiresome ingenuity—among them I would reckon *Atonement*—a poem
astonishingly clever, but with a wasted cleverness. Of
some other poems the ingenuity is even a little silly. I
hope, again, that Mr. Wolfe will give up altogether what
is called 'free verse'. He tries it once or twice in this book
—and elsewhere; but neither is it verse, nor does it make
him free; always it seems to me to cramp and fetter him.
I could wish also that he would abandon lines of two

syllables—sometimes there is only *one* syllable to the line.
The Elizabethans, some of them, made such verses; and
they made them, I always think, badly. They have not
influenced Mr. Wolfe—I do not feel, indeed, that any
poetry has influenced him that was not written yester-
day. The French decadents, and their successors, have
obviously influenced him a good deal. But verse of the
order of Verlaine's *Song of Autumn* is outside Mr. Wolfe's
powers, perhaps outside the genius of the language. I
hope, once more, that Mr. Wolfe will abandon composition in octosyllabic couplets. He will find something less
simple far simpler. In the lighter lyric measures he is only
once, in *Humoresque*, at his best. I may be allowed to give
you this isolated success, p. 31:

> What was it that the soul did
> in the gold-coloured night,
> that stained the wings folded
> after their flight?

> What was met in that vagrance
> that left, as they fell,
> with the pinions the fragrance
> of asphodel?

> What wisp of what far light
> is driftingly drawn,
> like the ghost of a starlight
> surprised by the dawn?

> What word, that was played with
> no flute that we guess,
> has left us afraid with
> dark loveliness?

> What voice of a lark has
> been threaded through thunder?
> What kiss in the dark has
> split heaven asunder?

That is Mr. Wolfe at his best, for this species of lyric.
Even so, he has done his worst in the last two lines—

> What kiss in the dark has
> split heaven asunder?

I verily fear, some vulgarly smacking kiss; and it has come near to splitting, or spoiling, all the beauty and music that went before. I have to note this, because it is the kind of thing that Mr. Wolfe does too often; too often, when he is flying well and strongly, some kink in judgement disarrays his wings, and he drops plumb.

All this notwithstanding, I think *Humoresque* a much better book than *News of the Devil*. *News of the Devil* has had a great deal of praise. But there has been one adverse criticism of it, which may very well prove fatal to it— I mean Dryden's *Absalom and Achitophel*. The criticism of *Humoresque* and of *Requiem* has yet to be written. I have the hope that Mr. Wolfe will live to write it himself; and indeed, I think it likely. In *News of the Devil* Mr. Wolfe is doubly hampered. He knows what he wants to say; and he wants to say it in a way which does not suit him; I mean an English way. I like him very much better, first, when he is a degree foreign; and, secondly, when he does not quite know what he wants to say; when I do not quite know what he has said. Not that I do not want to understand him; but because, when I fail to, then especially I feel that he *has* something to say; and that, one day, he will find it difficult to say, and not, as now, easy, too easy. One day, I hope, he will falter and stammer; and of that divine embarrassment I shall be the intensely interested witness, and 'Speak,' I shall say, 'for thy servant heareth'.

Meantime, I am content to observe that the best of *Humoresque* preludes the best of a better book, *Requiem*. Already in the best poems of *Humoresque* Mr. Wolfe is discovering, I will not say his true lyric gift, but the proper instrument of it. Already in *Humoresque* he touches to new and fine issues the decasyllabic line. I do not know that decasyllabic verse has been quite so fully *lyricized* before. Whether Mr. Wolfe uses the old elegiac stanza, or some stanza of his own—whatever arrangement of decasyllabic lines he employs, he manages to impart to verse and line a lyric quality which, at least in the sum of

its effects, may be accounted, I think, new and individual.
I am anxious to avoid exaggeration. Mr. Wolfe knows
that the decasyllabic line is scanned, not by syllables, but
by breaths. I do not know how many syllables he has not
crowded into some of his decasyllabic lines; nor how many
syllables he has not, from time to time, left out. If you
count your feet on your fingers, he is a very licentious
versifier. But if you count in breathings, and are satisfied
with that equivalence which relates expense of breath to
the expense of spirit, I should not be surprised if he were
found a very exact metrist. The only measure of verse,
I mean, is the leap or delay of spirit. This is so far a secret
that it is better not to talk about it; not because anybody
will repeat it, but because there are persons to whom it
will mean nothing at all.

> Look! we have loved all day, without asking or thinking,
>   and, like Joshua, love has held back the sun,
> now when for all the Western world it is sinking:
>   for the long day of our beauty can never be done.
>
> Never, because the moments and hours it is made of
>   have ceased to be time, and have become a part
> of the one impulse of life that death is afraid of,
>   the unsubstantial fictions of the heart.

—you wait for the last line before you so much as discover
that these *are* decasyllables—that this is the old elegiac
metre, the metre of Sir John Davies and of Gray, but
adjusted, no longer to philosophic or sentimental reflection, but to lyric passion. You wait for the last line; but
the accident that it has betrayed him is not going to hold
Mr. Wolfe back:

> This is a world outside the world, whose daylight
>   is a dream some Trojan dreamed, a Roman kiss,
> a tune that Villon sang in France's May, light
>   as all these, immortal with all this.
>
> And if you say to me, 'Though this day is beating
>   into all beauty, yet we in whom it was born,
> we do not endure with it, we, who are fleeting,
>   torn from its light as a flower is torn.'

If you say, 'We see the splendour and lose it.'
If you say, 'How are we better thus?'
I shall answer, 'Because we did not refuse it,
we are one with this, and this is one with us.'

That is all from a poem of *Humoresque*. The book has
better poems; but this better than some others illustrates
the variety of Mr. Wolfe's verse. The best poem in the
book is *The Incommunicable Surd*—I am sorry that I have
not time to read it to you. The best stanzas in the book
are two from the Prologue of it—I may give at least these.
'Any Girl to any Artist' they might be called:

I made a fetch of my own joys and grief,
    and mixed them with the leaves, and moon, and song,
I made a lover of a tumbled leaf,
    and dreamed that I could love him, and was wrong.

.   .   .   .

You were yourself, not made for praise or blame,
    and, in your music lonely and content,
between two snatches of a song you came,
    and in the silence after song you went.

The verse of *Requiem* is, the best of it, in the same
kind, and of the same order; yet drawing out, I think,
new stops; the two books together exhibiting a metrical
accomplishment well worth our wonder for the breadth
and height of it. The metrical technique of *Requiem* certainly marks an advance on that of *Humoresque*; and the
diction of it strives after a grandiloquence of which Mr.
Wolfe's earlier work is careless. On the other hand, the
transition from the one book to the other marks, I fancy,
a transition from a greater to a less *humanity*. The persons
of *Humoresque* purport to be very unreal creatures, not
able to compete with a world

Where every man of us is once Pierrot,
    and every woman always is Pierrette.

But, slightly as they are sketched, they are a better and more
likeable and more living set of creatures than the common
and uncommon men and women and soldiers and harlots
and hucksters and what not who furnish the dramatis

personae of *Requiem*. The truth is that the fairies, or
angels, who, when Mr. Wolfe was born, brought to his
cradle an astonishing variety of gifts, forgot to give him
a subject-matter. At some later date, an imp of mischief
whispered to him that he had better be no better than
his age; and he betook himself to that last refuge of poets
out-at-elbows, real men and women. *Requiem*, accordingly, is not only a little inhumane, but a great deal more
obscure than Mr. Wolfe can expect us to bear. It is, perhaps, the most obscure poem since *Sordello*. I mention
Sordello for the reason that Mr. Wolfe is old enough to
have read Browning, and young enough to betray, by
many echoes, that he has done so. The best of his Men
and Women are, I think—though I doubt whether Mr.
Wolfe will wish to be told so—the reputable ones. The
best poems of *Requiem* are *The Soldier*, *The Nun*, and
The Respectable Woman. About the Respectable Woman
Mr. Wolfe has his own ideas; and when she sings her
respectabilities, it is not altogether certain that she does
not feel herself to have missed the true singing. But hear
her; for here Mr. Wolfe sings clearly and well, almost
throughout:

> They are singing, but I have not listened
>   in the open spaces in spring.
> Their white feet in the dances have hastened,
>   but mine are not hastening.
>
> They have loosed their hair that is golder
>   than laburnum's gold in May,
> and the birch in the rain is their shoulder—
>   but I have looked away.
>
> They have bound their breasts with rushes,
>   they have dived in the forest lake,
> but the foot of the satyr crushes
>   the lilied reeds in the brake.
>
> The sound of a flute drifts over,
>   (but I have closed my ears)
> and the air is sweet with the lover,
>   and the cry of the fugitive years.

I have not heard nor seen them,
    I have not danced nor sung,
and when love passed between them
    he left my heart unwrung.

They have wasted their lives by spending,
    and are with death rewarded,
but I shall find no ending
    of the life that I have hoarded.

I saved the source of living,
    Thou knowest at what cost,
and, therefore, All-forgiving,
    now give me what I lost!

There is something lost from *Requiem*. But I have the
fancy—so finely does Mr. Wolfe use rhythm and words—
that, before long, some power will give it back to him.
He calls *Requiem* his 'high song'; and over large tracts of
it, certainly, he soars and sings; and it would be a dull ear,
I think, which missed hear the pulse of true poetic flight.
But I am not sure that he yet fronts the sun with steady
eyes. I can admire the high and sonorous unrealities amid
which he moves. But I am not sure that he has yet found
his subject-matter—or himself. I should not be surprised
if the two things proved one and the same; nor, yet again,
if Mr. Wolfe one day merged both in the Catholic Church.
Let me end with the epilogue of his 'High Song':

The high song is over. Silent is the lute now.
    They are crowned for ever and discrown'd now.
Whether they triumphed or suffered they are mute now,
    Or at the most they are only a sound now.

The high song is over. There is none to complain now.
    No heart for healing, and none to break now.
They have gone, and they will not come again now.
    They are sleeping at last, and they will not wake now.

The high song is over. And we shall not mourn now.
    There was a thing to say, and it is said now.
It is as though all these had been unborn now,
    it is as though the world itself were dead now.

The high song is over. Even the echoes fail now;
  winners and losers—they are only a theme now,
their victory and defeat a half-forgotten tale now;
  and even the angels are only a dream now.

There is no need for blame, no cause for praise now.
  Nothing to hide, to change or to discover.
These were men and women. They have gone their ways now,
  as men and women must. The high song is over.

Perhaps if Mr. Wolfe had left out all the 'nows', it would
be a better poem. It is in any case, perhaps, a *truer* poem
than Mr. Wolfe meant it to be. 'These were men and
women', he says; and 'they are only a theme now'. Was
Mr. Wolfe, when he wrote his epilogue to *Requiem*, vexed,
I wonder, by some uneasy sense that its realistic and seem-
ingly full-blooded personages are in fact rather paler and
more anaemic than they had any business to be?

I dare say that his next book [1] will furnish an answer.
It will be a very interesting book, in any case. Meanwhile,
I wish that Mr. Wolfe would give up translating—whether
the Greek Anthology or something else. For disappointed
literary talent, translation is a good enough anodyne. But
it is not a man's job; not, I mean, a poet's job. I cannot
think that the Greek Anthology will help Mr. Wolfe to
do what I want to see him do—to find himself.

I may perhaps be allowed to conclude, after the manner
of Hazlitt, by satisfying that curiosity which we all have
about the form and feature of eminent persons. Mr. Wolfe
is in figure slight, and somewhat below the middle stature.
He is of a dark complexion, with features of a foreign and
distinctly Jewish cast. You might pass him in the street
without noticing him; but if you happened to notice him,
you would think him noticeable. His head is well shaped
and well carried; and he has long hair which he can toss
with effect. He at one time wore those short side-whiskers

[1] It proved to be *This Blind Rose*. I do not like the affected title (I had
to read the book to know that *Blind* was not a substantive nor *Rose* a verb).
I find in it too much of the old manner. I can admire the brilliancy of
its technique—*quamquam O!* (Nov. 1928).

which are more easily admired than understood. His voice might be called golden rather than good; but when he reads his own poetry, his tones are finely modulated, expressing soul. His conversation has more of flippancy than is just to himself. But if it sometimes makes enemies for him, that is partly their fault. His friends believe in his fundamental seriousness; but they sometimes wonder where it will lead him. Much might be affirmed of him; very little, with certainty, predicted. Time, says Pindar, is the only sure test of truth. But it eats like acid into all poetry except the best.

MR. A. E. HOUSMAN

I HAVE confessed before to a fondness for the poetry of Fellows of colleges. I have not observed that the world in general shares it with me; but I have not allowed that to worry me. I like Matthew Arnold; and, as he did, I like Gray: Gray not too much, but I like him. I even like old Tom Warton, who was contemporary with Gray, and has some of Gray's merits. Warton, I suppose, unlike Matthew Arnold, will be remembered, not as a poet, but as a professor of poetry, and as the first historian of our poetry. He belongs, in any case, to an order of Fellows of colleges which has gone beyond recall. He loved the tavern better than the lecture-room. He was the last of the 'jolly' dons. But coming to a period nearer my own, and, I suppose, a more respectable one, I like the poetry of Rupert Brooke, who was a Fellow of a Cambridge college. I like the poetry of J. S. Phillimore, of Gerald Gould, of Godfrey Elton, all of them Fellows of Oxford colleges. And yet again, I like the poetry of Mr. A. E. Housman. Mr. Housman is a Fellow of Trinity College, Cambridge. Even so, the Latin that he teaches there he learned in Oxford. Two terms ago, speaking of Mr. Humbert Wolfe, I put it to his account that he was the only poet I knew who had taken a first in Greats. I believe I was one out; and though that should teach me caution, yet Mr. Housman, I verily believe, is the only great poet who, taking the same school, has ever been ploughed outright. I do not say that from malice; though, if I wanted to be quietly malicious, I do not see why I should not. But I record it as a material circumstance. I put it in as evidence—if we knew what it was evidence of, we should know all about poetry; of which at present we may sum all our knowledge by saying that the spirit bloweth where it listeth. However, here is a poet, the most considerable of his generation, who refused learning in his youth, and has since dedicated himself to it with deadly austerity. He stands to-day the first scholar in Europe; if this country has had a greater scholar, it will be only Bentley. The sum of his achievement in poetry is two small volumes of verse, separated from one another by an interval of near thirty years; and the title and Preface to the second of them intimating to us that we must expect no more. It is not often that a man may sit and choose which of two immortalities he will. Mr. Housman, I truly think, has had this singular privilege; and to a good many people, perhaps to most, he will seem to have used it perversely. As plainly as what a man does can tell us what he thinks, he has told us that he thinks more highly of scholarship than of poetry, that he prefers to be immortal along that line. For the perpetuity of his fame as a scholar, he has laid the foundations deep and broad; and has done all his work as though only that mattered. What he has done for, and in, poetry, he has done with a savage insouciance, as though he could say all that he had to say in verse by biting his lip. I suppose that there will always be scholarship in the world; and the hard and narrow immortality that comes by it Mr. Housman can count on. But I am not sure that, biting his lip at poetry, he has not been caught in the act: arrested and frozen into a second immortality.

Meanwhile, one of the facts of his poetry is his contempt for it. He is the only poet I know whose primary interest is exact knowledge. That he is a scholar most persons are aware who read his poetry; but they are aware of it in a rather dim and careless fashion: as though it were an accident and an irrelevance. Of no man's life can nine-tenths be irrelevant; least of all of a poet's life. I cannot think it a matter of indifference that Mr. Housman is a scholar, nor that he is the kind of scholar that he is. He is the kind of scholar that bad scholars call a 'mere' scholar; that is to say, he mixes with his scholarship nothing that appeals to any other instinct than the instinct for knowledge. The drier the knowledge, the better: the less it leads anywhere, the safer. Much of his time has been given to editing Latin poets. But you will search his works in vain for any expression that betrays a sense in him that poetry is what it is, or that the scholarship of poetry is, in any respect, different from, or better than, entomology, palaeontology, or the geometry of hyper-space. His favourite poet is a writer so difficult and obscure that, of persons in this room, perhaps not ten have heard his name, and, of living Englishmen, I vow that Mr. Housman and myself alone have read him from cover to cover, and only Mr. Housman has understood him. I do not mean that Mr. Housman's scholarship is not, often, very lively. Mr. A, an eminent living scholar, had a disciple, Mr. B; and Mr. B was so unwise as to publish a book. 'I suppose', writes Mr. Housman, 'that Mr. A, when he perused Mr. B's book, must have felt somewhat like Sin, when she gave birth to Death.' That is what I call being lively—you will see that it is not very different from being deadly. Mr. Housman's scholarship has these emotional passages. But they are so far proper to his purely scientific temperament that they are provoked only by the unscientific behaviour of other scholars. For him scholarship is a science, as much as any other of the sciences; and the death of it is the intrusion into it of qualities proper to other departments, those qualities, in particular, which belong to *belles lettres* and to poetry. Across the page of Mr. Housman's scholarship there falls never so much as the shadow of literary appreciation. You could no more suspect him of poetry than you could suspect Darwin or Linnaeus.

So much about Mr. Housman's scholarship I have felt obliged to say. For myself, like other people, I am more interested in his poetry. I think he would think us all wrong; though not, I fancy, for the right reasons. In any case, I have no wish to disparage scholarship. Bad poets are at least worse than bad scholars, and they are infinitely more numerous. And touching good poets and good scholars, let me say at any rate this much. We do not, I think, sufficiently reflect how rare, in comparison with

genius, is consummate learning. That learning should be
less admired than genius is natural enough. Men admire
what is grand most of all when it seems to be done easily,
and the mark of genius is its divine facility—it may endure
agonies, but it does *not* take pains. Learning, on the other
hand, must both take pains and give them. Mediocrity,
or less, can appreciate genius. But learning can be known
only by its like. The effects of genius are easily appre-
hended. It is sensibly known in the quickening of the
blood, the tension of the nerves, the fine thrill of the whole
being. It does not merely move us; it drives us before it,
as the wind the leaves. It has something stinging and
compelling. It accomplishes its end in being felt. We
never inquire—or we are foolish if we do inquire—what
it would be at. There *is* a sense in which genius, mysterious as it is, is the most intelligible of all things. But
learning is at once less direct in its aims and less clear in
its effects. One thing only it seems to share with genius—
its unhappiness. It rises up early and late takes rest.
There is a pallor upon its cheek, and in its eye a latent
fever; and over all its attainment there broods the shadow
of something missed and desired.

I hope that these reflections, general as they are, will
not seem too distant and irrelevant. I cannot think them
so. I was brought up in what is called scholarship; and
I was familiar—if my memory serves me rightly—I was
familiar with Mr. Housman's scholarship before I read his
poetry. There is an unhappiness in his scholarship, just
as there is in his poetry. He edits poets in the manner of
a man hating poetry. He criticizes critics with an in-
humanity grounded on the fierce conviction that there is
no truth in man. Speaking of the difficulty of arriving at
a good text of his favourite Latin poet, 'the faintest of all
human passions', he writes, 'is the love of truth'. Take
truth in what sense or in what connexion you will, Mr.
Housman, I think, really believes that. There is no truth
in man or woman. This gloomy persuasion informs his
scholarship. This gave birth in him to his poetry, his hate

of poetry, his fear of poetry. For really and truly, as I
think, Mr. Housman does hate poetry—poetry and all
those parts of life which make up into poetry. He is a
scholar because he hates poetry; seeking from scholarship
an anodyne for the wounds which poetry has wrought in
him; not expecting to find here, any more than in life,
truth in other men; but finding, here as elsewhere, a
savage satisfaction in detecting, and blazoning, other
men's falsehood, the intellectual dishonesty and incom-
petence of all the world save himself. Of his fellow
scholars he is pleased, in one place, to sum the merits by
a sentence from Swift: they are 'as little qualified', he
says, 'for thinking as for flying'.

To Swift Mr. Housman bears a considerable likeness;
save that, firstly, he is a better poet, and secondly, he is
more mysterious. Like Swift, he waits for a world 'ubi
saeva indignatio cor ulterius lacerare nequit'. Life has
done him some injury; the nature of which I am not
curious to inquire beyond what his poetry tells us. If we
may believe what it tells us, once 'in glory and in joy' he
'followed his plough along the mountain-side'.

> Is my team ploughing
> That I was used to drive?

Once he had loves, who now has only hates. There is no
truth in man or woman.

> His folly hath not fellow
> Beneath the blue of day,
> Who gives to man or woman
> His heart and soul away.

But there was truth in himself:

> If Truth in hearts that perish
> Could move the powers on high,
> I think the love I bear you
> Should make you not to die. . . .

But now 'all is idle'. Once he had loves. Once, like other
men, he had friends; and drank with them from sheer
good-fellowship, who drinks now in no better cause than

that of self-forgetfulness. He had friends. But they were
even more unlucky than himself. 'Souls undone, undoing
others', the more respectable of them were murdered, the
less engaging were hanged. Ned, and one or two others,
lie long in Shrewsbury gaol. Here and there a lucky one
got away, and enlisted for foreign service. 'The enemies
of England' saw these and were sick. Of these 'lads' and
'chaps', as their poet calls them, some found a second
service, in 1914, in that army of mercenaries who, 'in the
day when heaven was falling', 'held the sky suspended',
defending 'what God abandoned'. These 'took their
wages and are dead'. It is odd that the most striking
poem which the war produced should have this sardonic
ring. These 'chaps' were the lucky ones: though their
girls walk now with other 'chaps'. Next blest were those
who took a pistol and put a clean ending to the sickness
which was their soul:

> Oh soon, and better so than later
> After long disgrace and scorn,
> You shot dead the household traitor,
> The soul that should not have been born
>
> .   .   .   .
>
> Now to your grave shall friend and stranger
> With ruth and some with envy come:
> Undishonoured, clear of danger,
> Clean of guilt, pass hence and home.

A fine funeral march. For the morality of it, God knows.
  Some few more tender memories, indeed, this poet's
youth offers; but the sweet tenderness of them makes only
chaplets for headstones:

> With rue my heart is laden
> For golden friends I had,
> For many a rose-lipt maiden
> And many a lightfoot lad.
>
> By brooks too broad for leaping
> The lightfoot boys are laid;
> The rose-lipt girls are sleeping
> In fields where roses fade.

Those golden friends will outlast, I think, the gaol-birds, and suicides, and chaps that were hung; for they have met that immortality which there is in a commonplace when it is handled by a master of the classical manner. Of the golden lads that were swift of foot, there was one who merited an individual elegy; and for him, summoning again his purest classical manner, Mr. Housman has woven this unfading laurel:

> The time you won your town the race
> We chaired you through the market-place;
> Man and boy stood cheering by,
> And home we brought you shoulder high.
>
> To-day, the road all runners come,
> Shoulder-high we bring you home,
> And set you at your threshold down,
> Townsman of a stiller town.
>
> Smart lad, to slip betimes away
> From fields where glory does not stay,
> And early though the laurel blows
> It withers quicker than the rose.
>
> Eyes the shady night has shut
> Cannot see the record cut,
> And silence sounds no worse than cheers
> After earth has stopped the ears:
>
> Now you will not swell the rout
> Of lads that wore their honour out,
> Runners whom renown outran
> And the name died before the man.
>
> So set, before its echoes fade,
> The fleet foot on the sill of shade,
> And hold to the low lintel up
> The still-defended challenge-cup.
>
> And round that early-laurelled head
> Shall flock to gaze the strengthless dead,
> And find unwithered on its curls
> The garland briefer than a girl's.

Of this beautiful elegy I am ashamed to qualify the

praise. Yet I cannot let it pass without voicing an uneasiness and embarrassment which the first two stanzas of it
create in me. The poem as a whole has been so truly felt,
and to the verse and the diction so much art has been
brought that it would be pedantic to prefer nature; and
yet these perfections have been framed, I feel, in a setting
not only false but preferred for its falsity.

The time you won your town the race . . .

Mr. Housman was at an English public school; he was an
undergraduate here in Oxford; he speaks of himself somewhere as a 'Son of Sorrow' playing, or playing at, cricket
and football, and I dare say he played at running races.
But the athlete of his poem is his fellow-townsman; the
scene a market-place; the prize a municipal challenge-
cup; the victor was 'chaired' shoulder-high. I am even
prepared to believe that the victory was celebrated in
'pints and quarts of Ludlow beer', and that the poet and
his friends (I draw inferences here from other poems) lay
down in the road 'in lovely muck' and went home leaving
their neckties God knows where. I say 'I am prepared to
believe' that. But no: I am prepared to be told it. But
it will not do. And why does Mr. Housman do it? Do
you really see him all that degree interested in the Ludlow
sports—if in Ludlow they hold sports? This false-pastoral
twist is altogether too tiresome. I hate vulgarisms; but
I hate 'fakes' still more; and I do not know what to call
this false pastoralism if I am not to be allowed to call it
a not too clever fake.

The trouble pervades nine-tenths of the *Shropshire
Lad*. The very title prepares you for a false world. I do
not mean that Mr. Housman is not so far a Shropshire
Lad that he has vivified and glorified large tracts of that
pleasant country-side—I reckon it with my best luck that
I first made acquaintance with these poems in a village
not twenty miles from Ludlow. But the rest is fake: the
town-and-county patriotism; the lads and chaps with
their ploughshares and lost neckties; the girls with their

throats cut, and their lovers that were hanged for it. I call it false pastoralism. It is not quite the pastoralism, it is true, of Mantuan or Spenser or Pope. Since those days, there has flowed under the bridges of pastoral a good deal of Villon and water, of Verlaine and absinthe. But I do not know that it has made the pastoralism of Mr. Housman either more intelligible or less false.

Utterly false this world of his, of course, is not. Open his heart, and you will find written there, I do not doubt, not Cambridge, but Clunbury and Clun. Nor do I question that the stuff of his poetry is the stuff of a real experience. I believe it of him more readily than of some other poets; because only so could it have happened that his best work should, in this false setting, yet shine so true—perhaps *glower* so true would be nearer. When Mr. Housman lifts his eyes to the hills whence the strength of his youth came, sure enough (we might wish it otherwise) he sees gaols and gibbets and ditches strown with 'lovely lads and dead and rotten'; and sure enough Ned and Dick and himself are or were, all of them, of all men most miserable. But was it not enough that they should be that, without being dressed, or undressed, into tiresome allegoric personages? If there be no truth in man nor woman, if the heart be so made that every wind which blows through it clanks chains and shakes a gibbet, must we none the less make a charade of it?

I suppose we must leave poets to do things in their own way. Very likely Mr. Housman uses these veils and pretences out of some mercy to himself and others. Yet he rarely writes like a merciful man; and I am inclined to seek a different explanation; and to find it in what I have already said. Mr. Housman hates poetry, and he believes that all men hate truth. His poetry is wrung from him, as from so many poets, by some pain of life:

> Und wenn der Mensch in seiner Qual verstummt,
> Gab mir ein Gott zu sagen was ich leide.

Some god gave it to him to say what he suffers; but he

would rather have been given the power to hold his tongue. He hates poetry sufficiently, and he so little credits men in general with any genuine taste for the truth, that he will not be persuaded to take pains enough to deal truly with his material. He will not be more true with it than he thinks good enough for his readers; and he knows what he is doing. His gaol-bird stuff, the cruder of his macabre pieces, the curiously elaborated perversity of such poems as *The Immortal Part*—these nine-tenths of his readers have preferred to his best work; and he knew that they were going to do so. That some of these poems are absurdly false, he knows, without caring. Even so, into all of them he has put—from an instinct for truth which he is never quite able to suppress in himself— enough of truth to make them poems not to be dismissed without consideration. If I call Mr. Housman's poetry an astonishing medley of false and true, in the long run I am praising it; for it is a marvel that it should be so true as it is, under the conditions which he has deliberately imposed upon it.

Lest I should be misunderstood, the best of it—much of it, that is—is wholly true and set beyond cavil.

When I watch the living meet
  And the moving pageant file
Warm and breathing through the street
  Where I lodge a little while,

If the heats of hate and lust
  In the house of flesh are strong,
Let me mind the house of dust
  Where my sojourn shall be long.

In the nation that is not
  Nothing stands that stood before;
There revenges are forgot,
  And the hater hates no more;

Lovers lying two and two
  Ask not whom they sleep beside,
And the bridegroom all night through
  Never turns him to the bride.

There is no gainsaying perfections of that order; and perhaps I could find near a score of pieces equally adequate in feeling and expression. I suppose none of us were ever very happy about our war poetry, the patriotic verse, I mean, of the Great War. Simonides, Horace, Wordsworth —take any of it to these high tests, and it seems almost sordid. Let me take a poem of an earlier war—which of our wars I know not; but it must have been somewhat earlier than the Boer War. What a great war we thought that, and how little and provincial it looks since! This was a yet littler war. But here are some lines of Mr. Housman's which it provoked, neither little nor provincial, but sufficiently answering high needs:

> On the idle hill of summer,
>   Sleepy with the flow of streams,
> Far I hear the steady drummer
>   Drumming like a noise in dreams.
>
> Far and near and low and louder
>   On the roads of earth go by,
> Dear to friends and food for powder,
>   Soldiers marching, all to die.
>
> East and west on fields forgotten
>   Bleach the bones of comrades slain,
> Lovely lads and dead and rotten;
>   None that go return again.
>
> Far the calling bugles hollo,
>   High the screaming fife replies,
> Gay the files of scarlet follow:
>   Woman bore me, I will rise.

The *Shropshire Lad* was first printed in 1896. The greater part of it was written early in 1895. Mr. Housman tells us so much himself, in the Preface to *Last Poems*. That Preface contains some few words of self-revelation such as its author is commonly shy of. Most of these early poems, he says, were written in the early months of 1895, under the condition of a 'continuous excitement'. Of the nature of this excitement nothing is said: save that it was such that it is not likely to revisit its poet; 'nor indeed', he says, 'could I well sustain it if it came'. Let us not ask too many questions, therefore. But I had this passage in mind when I said that Mr. Housman, besides hating poetry, feared it. He has a real superstitious fear of it, I believe. The same superstitious fear of his own poetry haunted Byron, as I have noticed elsewhere. And both poets react upon their fear in the same fashion. They meet it with a kind of gloomy insolence; and it deprives both of them of the power of being perfectly sincere; and even of the will to be so. They are only perfectly sincere in their best moments; and in despite of themselves. But I have a further, and not illegitimate, curiosity about the 'continuous excitement' which brought to birth the poems of the *Shropshire Lad*. For I take Mr. Housman to mean that these poems were written in, and from, the passions or emotions which they treat. That is interesting, because it has not been the way of some great poets. It was not the way of Byron, who speaks of his poetry as the language of his *sleeping* passions—when his passions were awake, the poetry in him died, he tells us. It was not the way of Wordsworth. Wordsworth's way was Byron's way; he had to set some interval between his emotion and the expression of it. But we must take poets as we find them; and it is interesting when they reveal anything of the conditions in which they work.

Between Mr. Housman's *Shropshire Lad* and his *Last Poems* there lies, as I have said, an interval of nearly thirty years. But it is a less real interval than it seems. Three-fourths of the *Last Poems*, he tells us, were written between 1895 and 1910. They are the belated reverberation of the shock, or excitement, of the *Shropshire Lad*. The other fourth part of the *Last Poems* belongs to the April of 1922. About that month and year, again, I would not wish to show an impertinent curiosity; but the mention of it by Mr. Housman may serve to remind us how unpredictable are the comings and goings of poetical inspiration. Most of us, I suppose, who had read the

Shropshire Lad somewhere near the time at which it first
appeared felt some sense of disappointment with *Last
Poems*. That was wrong. We looked for some advance in
art, some new curiosity of theme, some widening of range.
We forgot that we were dealing with a poet who had a
strong distaste for poetry—for his own poetry a distaste,
if I may say so, almost insolent. Very instructive, in this
connexion, is the reason that he gives for printing these
Last Poems; he thinks that he had better print them while
he can himself see to the spelling and punctuation. If you
know his scholarship, its savage absorption in the minutiae
of pointing and orthography—and, indeed, in all minutiae—you will know that this is not affectation; but that
what truly interested him about this last volume was that
it should have deadly accuracy. For one or two of the
pieces in it I have a liking beyond what I have for a good
many of the earlier poems; one or two of them seem to
me softer, more tender, more feminine. Too much of the
Shropshire Lad is marred by what I will call a sham masculinity. The trick of this sham masculinity Mr. Housman
learned, I have always fancied, from Stevenson. The
pessimism of Mr. Housman, like the optimism of Stevenson, has an exaggerated masculinity which alienates. I
cannot but think, I may add, that Mr. Housman owes to
Stevenson something of both the verse and the diction of
his poetry. And there are other likenesses: such, however,
as may perhaps be explained out of the interest both have
in some French poets.

About Mr. Housman's verse and diction—both so individual in their melancholy bareness, in their damped-
down fire—I had wanted to say something—indeed, a
good deal; but I have left myself no time. I am not
sure that, fifty years hence, he will not be principally
esteemed for the classical finish of his best work; that this
will not be the 'immortal part' of him, 'the steadfast and
enduring bone' surviving 'the man of flesh and soul' who
to-day is so interesting to us. Indeed, I do not know why
else he writes. Who despises more than he all that 'fire

of sense' and 'smoke of thought', as he calls it, which has made his poetry so interesting to his contemporaries? Why any writer writes, perhaps no one knows. The simplest explanation is that we write because we want to, and there is nobody to stop us. That does not, of course, explain why we do it so badly. But here is a writer, a poet, who does not want to write at all; and indeed he has sworn never to do it again. But Jove laughs at 'last poems'; he scents from afar yet more last poems. From Mr. Housman I do not know whether we shall get them. But he has written, and he may do so again, in his own despite; hating poetry, thinking life a false thing, cursing the flesh and blood in him. But there is no lust of the flesh quite so strong as the craving of art. Among many false obsessions, that, I think, is real with Mr. Housman, the veritable tyrant of his mind.

Of all this I could have wished to say a good deal more. I have lost myself—which of his contemporaries has not? —in the enigma of the man. What matters, and what will outlast curiosity, is the pure and cold art of his good work. But we are human creatures; and this enigmatic figure—one of the most notable of our time—this enigmatic figure, lonely, irresponsive, setting us so many questions and answering none of them, crediting none of us with truth or intelligence, but allowing us to make what we can of the fire and ice that contend in his nature, the Byronic and the donnish—we may be forgiven if we look at him a little like men who have forgotten good manners. It is his fault if we stare.

MASSINGER[1]

I WOULD ask that this lecture should be conceived as an act of piety. Certainly it proceeds, like most of our piety, from a spirit improperly prepared, joyless and reluctant. When I say 'improperly prepared', I mean, not merely that my lecture was, as happens with the lectures of better men, put together in a hurry, but that I came to it in a mood altogether alien from that Christian charity which makes the success of pious ceremonial. For I am here only by the unforgivable default of two distinguished persons—whom I will not more nearly indicate than to say that the one of them would have brought to the subject of Massinger a knowledge which has no lacunae, and a judgement supernaturally impeccable, the other a delicate gaiety of temper and that skill in phrase which has made the Oriel stylists notorious. These two should be here in white sheets, not I in this academical sub-fusc.

The appearance of the first quarto of Massinger's *Duke of Milan* is not, it may be allowed, an event in the same order of importance as the publication, roughly synchronous with it, of the first Folio of Shakespeare. It may perhaps be allowed, too, that centenaries, or even tercentenaries, have become of late too numerous for the comfort of literature. Yet in this matter Oxford at least has not sinned greatly. Indeed, she has mostly taken her great men for granted, preferring that they should not be praised at all rather than that they should be praised *fussily*. In the last quarter of a century I can recall but two full-dress ceremonials in this kind, both of them, by a flattering accident, in connexion with Merton men: the Bacon sexcentenary and the Bodley tercentenary. The

[1] A lecture delivered in 1923 on the occasion of the tercentenary performance in Merton College of Massinger's *Duke of Milan*.

connexion of Bacon with Merton, has, it is true, been questioned.[1] But Sir Thomas Bodley no man can take from us—nor deny his connexions with the drama in this college. Not many years since I was so fortunate as to find, in a long-neglected beer-barrel in a long-disused attic, a document written in Bodley's autograph in which he makes gratified mention of the successful performance in Merton of the tragicomedy *Damon and Pithias*. The College paid for the performance, and the Warden lent his house for it. The author was a Corpus man, Richard Edwards; and it is not certainly known that the play—our earliest English tragicomedy—had ever been performed before.[2]

Merton has earlier connexions with the drama, which are perhaps worth mentioning. Nicholas Grimald, the editor and part-author of that most famous of Anthologies, *Tottel's Miscellany*, was a Fellow of Merton; and, albeit in the Latin tongue, he was a dramatist whose plays, wedding Senecan form to Christian matter, assisted to naturalize Renaissance influences in England. His *Christus Redivivus* was performed here as early as 1542; and another of his tragedies, *Archipropheta*, dealing with the story of John the Baptist, was published at Cologne in 1548. He is credited also with two comedies. More interesting to us, perhaps, are his rhyming dodecasyllables *The Garden*—was it *our* Garden?—and the fact that he was sentenced to be hanged, drawn, and quartered. He escaped this fate; but a complete edition of his works is, I believe, to appear shortly in the United States.

Grimald's publisher, Tottel, was also publisher to another Fellow of Merton, a man whose work was destined to influence in an indirect, but very powerful, fashion the

[1] But it was allowed to pass on the occasion of the sexcentenary: and I recall that among those who honoured Bacon by lunching in Merton was the present Pope.

[2] This may pass—for a local audience. But really it would be unreasonable to doubt that the reference in the Revels Accounts for 1564 to 'Edwardes tragedy' is to a court performance of *Damon and Pithias* three years earlier.

development of the English drama—Jasper Heywood. Jasper Heywood was a son of the more famous John Heywood the 'interluder', the author of the *Four PP*. In 1559 Tottel published for him his verse-rendering of the *Troades* of Seneca. The publication of this book truly, and not conventionally, marks an epoch. An influence was liberated which is felt throughout the Elizabethan drama, and which may be felt still in Massinger, and in Massinger's *Duke of Milan*. 'Cresce, cruor: sanguis satietur sanguine.' [1] 'Moral edification' it has been well said [2] in this connexion 'is dear to the heart of the British public, and violent and bloody actions are dearer still.' No author so fully fed these ruling tastes as Seneca. Heywood followed up his *Troades* in the very next year with a translation of the *Thyestes*; and to that, in the year succeeding, he added the *Hercules*. He had lighted a torch not to be put out: within less than a quarter of a century, the whole decade of Senecan tragedies was available in English, and thereafter that vein of talent which Shakespeare has christened 'Ercles' vein' flowed freely.

Nothing that Heywood wrote is to be found in the Merton library; and it is not difficult to guess why. The fact is that the authorities found it necessary, after repeated admonitions, to get rid of Heywood. Amateur theatricals, it is believed, were his undoing: his conduct in the celebration of the Christmas mummeries then traditional in the college was of such a nature that these performances were, for good and all, closed down. His persecuted talents found a home in the more liberal environment of All Souls; but to no purpose; for very soon he turned Jesuit. Yet he deserves to be remembered here as the liberator of forces greater than himself; as a

[1] *True Tragedie of Richard the Third*, init. The Ghost's Latin should be written and punctuated thus:

> cresce, cruor: sanguis satietur sanguine: cresce:
> quod spero sitio: sitio, sitio vindictam.

[2] A. D. Godley, in Gordon's *English Literature and the Classics*, p. 244.

forerunner to whom alike Kyd and Marlowe and Shakespeare and Webster and Massinger, at whatever distance, look back. In the endless *lampadephoria* of our dramatic development, he is the first link.

'Seneca his tenne tragedies translated into Englysh' appeared in 1581. The birth of Massinger falls three years later. Go forward another three years, and you hit a date and incident depressingly suggestive. In 1587 the University paid 20*s.* to the company of Players to which Shakespeare—and subsequently Massinger—belonged, to act their plays anywhere but in Oxford. In 1602 Massinger entered St. Alban Hall. His father had been educated in the same Hall, and had passed thence to a Fellowship at Merton. No doubt, the son was marked down by the ambition of his father for a like course—Merton under the great Savile was then at the top of its prestige. It is a Merton man, Antony Wood, who tells us that the young Massinger fell short even of that measure of industry which is required for the degree of Bachelor. In this connexion, however, it is worth remembering that Massinger's plays are founded on a reading notably wide; and it is difficult to conjecture where, and when, if not during his period at Oxford, this foundation was laid. It has been inferred from his plays that he was a convert to Catholicism; and it has been sought to connect his premature departure from Oxford with this surmised Catholicism. When we remember that Grimald came near being hanged for a Protestant, Heywood for a Jesuit, the surmise is an entertaining one. On the other hand, there are many ways of getting sent down. Discipline and the drama, as we have seen, were not the best of friends in Heywood's time; perhaps they were not so in Massinger's; perhaps they are not so even to-day. Be the facts as they may, Massinger left Oxford without a degree in 1606. Thereafter he disappears completely from our knowledge until 1614–15. Among the Alleyn papers in Dulwich College are preserved two documents belonging to those years which attest loans of £5 and £3 made to Field, Daborn and Massinger by the great theatrical manager Henslowe. The borrowers speak of their 'pitiful request'; and when the first loan was made they were in fact in prison. These papers attest a literary collaboration between the three playwrights concerned, and, incidentally, between Massinger and Fletcher. Save for these two documents, we possess no information about Massinger earlier than the year 1621—in that year *The Virgin Martyr* was entered upon the Register of the Stationers' Company as the joint work of Massinger and Dekker. We have no certain record of any earlier work of Massinger; but that he had for some time collaborated with the three friends already mentioned seems certain—one of the best of his plays, *The Fatal Dowry*, was written in conjunction with Field, and, therefore, before 1619. That he had written plays independently of these collaborators is likely. A good deal that he wrote has been lost: that notorious personage, 'Mr. Warburton's cook', is said to have used the manuscript of no less than twelve of his plays in the processes of her cooking. *The Virgin Martyr* appeared in quarto in 1622. The play has been variously judged; but it is perhaps best judged—for Massinger above all men wrote for the stage and age that he knew—by the fact that it went through four editions in less than forty years. Not many of the Shakespeare quartos—in fact, five only out of nineteen—did better than that. It is now generally agreed that the more objectionable parts of this play proceed from Dekker. Yet, if I am to speak frankly, Dekker had far more of the real fire of poetry in him than Massinger— Massinger could never have written the first act of *The Honest Whore*, nor Candido's last speech in Part I of that play. I suspect that what has been justly called 'the thrill and the glamour in the style of *The Virgin Martyr*, Massinger caught somehow from his collaborator.

Between 1621 and 1640, the date of his death (he was buried in one grave with Fletcher), we know, in effect, nothing of Massinger save what may be known, or inferred, from the extant plays. *The Virgin Martyr* was followed in 1623 by *The Duke of Milan*, the earliest independent work of Massinger which has come down to us.[1] Of this play alone I shall speak in detail: of the others, and only of some of them, incidentally and cursorily. The story of it may be put in a few words.

Sforza, Duke of Milan, has taken sides with the French king against the Emperor Charles. The French forces are defeated, and Sforza believes that, not only his kingdom and his life, but what is dearer to him than either, his wife Marcelia, stands in the direst danger. On the advice of the wise and neutrally-minded Pescara, he sets out for Pavia, to make his submission to the Emperor. But before he goes, he appoints as regent the *parvenu* Francisco. Some years before he had injured irreparably Francisco's sister, Eugenia; and upon the ruin of his sister, gossip said, was Francisco's greatness raised. But Eugenia has long since been forgotten; and Francisco, as Sforza thinks, is enough man of the world to understand, in such matters, the temperament of princes. Yet Francisco—as we shall see—is, in his own fashion, an idealist. Meanwhile Sforza's only care is for his wife, Marcelia. On his departure he exacts from Francisco a monstrous oath: should any misfortune befall him, Francisco is to kill Marcelia, that there may be no successor to the great love of Sforza; and he gives his regent written authority to this end. Francisco, while the duke is absent in Pavia, endeavours to seduce Marcelia; and when his advances are indignantly rejected reveals the covenant with the duke, without, however, making plain its conditional character. Subsequently, he tells Marcelia the whole truth, and, expressing penitence, receives her pardon. The duke, meanwhile, has achieved an accommodation with Charles; but on his return he discovers in Marcelia a mysterious coldness. The tongues of the women wag, hinting plainly that Marcelia loves Francisco; and to the duke Francisco presently allows as much. The duke kills Marcelia with his own hand,

---

[1] Unless, as is thought likely, *The Unnatural Combat* be earlier.

discovering from her as she dies both her own innocence and the villainy of Francisco. Francisco flees from
Milan.

Only in the fifth Act do the motives of Francisco's
behaviour become gradually intelligible. Whether he in
fact loved Marcelia, or merely sought her ruin, we do not
discover—that Massinger leaves to his reader, or his actor.
But in either case, the over-mastering motive of his actions
throughout has been the thought of avenging on the duke
the wrong done to his sister Eugenia. Brother and sister
now come disguised to the ducal court; and Francisco
undertakes, by the aid of magical medicaments, to revivify
the body of Marcelia. To sustain his promise he paints
the face and hands of the dead duchess to a similitude of
life. The duke, whose reason grief has already overset,
lavishing kisses on the form of his dead wife, conceives
from the contact—for Francisco's pigments were deadly
—a poison which acts upon him like a Nessus shirt. The
play ends with his death-agony, and the discovery and
arrest of Francisco.

The plot, as may be seen, is ingenious, and not a little
horrible. Where it is most horrible, let it be said at once,
it did not originate with Massinger—the incident of the
painting of the corpse is taken by him from an earlier play,
The Second Maiden's Tragedy. The duke's death is, very
literally, in the 'Ercles' vein'—it comes straight from
the *Hercules* of Seneca, via *The Second Maiden's Tragedy*.
These grim effects are only justly judged in performance;
and even so it is fair to remember that Massinger addressed
himself to an audience strongly 'italianate' in taste and
temperament. For myself, the element of the horrible in
The Duke of Milan does not greatly offend or frighten
me: another play of Massinger, *The Unnatural Combat*, is
a great deal more horrible. Yet even there, the horror,
to my mind, comes nowhere near to that of the scene with
the lunatics and the executioners in Webster's *Duchess of
Malfi*. The Elizabethans and the Jacobeans alike were, in
fact, prone to that error which Aristotle condemns in the

audiences of his own day: they sought from tragedy, not its proper satisfaction, but every kind of satisfaction. In the complex passions, let it be said in fairness, the border-line between health and morbidity is not easily determinable; and if any one likes to urge that in the determination of it tragedy itself dies, I will not stop to quarrel with him. That tragedy should excite pity and fear, but not repulsion, is easily said. But there was never yet philosopher who did not like a play which made his flesh creep.

But here I touch speculations beyond my competence. More manageable is the problem, as Massinger presents it, of the relation between plot and character. In *The Duke of Milan*, and elsewhere, it is impossible to deny to Massinger immense skill in the construction of plot. If it be true, as the greatest of dramatic critics has said, that the plot is 'the soul of tragedy', and that the characters 'enter in for the sake of the plot', then undoubtedly Massinger is among the great tragic artists. But this dictum has not escaped criticism; and it may with reason be urged that both Aristotle in his theory, and Massinger in his practice, make between plot and character a distinction which, like that between body and soul, form and matter, is ultimately unreal. At least we may urge that in the greatest examples of tragedy these two elements of drama drop their duality—what a man is, that he does, what he does is himself. But it was not in the Elizabethan drama to hunt an ideal technique, to die for aesthetic canons; and so it is in general true that Shakespeare is supreme in characterization, weak in the construction of plot. Massinger's plots, on the other hand, are almost uniformly good; and we can read his plays, as Coleridge said, with the same kind of interest as that with which we read a novel; and this, it may be, is, of his various merits, the most welcome. His plots have in fact only two faults. Sometimes the presuppositions of the action are improbable; and here *The Duke of Milan* furnishes a relevant illustration. The whole plot hangs upon the resolution of

Sforza to kill his wife; and there is a good deal in Hazlitt's criticism when he says that this resolution 'is as much out of the verge of nature and probability as it is unexpected and revolting, from the want of any circumstance of palliation leading to it'. Secondly, Massinger's plots fail now and again in clearness: at least when the play is read, for on the stage it may, I suspect, be otherwise. This occasional obscurity in the action is, in general, a direct result of Massinger's neglect of characterization; though in some degree it arises from his fondness for tragedies with an Aristotelian discovery, or recognition, and he tends to defer the discovery unduly. In *The Duke of Milan*, from both causes, it needs, unless to-morrow's performance prove me wrong, four and a half acts to divine what Francisco would be at. The same defect shows itself in Massinger's comedy; indeed in the greatest of his comedies. The close of the first Act of the *New Way to Pay Old Debts* does not grip as it should from the difficulty, I would even say the impossibility, of discovering what motives govern Lady Allworth's change of behaviour towards Wellborn. Yet I am inclined to believe that Massinger's neglect of characterization is, at any rate in a large measure, studied. He lived with the actors for whom he wrote; and from his Paris (in *The Roman Actor*) we may suspect that he had a greater admiration for the profession than is common among playwrights. He was content to give them the story they wanted, and in good, indeed excellent, verse and words. But just as he has too much confidence in their spirit and sense to underline their words for them, or to point their rhythms, so he is content to give them the widest possible freedom in the interpretation of character. He wishes to be neither the master, nor the bully, of their intonation, look, gesture, or of any of those elements of the histrionic art by which an actor makes it clear that he is this or that kind of person. Perhaps this is not the way of dramatists who write for that large public which time and eternity supply; it is not perhaps the way of genius—which tends to a greater self-assertion. But it is a sensible and friendly way of going to work; and a large part of Massinger's greatness—I should suspect—lay in a plain appreciation of the conditions under which he wrote. I say 'Massingers' greatness'; but I know—and Massinger knew—the limitations of that greatness. It is such a greatness as Browning might have celebrated in a pendent to the *Grammarian's Funeral*. Loftier designs close often enough in less effects. Massinger is the greatest of dramatic hacks.

I have just said that Massinger's plots have only two faults; and I have no sooner mentioned them than I think of a third, and am too honest to suppress what I think. There is that in the telling of a story which, like charity in the living of our lives, redeems everything where it is present, and, absent, mars all. It is easily known when I say that even the worst of Shakespeare's stories is instinct with it. Shakespeare writes always, even when he writes badly, with gusto. He has the palate for his own stuff. But with Massinger I feel that never man constructed a story so well, and yet put it to us with so little of zest, so little rush of temperament, so little pleasure in the rhetoric of his own action and invention. Never does he fill himself really generously with the cakes and ale of comedy, nor is the ginger of his own melodrama hot in the mouth to him.

The Duke of Milan is, like *Othello*, a tragedy of conjugal jealousy; and to ask us, when we read the one play, to forget the other, is perhaps a degree naive. *Othello* was first published in the year preceding that in which *The Duke of Milan* appeared. Its composition, it is true, dates pretty certainly from a period some fourteen years earlier: Massinger might have seen it acted while he was still an undergraduate, and it is likely enough that he saw it performed—as it certainly was—in 1610. I cannot suppose that, like Pepys later, he thought it a 'mean thing': it is difficult not to believe that it was, in fact, the publication of *Othello* which supplied the stimulus for *The Duke*. It is

possible, indeed, that the first Folio had already appeared
before *The Duke of Milan* was composed. I say this
because the play owes something, I would suggest, not
merely to *Othello*, but to *The Winter's Tale*. I should be
surprised also if, when he wrote it, Massinger did not carry
in his mind *Measure for Measure*. The Lord Deputy
Angelo and the Lord Deputy Francisco are close kin: they
use to similar ends a similar accident of position. *Othello*
is a tragedy which many persons put above all other
tragedies, whether of Shakespeare or of other dramatists.
For *The Duke of Milan* no one is likely to claim that it
is a masterpiece either of drama or of literature. That
Massinger intended a challenge to Shakespeare, I do not
for a moment suppose. *Othello*, when it appeared in
quarto, no longer kept the stage—publication was allowed
just because the play was no longer running. The character
of *Othello*, again, had been one of Burbage's great parts;
and Burbage had died three years previously. Tragedies
having for their theme uxorious frenzy were in favour at
the moment—Massinger tried his hand with this theme
again next year in *The Bondman*, yet again in 1629 in *The
Picture*, and Ford a few years later in *Love's Sacrifice*.
There was an opening here for the race of *epigoni*, for a
lesser actor than Burbage, and for a dramatist who, shy
of the crowded stage of Shakespeare, might follow securely
his natural bent for simplification, coherence, symmetry.
Othello, it is true, is, in the structure of its plot, far better
managed than most of Shakespeare's tragedies. Even so,
the muddle of time in *Othello* is inextricable—in an age
which finds the cause of the unities not particularly
agitating, serious critics still feel obliged to discuss, in
connexion with it, Wilson's ludicrous theory of the two
clocks. The bad clockwork, it may be added, of *Othello*
connects with a disturbance of the unity of place which
to Massinger, it is likely enough, would have appeared
gratuitous—it would not have been a day's work for
Shakespeare to fix the scene of the action throughout in
Cyprus. If, when he wrote *The Duke*, Massinger had in

mind also *The Winter's Tale*, it is worth observing that, though that play runs by one clock, Shakespeare allows himself, light-heartedly, at the end of the third Act, to put the clock forward sixteen years. In *The Duke of Milan*, and elsewhere, Massinger aims, not at a better type of tragedy than the Shakespearian, but at a more convenient one; one better adapted to his actors, his audience, his own talents, the tendency of the times—in many respects he prepares the way for Dryden.

Twice and thrice recently I have seen it said that *The Duke of Milan* is the best of Massinger's tragedies. With a proper deference to persons younger than myself, and with infinite deference to Mr. Nigel Playfair—who not only knows good from bad, but has spent himself here most generously in communicating his rare knowledge [1]— I think *The Bondman* a better play; and I fancy that Massinger agreed with me. I only mention this play for the reason that it was written just after *The Duke of Milan* was finished; and that in it Massinger to some extent uses over again the plot of *The Duke*. Leosthenes's jealousy for Cleora, in *The Bondman*, repeats with differences the exacting amorousness of Sforza—Cleora, while her lover is at the wars, is made to immure herself in her chamber, blindfolded and gagged, for fear a new lover should supplant Leosthenes. Leosthenes, again, has wronged the sister of Marullo, exactly as Sforza wronged Francisco's sister Eugenia; and the discovery in both plays is deferred as a surprise for the fifth Act. The worldly women of *The Bondman*, once more, have considerable likeness to Isabella and Mariana; they use their nails; and even the pert Gracculo seems to echo in character, as in name, the earlier Graccho. Throughout *The Bondman*, I fancy, Massinger was consciously endeavouring to better *The Duke* by something in the same kind. Unhappily two scenes gratuitously offensive make impossible for representation on the stage a play which contains an excellently de-

---

[1] Mr. Playfair was the producer of *The Duke of Milan*.

veloped plot and a good deal of genuine poetry. Indeed,
I am not sure that it might not be contended that, as
a tragedian, Massinger is at his best in the plays of which
he derives the material from ancient history—*The Bondman*, *The Roman Actor*, and *Believe as You List*. The
merits of the first two of these plays are emphasized by
the fact that they were, in the Restoration period, successfully revived by Betterton. The mention of the last
two of them leads me to remark upon a characteristic of
Massinger which deserves generous recognition: his fine
English courage. *Believe as You List* brought him into
conflict with the Licenser of Plays: so did another piece,
now lost, *The King and the Subject*. In a well-known passage of *The Roman Actor* he vindicates nobly for the
dramatist the right to indulge political criticism, to 'search
into the secret of the time'; and he himself exercised
this right with a freedom beyond that of any other
dramatist.

I have said nothing of that quality of Massinger which
has been most generally selected for praise, his versification; nor again of his diction. I hope that in to-morrow's
performance the versification will be faithfully given; for
of all our dramatists Massinger is the most accurate versifier; in him alone you will find no faulty line. His
characters may spit fire in half-lines; but the two halves
make always a perfect whole. Whether this is in nature,
I do not know; nor whether, if it is not, it matters.
Coleridge thought Massinger's verse a better pattern for
the graduate in dramatic honours than Shakespeare's.
Swinburne has bestowed on it an equal, but different,
praise; praising it—I think—more truly; for Coleridge
should mean that Massinger's verse can be imitated. Massinger's style, says Swinburne, is 'a style as unlike that of
any other English poet as that of Dryden or Pope; as
tempting to imitators as it is inimitable by parasites, and
as apparently easy as it is really difficult to reproduce . . .
serviceable . . . business-like . . . eloquently practical . . .
rhetorically effusive, yet never effusive beyond the bounds

of effective rhetoric'. Some part of this praise, if my hour-
glass had not already run low, I could wish to qualify.
The easy accuracy of Massinger's verse, its pleasant diffusion, its serviceableness, are certainly more individual,
more artful, and far less easily imitable than, either in
reading or as rendered on the stage, they seem. Yet I feel
many embarrassments of judgement; and indeed, to speak
freely, I am not satisfied in my own mind that there is
not, in fact, an unhealable breach, at any rate in many
of Massinger's plays, between plot and style. Often to
an action irredeemably 'italianate' he weds a verse and
diction which are more truly proper to the comedy of
manners. Something of the same sort Euripides did. Is
it over-fanciful to trace in both poets the same motive?
Can it be that Massinger was a little tired of these
'italianate' plots, just as Euripides was not a little tired
of the heroic myths? that both poets bring to the themes
offered to them a good measure of scepticism? Some one
asked Matthew Arnold, 'Are you always quite serious?'
Is Massinger always quite serious with us? Or at the top
of his tragedy, sometimes, is he, in very homely phrase,
'getting at' his public? When, to take a near example, he
paints for us the corpse of Marcelia, are we quite sure that
it is not, in some degree, what is called a 'put-up thing'?
If Mr. Playfair will forgive me for telling tales, I have
heard him say that *The Duke of Milan* 'bubbles with fun'.
I will not go so far as that; but if we knew a little more
of Massinger, the man, we might perhaps find it conceivable that when, in the fifth Act of *The Duke*, he came
to the corpse scene, he rubbed his friendly hands in pro-
spect of a calculated burlesque. Let it be added that the
greater part of his tragedies in fact end happily.

Of the man we know nothing. Of his verse we have
plenty; and to what I have said of it I will add this last
word. Allow it all the excellences that Mr. Swinburne
claims for it. Yet *there is something the matter with it*;
and the something, I strongly suspect, is the man, that
unknown factor. The question is asked, whether

Massinger had a hand in the last Act of *Henry VIII*.
Here is the answer—from the play itself: [1]

> But we are all men,
> In our own natures frail, and capable
> Of our flesh; few are angels.

Just what makes the greatness of that is what is everywhere wanting to Massinger. This kind never comes by
hack-work.

[1] *Henry VIII*, v. iii. 10. I take the example from Mr. Cruickshank's
Philip Massinger, p. 86.

MILTON AND OXFORD[1]

NO doubt, when you saw my title, you supposed 'Oxford' to be a mistake for Cambridge. But no! Cambridge was Milton's mistake for Oxford; and, if we may believe his enemies, he paid dearly for it. True, it is an Oxford man, Aubrey, who is responsible for the story that Milton was whipped at Cambridge. But it is certain that he was sent down; that he quarrelled with his tutor; that he had a good many enemies among his fellow-undergraduates; that he failed to get a Fellowship; and that, in later life, he felt for Cambridge less affection than is consistent with his having been happy there. When it came to finding a college for his nephew and biographer, Edward Phillips, it is significant that he sent him, not to Cambridge, but to Magdalen Hall, Oxford. I do not know whether it was mere accident; but to Oxford went also the most distinguished of all Milton's pupils, Richard Jones, first Earl of Ranelagh.

I understand that, before coming to Oxford for a vacation sojourn which I hope will be full of pleasant experiences for you, you have all been making some study of Milton, and it occurred to me that here was an opportunity too good to miss of putting together some notes upon Milton's connexions with Oxford. These connexions are few and rather slight: but some of them are interesting; and to the studies of any one studying Milton in Oxford may add a certain reality. Let me say at once that I have nothing new to offer you. But thirty years of teaching have taught me that old things are never as well known as they should be; and that nothing is so old but that a local setting makes it new. How much of each of your days here you are obliged, or expected, to spend in the lecture-room, listening to persons like myself, I do

[1] For the occasion of this lecture, and that immediately following it, see *Preface*, p. v.

not know. It is a secret between you and the Board of Education which I shall not try to penetrate. But I hope you are sometimes more happily employed; that you have the earlier part at least of the afternoon to yourselves, and the chance to see something, not only of Oxford, but of the country round. If you have, and are interested in poets and poetry (and you would not be here if you were not), there are two walks which I want to commend to you. The first has nothing to do with Milton. But it has much to do with poetry and with the sentiment of Oxford. The first walk to take is that into the Hinksey country—the country of Matthew Arnold's *Scholar Gipsy* and *Thyrsis*. It is not Oxfordshire, it is true, but Berkshire. But Matthew Arnold's two poems have made it Oxford for us. No one who wants to catch the spirit of Oxford must miss it. Let me add that scholar-gipsies, real and living poets, yet wander there on the hill-side; and that if one of you is particularly lucky he may chance upon a sight of Mr. Bridges or Mr. Masefield.

But that is not the only poetical ground. The Hinksey walk takes you south-west of Oxford. I want to recommend to you a walk in exactly the opposite direction. Go down the High Street, cross Magdalen Bridge, bear to the left, and you will find yourselves on the Old London Road, with Headington Hill facing you. You will not miss it, for it is one of the few hills we keep. Climb the not very formidable ascent of Headington Hill, and go straight on, until, about two miles from Magdalen Bridge, you find on your left a by-road, pointing you to Stanton St. John. Follow it. For a mile of your way you will be following the line of a Roman road—the old Roman road which connected Dorchester-on-Thames with the Roman station of Alchester, some two miles south of Bicester. Let me say, in parenthesis, that Dorchester itself is worth a visit. A motor bus will take you in half an hour right to the doors of the magnificent Abbey there. A few hundred yards this side—the Oxford side—of the Abbey, you will see the Dorchester end of the old Roman road I speak of—

a broad grass track which you cannot miss. However, I am concerned here with this Roman road as you meet it just beyond Headington. When you have found it, follow it for just about a mile, then turn east—take the turning, that is, to your right, and a quarter of an hour's walk will bring you to Stanton St. John. The church there is worth looking at for itself—though the same is true (if people would only remember it) of nearly every village church in England. The main body of it belongs to what is called the Decorated period of our architecture—it is a little later in date than the choir of Merton Chapel. But the chancel arch is Norman, and the tower perpendicular, coeval with, say, New College. The chancel windows contain the remains of some good painted glass; and the poppy-head carving of the pews is worth looking at.

In any case, you will be looking at a church at which Milton must often have looked with a rather wistful curiosity. Ancestry he had none worth speaking of, or that can be traced certainly beyond the fourth generation. But to Stanton St. John belonged his great-grandfather, his grandfather, and his father. 'He is said to have been descended', writes his nephew, Edward Phillips, 'of an ancient family of the Miltons of Milton near Abingdon in Oxfordshire [Abingdon is, in fact, in Berkshire]; where they had been for a long time seated, as appears from the monuments still to be seen in Milton church [Milton church contains no such monuments]; till one of the family, having taken the wrong side in the contests between the Houses of York and Lancaster, was sequestered of all his estate but what he held by his wife.' Antiquarian research makes it likely that most of this is mere legend. Milton near Abingdon is probably a blunder for Great Milton in Oxfordshire. Great Milton is some five miles south of Stanton St. John; and from Great Milton members of the poet's family may well have migrated to Stanton, where his great-grandparents were certainly located in the middle of the sixteenth century. As for their estate, it was very small indeed—the total fortune of the great-grandfather amounting at his death to less than £7. The grandfather, however, greatly improved upon this, and became a substantial Oxfordshire yeoman, the first of the family to rise out of poverty and obscurity. He was a zealous Catholic; and for non-attendance at the church of Stanton St. John he was twice fined so large a sum as £60—worth then perhaps six times what it is now. He was, in fact, one of the churchwardens of this church. Milton's nephew, and others, tell us that he disinherited his son—the poet's father—'for embracing, when young, the protestant faith, and abjuring the Popish tenets'.

Milton's father seems not to have been much disadvantaged by being disinherited. He became a prosperous business man. But more important, either with or without his father's assistance, he acquired, not only a good education, but, what is much rarer, a belief in one. He was, as you know, an accomplished musician, whose compositions were printed with those of the best composers of the time. In that connexion, it is interesting that a tradition—for which I do not know the authority—makes him a scholar of Magdalen School: the school which, near a century earlier, had educated the great Tyndale. In Elizabeth's reign Magdalen School and College were alike strongly Protestant.

That Milton himself sometimes visited members of his father's family in Stanton seems likely from the circumstances of his first marriage. Let me remind you of these. I can best do so by continuing my guide-book manner. When you have finished looking at Stanton church—the church of which Milton's grandfather was churchwarden, but the services of which he refused to attend—you should set your faces to return by a different route from that by which you came. You should leave Stanton by the road that points south-east to Wheatley. Following it, less than a quarter of an hour will bring you to the village of Forest Hill. Again the church, late Norman, is worth looking at—the bell-tower is especially interesting. Near the church stood, in Milton's time, the Manor House, now no longer to be seen; but the property then of Richard Powell, the father of Milton's first wife. If you make friends with the gardener at the Rectory (in my experience, not a difficult thing to do), he will show you at the west end of his garden 'Milton's Gateway'. It is reputed to be, and very well may be, a gateway of the old Manor House. The gardener is a sentimentalist; and he believes that Milton and Mary Powell used to sit in the shadow of it o' summer nights. Powell, Milton's father-in-law, was a prosperous squire, of royalist sympathies. But he had become indebted to Milton in a sum of something like £500—Milton seems to have had a kind of mortgage on the Forest Hill estate. On some day in May 1643 Milton left London, in a fashion full of mystery, and descended upon Forest Hill. The Civil War had already begun; Oxford and the country round was held by the King. Powell and Forest Hill were for the King. Milton was not only a Parliamentarian, but, by reason of his recent pamphlets, a particularly notorious one. How he was able, and why he wished, to make his way under the conditions given from London to Forest Hill is past finding out. His nephew, who lived with him at the time, was no wiser than we are. It has been suggested that he went to try and extract from Powell the money owing to him. It has been suggested that Mrs. Powell offered him, in lieu of his money, Mary Powell. At any rate a month later Milton and Mary appeared again in London, man and wife. They were not married in Forest Hill—where the Register knows nothing of them. Masson (whose *Life of Milton* is our standard biographical authority), Masson thinks it likely that they were married at some church in Oxford. The rest everybody knows. Within a month Mary was back with her family at Forest Hill; and even before she left him Milton had begun the composition of that scandalous treatise of his, *The Doctrine and Discipline of Divorce*: one of the books which he described as 'more particularly necessary at that time, when man and wife were often the most inveterate foes, when the man often

stayed to take care of his children at home, while the
mother of the family was seen in the camp of the enemy,
threatening death and destruction to her husband'.
Nearly three years later, when Oxford fell before the arms
of Fairfax, the Powell family were in that city; from that
city they betook themselves for refuge to Milton's house
in London.

The road from Forest Hill to Wheatley comes out into
the old London road about four miles north of Oxford.
If you fear to miss one of your evening classes, there
are buses for those who are fortunate enough to find
them. Just before you begin to descend Headington Hill,
look away to your left. You will see the low range of
Shotover. Milton's grandfather, it is said, held the office
of Ranger of Shotover Forest. The green plateau that
crowns it was, when I was an undergraduate, a favourite
place for a gallop, for men who could ride horses, or
couldn't. To-day the undergraduate who wishes to
break his neck prefers mechanical transport and tarmac
roads.

That Milton knew Oxford itself we may be fairly certain. That he had a particularly good opinion of it I think
not likely. In 1656 he corresponded freely with his old
pupil Richard Jones, who was at Christ Church. 'You
tell me you rather like Oxford', he writes. 'That is not
a circumstance that would lead me to believe that the
place has made you wiser or better—for that I should
want very different evidence.' And elsewhere—in another
letter to the same pupil—'No doubt', he writes, 'Oxford
is as you describe it; a very pretty and a very healthy spot;
and it contains books enough to make it a university. If
its pretty situation advanced the intelligence of its resi-
dents in the same degree as it promotes their pleasures, it
would indeed be an ideal place. Even so its Library is
certainly very well furnished. But unless the minds of the
students become better furnished by using it, it may more
fitly be called a lock-up for books than a library.' This
was written after the Parliamentary Commission had sat

to reform the University—perhaps, like some other Commissions, it accomplished less than it thought to do.

Twenty-one years earlier, Milton had paid the University of Oxford the compliment of becoming incorporated M.A., receiving what we call an *ad eundem* degree. He hardly did this without some wish to establish, or strengthen, connexions with Oxford learning and learned Oxford men. It is likely, I think, that, during occasional visits to his father's kindred in Stanton St. John, he may have desired to make use of the Bodleian Library—the library of which he speaks thus doubtfully in his letter to Jones. The Librarian of the Bodleian at this time was a certain John Rous, whom we know to have been a friend of Milton's. You have read *Comus*: and you will know that Milton prefixed to *Comus* a letter written to him by Sir Henry Wotton in 1638; a letter in which, thanking him for a copy of an earlier edition of that poem (Lawes's edition of 1637), Wotton says that he had in fact already had a copy of the book from 'our common friend Mr. R.'. There is ground for believing that 'Mr. R.' stands for John Rous, Bodley's Librarian. And Milton's acquaintance with Rous furnishes a good reason for sending you to the Bodleian Library, which contains a number of Milton treasures. In the show-cases you may see Milton's snuff-box, and other like bric-à-brac. Whether these are proper objects of interest—more proper than, say, the cherry-stones of Calverley's poem which 'once dallied with the teeth of royalty itself'—I should not like to say. (I hope you know Calverley's poem. It is called *Precious Stones*, and describes a luncheon attended by a royal person at which cherry tart was eaten. After the luncheon, there was a loyal, but undignified, rush for the cherry-stones which the royal person had ejected on to his plate (instead of swallowing them like a gentleman.)) Well, there these trivial memorials of Milton are; and, truth to tell, to the snuff-box I attach some sort of importance. I like to think of Milton taking snuff; just as I like to recall that, in his old age in Bunhill Fields, he used to smoke a pipe of tobacco before going to bed; that he was 'of a very cheerful humour—he would be cheerful even in his gout-fits and sing' (says Aubrey); just as, again, I like nothing better in his nephew Phillips's recollections of him than the circumstance that, when he lived in Aldersgate Street, 'once in three weeks or a month he would drop into the society of some young sparks of his acquaintance . . . the beau's of those times, but nothing near so bad as those nowadays; with these gentlemen he would so far make bold with his body as now and then to keep a gawdy-day'.

So much for the snuff-box—slight but treasurable evidence of a Milton more humane, more *human*, than we are easily able to think him. But somewhere near the snuff-box may be seen a bound volume of eleven pamphlets, with an autograph inscription by Milton. The volume contains all that he had written in prose up to the year 1645; and was presented by himself to the Bodleian. With it he had sent to the Library a copy of his *Poems*, the 1645 volume. But the *Poems* became lost in the post. Milton seems to have learned of their loss almost immediately; for a week or two later he forwarded to John Rous a second copy of the book. This second copy the Bodleian has to-day; and bound into it is a Latin poem of Milton, addressed to Rous, setting out the circumstances under which the book was sent. The poem is in manuscript, and there are those who will tell you that the manuscript is written in Milton's own hand. Other people know better; and I confess myself among the sceptics. The book is not in the show-cases; and indeed access to it is rather jealously guarded. It is, I think, worth noticing that, despite the loss of the first copy of Milton's *Poems*, the posts between Parliamentary London and Royalist Oxford were surprisingly good. The *Poems* (though they bear the date 1645) were in fact not published until 2 January 1646. By 23 January Milton had heard from Rous of the loss of the first copy; for it was on that day that he forwarded to him the substitute copy—the copy which the

Bodleian still has. It would seem that, in that war too, there was 'business as usual'. I may notice that at this time it was, by a decree of the Star Chamber of 1637, the duty of every printer to deliver a copy of any book printed by him to the Stationers' Company 'before any public venting of it'; and by the same decree the Company was obliged 'under paine of imprisonment' to forward the copy to 'the Librarie at Oxford'. But the days of the Star Chamber were done; as for the Stationers' Company, Milton had already shown his contempt of it. We must suppose his gift to the Bodleian to have been something in the nature of a *personal* offering.

For printing his *Poems* a licence was required. It was required by a parliamentary Ordinance of 1643, the Ordinance, in fact, against which Milton had directed his *Areopagitica*—his great Plea for the Liberty of Unlicensed Printing. The official from whom Milton obtained his licence was the Head of an Oxford college. I take pleasure in thinking that but for one of the Wardens of my own College the world might never have had *L'Allegro* and *Il Penseroso*. The book was licensed by Sir Nathaniel Brent, Warden of Merton—who also licensed, I like to remember, Waller's *Poems* and Lovelace's *Lucasta*. At the moment Brent was out of Oxford and out of office. The King at Oxford had caused him to be deposed, and had, in effect, appointed a Warden of his own, the celebrated Dr. Harvey. But Harvey's tenure of office was destined to be brief and unfortunate. Within a few months Oxford surrendered to Fairfax, and Brent returned. He came back as Warden of Merton—and to a position even more invidious; for it fell to him to be Chairman of one of the first University Commissions of which our troubled annals hold record. However, in 1645, he sat in London licensing books for the parliament. Masson suggests that some special caution was employed in the licensing of Milton's book. Twice already, it is true, Milton had been in trouble for unlicensed printing. But on each occasion he would seem to have found

powerful protection; and the real difficulty, I should suppose, was, not in giving him a licence, but in getting him
to ask for it. His Oxford connexions make it not unlikely
that he was personally known to his licenser. He may very
well have known him through John Rous, or, again,
through the well-known parliamentarian, Francis Rous,
M.P. for Truro. Francis and John Rous were, it is probe-
able, related; and Francis Rous's son (also called Francis)
was a student at Merton under Brent—to whom he
dedicated 'from his study in Merton Colledge' his book on
the Antiquities of Attica (*Archaeologiae Atticae Libri vii*).
Or, again, Milton may have been known to Brent through
another Merton man, John Hales. Hales was a Fellow of
Merton and professor of Greek; he became subsequently
a Fellow of Eton. It is generally supposed that he is
the 'Mr. H.' of Sir Henry Wotton's letter to Milton—
the letter, prefixed to *Comus*, which I have already mentioned. The connexion with Hales is of interest for the
reason that he was the friend of a poet one of the most
accomplished of the time, albeit in the lighter genres,
Thomas Carew, also of Merton College. It would be interesting to know whether these connexions ever brought
together Milton and Carew, Puritan and Cavalier,
but poets both. I hope I may be easily forgiven for
straining thus at the slender threads that connect Milton
and Merton.

I do not know whether Milton ever set foot in Trinity.
To Trinity belonged the two persons whom I should suppose to have been the most intimate friends of his youth.
The one of these was Charles Diodati, Milton's school-
fellow at St. Paul's; in whose memory Milton wrote the
Epitaphium Damonis, a Latin elegy in which critics profess
to discover more personal feeling than can be found in
Lycidas. The other was Alexander Gill the younger, one
of Milton's schoolmasters. The elder Alexander Gill was
High Master of St. Paul's; and his son acted as his assis-
tant. Milton had a respect for his schoolmasters which
he never had for his dons. With the younger Gill he

maintained a familiar correspondence, from time to time exchanging verses with him. There are still extant two letters which he wrote to Gill in the summer of 1628. It was a disastrous summer to Gill. In the first week of September occasion took him from London to Oxford, and to his old college of Trinity. I do not know but what Diodati also was in Trinity—he had only recently gone down. A few days before had occurred the murder of Buckingham by Felton; the country was excited, the government alarmed. Gill enjoyed himself in Trinity more than was proper in a Doctor of Divinity; he drank more than a divine should, and he talked more than becomes a man of sense. Amid other loose talk, he spoke of Felton as a hero; drank his health, and indulged in conversation about the King something between silly and treasonable. Among the junior Fellows of Trinity was William Chillingworth, later a celebrated divine, but already a man of tender conscience. He seems upon this occasion to have undertaken the office of tale-bearer; and, on information furnished by him to Laud, Gill was arrested and put in the Tower. His case excited almost as much sensation as that of Felton; and the examination of his correspondence brought some of his friends into danger. Masson speculates whether, when he was searched, there may not have been found in his pocket-book the two letters he had recently received from Milton. They were not, I think, in any case, of a character to excite suspicion. But this Oxford sensation was certainly a sensation in Cambridge also; and Masson is no doubt right in thinking that it brought distress and anxiety to Milton. Gill was kept in prison for two years, fined £2,000, sentenced to lose his ears, and deprived of his orders and his degrees. The greater part of this punishment was subsequently remitted, and Gill lived to succeed his father as High Master of St. Paul's. Later he was ejected from his office for cruelty to the children under his charge.

So much for Trinity. Whether Milton ever visited it,

with Deodati or Gill, there is no knowing; nor again whether he knew the tale-bearing Chillingworth—he may very well have done so: for Chillingworth was born and bred in Oxford.

Another college, in part an Oxford college, in which Milton must have had a considerable interest was the so-called Invisible College. You will not find the Invisible College in the guide-books, and it may be that you have never so much as heard of it. Its members and promoters were located partly in Oxford, partly in London; and the college itself for some time hung uncertainly between a Utopia and a chemical laboratory. Prominently connected with its beginnings was Milton's friend Samuel Hartlib, the whimsical idealist to whom he addressed his tractate *Of Education*. A more important member of it was the celebrated Robert Boyle, the soul of the Oxford, as distinct from the London, branch of the college. Boyle was the brother of Milton's friend 'the incomparable Lady Ranelagh', and the uncle of his old pupil Richard Jones. Another friend of Milton's who was a member of the college was Henry Oldenburgh, who acted for a long time as Jones's tutor. Jones himself was a candidate for membership. Other members were Christopher Wren, John Evelyn, and Abraham Cowley. The Invisible College became ultimately the Royal Society, the foundation of which is one of the few deeds of light that lighten the darkness of the reign of Charles II. This was not the Invisible College which its promoters had envisaged. They had envisaged a college somewhat like an Oxford college, but given over to the study of what we call Natural Science—which was then called 'philosophy'. According to the scheme of Cowley, it was to be situated within two or three miles of London—doubtless to keep it in touch with the realities of life. There were to be twenty professors and 'sixteen young scholars, servants to the professors'. There were to be 'four old women to tend the chambers', and so on. The luxurious ideal of a college where the teachers had less than one pupil apiece, and could use their pupils as servants, contrasts remarkably with the reality we most of us know, where the teacher is the servant of anything from twenty to forty pupils.

The Invisible College was not designed to supersede the colleges of Oxford and Cambridge. With some of the ideals of its promoters Milton had sympathy—already in his undergraduate days he had favoured the enlarged study of experimental philosophy; and in his tractate *Of Education* provision is made for this. But the Invisible College of the tractate leaves no place for other colleges than itself. Milton has in fact no use at all for either of the two great universities. His college is to 'be at once both school and university, not needing a remove to any other house of scholarship'. He would begin his experiment with 'a spacious house and ground . . . big enough to lodge 150 persons'. But he contemplates the erection later of 'as many edifices . . . as shall be needful in every city throughout this land; which would tend much to the increase of learning and civility everywhere'.

It is proper that we should recognize plainly that Milton, the most scholarly of all our poets, the English man of letters who owes more to study and education than any other, supposed both Oxford and Cambridge to have outlived their usefulness. He speaks of them, in the tractate *Of Education*, as lingering still in 'the scholastic grossness of barbarous ages'; of their students as 'mocked and deluded . . . with ragged notions and babblements, while they expected worthy and delightful knowledge'. When these students have finished their course, what careers are open to them? They pass, Milton says, some of them 'to an ambitious and mercenary or ignorantly zealous divinity'; others to 'the trade of law', but 'grounding their purposes not on the prudent and heavenly contemplation of justice and equity, which was never taught them'; others again to 'state affairs, with souls so unprincipled in virtue and true generous breeding that flattery and courtships and tyrannous aphorisms appear to them the highest points of wisdom'. The best of them, those

'of a more delicious and airy spirit', stay where they are.
He means the dons. They 'retire themselves (knowing no
better) to the enjoyments of ease and luxury, living out
their days in feast and jollity'. 'Which indeed is the wisest
and safest course of all', he adds bitterly. If you have been
educated at Oxford or Cambridge, he means, the best
thing you can do is to stay there. At least you will be
harmless. The real danger of Oxford and Cambridge is
when their dons issue forth into the world, and, without
understanding virtue and justice, undertake the government of Church and State. Milton's more particular
animosity is directed here, I think, against Oxford. At
any rate it is primarily of the University of Oxford that
he writes, in the same strain, so contemptuously in the
pamphlet *Of Reformation in England.* The Oxford dons,
he says there, 'beseech us that we would think them fit to
be our justices of peace, our lords, our highest officers of
state, though they come furnished with no more experience than they learnt between the cook and the manciple,
or more profoundly at the college audit, or the regent
house, or, to come to their deepest insight, at their
patron's table'.

A very ill-natured critic of Oxford I hope you will think
Milton. I hope that, before you leave, you will feel more
kindly than he did towards the cooks and manciples who
feed you and even the dons who lecture to you. You will
hardly attend an audit. But you will perhaps discover
that there are still colleges which brew their own audit ale.

HOW TO KNOW A GOOD BOOK
FROM A BAD

HOW do we know a good book from a bad? A contemporary of Shakespeare wrote a play, very popular in its time, bearing the title *How a Man may chuse a Good Wife from a Bad*; and, if it really answered the question, the play may be accounted one of the great books of the world. The right choice of books is, no doubt, in comparison with the right choice of wives, a subject of secondary importance. Only in the East is man polygamous; nearly everywhere he is polybiblous—a creature of many books. Always it is open to him to burn or sell, or, at the least, to criticize his books; an unsatisfactory wife can be neither burnt nor sold—and it is not often that she will allow herself to be criticized. On the other hand, a man, once married, is able immediately and certainly to formulate a reasoned account of those qualities in his wife which create in him dissatisfaction or uneasiness; but I have known many men who have lived all their lives with books of whom never a one could discover to me what, in a book, are those qualities by which it is confidently pronounced good or bad.

But let me say first what I mean by a book. A book of logarithm tables is not a book; nor a book of dates; nor a spelling book; nor a Latin grammar; nor Newton's *Principia*; nor Darwin's *Origin of Species*; nor any other book, of however great importance to mankind, which aims at instruction and information rather than at delight and edification. In a word, I call nothing a book which does not address a large part of its appeal to imagination and emotion. Among books so defined, how do we distinguish the good from the bad? For of both kinds there are plenty—though let me say at once that I think we grumble a great deal too much at the mounting tale of bad books. For myself, I can never enough admire that there should be that infinity of good books that there is in the world. Indeed, in a sense, all books are good. Have you ever reflected what a world of talents goes to the making even of what is admitted to be a bad book? It is sometimes said that it requires more talent and training to paint even a poor picture than to make a tolerable book. But this is to forget the infinite pains with which we learn speech itself, grammar, accidence, writing, spelling—there are long years of training here before we can even approach those higher exercises which consist in the rhythmizing of speech and that selection and ordering of fact and fancy called narrative. It requires some training and technique to ask for the butter; a great deal to write home for five shillings; an infinite deal to write a really good letter (an art almost dead); and that a man should write a book, just a tolerable book, even what is called a bad book, this may well be thought the top of miracle.

All books, then, may be called good, in virtue of the talent and technique necessary to the production of any book. And though I am here to commend to you, among books, the best, and to make suggestions as to how these may be known, I feel disposed to say a word on behalf of bad books. I am sure, at any rate, that the best critic of books, in the long run, is the man who brings to the study of them a large charity, and that the worst criticism is the 'highbrow', as it is called. There are a great many books in the world which are poor literature, but which afford none the less the means of agreeable and harmless recreation; and to brush them aside, to pretend that one does not like them, that they count for nothing in the sum of life's conveniences, is to be first pedantic and then dishonest. Robert Louis Stevenson loved what are called 'penny dreadfuls', and said so like a man. Study the sources of Shakespeare's plays, and you will find an infinite deal of poor literature which Shakespeare read with very obvious pleasure and edification. He was unscholarly enough to like blood and thunder; and honest enough to let us find it out. Our world has too many drab parts for it to be worth our while to disparage even an ill-written book if it gives us something of the colour of life. Perhaps, indeed, any book is worth having that quickens the pulse or softens feeling.

Let us hate pedantry, then, and, as we grow more and more educated, fight against literary pride; remembering that a bad book, at its worst, is not like a bad man. The chances are ten to one that it is the best part of the man who wrote it, and that he was a good enough fellow. Indeed, that is why he wrote it; it sprang—all literature springs—from the ineradicable instinct in man to communicate good; and thus almost all books assure us that the soul is divine.

None the less, it is well that we should be able, in a world too narrow for the books it holds, to distinguish, if we can, good literature from bad, and the best from the mediocre. For not to do so is, firstly, to waste time; and though life is longer than we commonly allow, the books really worth reading are, as I have said, so many. And secondly, though I have wished to say a good word for bad books, they are at least less good than good ones; and read by the wrong persons, or at the wrong season, they may easily prejudice our faculty of appreciating what is really best in literature. Reading a book is not like buying a piece of goods in the market; or, if it is, it is so with this difference—you take this particular kind of goods home, not in a parcel or cart, but in the soul. A moment ago I suggested that almost any book was worth having that softened feeling. I think that is true; but it needs qualifying. I have noted among persons who read novels, and see plays, that, in respect of a particular kind of play or novel, they tend to measure excellence by a tear-bottle: to suppose that, of literature which is tragic or pathetic, a necessary character is its power to make them cry. I am not sure that the truth is not just the other way. Of the most moving passages of Homer a great French critic said, I think properly, that what was marvellous in them was the fact that nowhere does Homer's voice tremble, nor his hand shake. I have cried, I can remember, to read Mrs. Henry Wood's *East Lynne*, and Canon Farrar's *Eric*. But God forbid that I should cry over *Lear* or *Othello*— I should know that there was something the matter with Shakespeare or with myself. I remember reading *East Lynne* in a crowded third-class railway carriage; and the manner in which the tears ran down my cheeks made me an object of general attention. So much so, that an elderly and benevolent clergyman seated opposite expressed the hope that I was not in any trouble; and I perplexed him, I know, not a little by telling him with perfect truth that I was only crying because this was so bad a book. Thereafter he left me alone, not because he saw that I had made him an inspired answer, but because he supposed me to be beyond his art, to be past praying for. Of tragedy, of that whole department of literature which we call the pathetic, the proper function is to steady us. It is life that shakes us and rocks us, literature which stabilizes and confirms.

Even as I say this, I am sensible of the many objections which can be raised against it; some of them very powerful; so powerful, indeed, that I am content here not to meet them, but to allow some parts of my case to go by default. Temperament is, from man to man, infinitely diversified; and the effects of literature depend often upon accidents of past experience, of situation, of physical health. And in general the critic who bids tragedy not make him cry courts the mortification of the king who bade the waves come no nigher. I will not say more, therefore, than that it is, as I think, true upon the whole that the great poet, the great artist in literature, rarely tempts us beyond what we are able to bear. We speak of him as 'swaying' our emotions; and sway is governance. In proportion as he knows his trade, he never drives the car of passion so as to let it get out of control.

I mentioned just now Shakespeare's *King Lear*. If you want to know how a poet truly 'sways' the emotions, look

at the last scene of the fourth act of that play. There is
no greater example in literature of artistic control; passion
is driven there urgently, but not cruelly; the restraining
hand is throughout present and felt:

Lear.　　　　　　　　　　　Pray, do not mock me:
I am a very foolish fond old man,
Fourscore and upward, not an hour more or less;
And, to deal plainly,
I fear I am not in my perfect mind.
Methinks I should know you and know this man;
Yet I am doubtful: for I am mainly ignorant
What place this is, and all the skill I have
Remembers not these garments; nor I know not
Where I did lodge last night. Do not laugh at me;
For, as I am a man, I think this lady
To be my child Cordelia.
Cor.　　　　　　　　　　　And so I am, I am.
Lear. Be your tears wet? Yes, faith. I pray, weep not:
If you have poison for me, I will drink it.
I know you do not love me; for your sisters
Have, as I do remember, done me wrong:
You have some cause, they have not.
Cor.　　　　　　　　　　　No cause, no cause.
Lear. Am I in France?
Kent.　　　　　　In your own kingdom, sir.
Lear. Do not abuse me.
Doc. Be comforted, good madam; the great rage,
You see, is kill'd in him; and yet it is danger
To make him even o'er the time he has lost.
Desire him to go in; trouble him no more
Till further settling.

That matter-of-fact Doctor has saved a break-down. A
lesser artist than Shakespeare would have been tempted
to take the dialogue between father and daughter too far,
to try over again something in the same pitch as Cordelia's
wonderful 'And so I am, I am'. But Shakespeare never
loses control.

I have sought an illustration from tragedy because,
from the time when literary criticism first begins, tragedy

has commonly been accounted the supreme literary form; and in any case it is from those parts of literature where tragic or pathetic incident is handled that the difference is most clearly discerned between the master and the amateur, between supreme work and second-rate work. It should be said, however, that, while the supreme effects are easily known, it is precisely in this department that, without a standard of comparison, we are apt to be taken in by inferior effects. The sentimental and the false-pathetic too often 'overcome us like a summer cloud'; and if they are good in the sense that everything is good that softens feeling, yet they encourage a prodigality of nature by which we may easily waste what is best and rarest in us on incidents and reflections not worthy of it, and by which, in the end, we may come to lose the distinction between true and pure feeling and feeling that is factitious and unreal. I suggest to you, therefore, that in this matter of tragic and pathetic effects—which are, as I say, the highest effects of literature—nothing is so likely to help us to distinguish the good from the bad as that we should satisfy ourselves that we are really 'swayed' by what we read, that we are conscious that the poet, or writer, not only drives, but controls, our affections and emotions. And this control which the great poet exercises is, if not easily defined, easily perceived, as I think. It is atmospheric, if you like. We are conscious of a presence— much as, in social intercourse, we are conscious, very often, in a chance-assorted crowd, of the domination of some individual temperament, drawing all eyes, compelling attention.

Where this sense of control manifests itself, it is, I suggest, the most distinctive note of great literature, the trademark of an inalienable excellence. What other marks are there by which we may know the good from the bad?

First, I would hazard the suggestion that there is no better test of excellence than to ask oneself of any book a very simple question: Does it speak to the point? The question seems, indeed, so simple that you may doubt whether the answer to it will carry you very far; you may even doubt whether one has any business to interrogate literature, especially romantic literature (with all of us the first of our literary loves), in a fashion so elementary, so matter-of-fact. But after all, good and bad are elementary distinctions, and are, if life has any meaning, very matter-of-fact indeed. Just now I mentioned in passing those classes of literature which we call 'exciting', and I said something in excuse of our untutored fondness for them. But what is it in them which alienates criticism? What is the matter with them? In part what is the matter with them is what I have already indicated—they spur what they cannot rein. But they have commonly a technical defect at once more obvious and less venial. The 'exciting' book nearly always accumulates episodes; it tends to pile incident upon incident without regard to necessary or probable connexions; it tends to be a series of sensational happenings which are not organically connected, which are a sequence and not a chain; any one of them might be removed without affecting any other or the disposition of the whole. The book, in other words, is, over large tracts of it, not *to the point*.

A large part of life, you will say, is faulty in the same particular—throwing together unrelated happenings. And you will be saying what is true enough; and, perhaps without knowing it, you will be saying why it is that literature exists at all. The end of literature is, truly enough, to present life; but to present it in such a fashion as to eliminate what is unessential, unrelated, inorganic; to present it as a whole of which all the parts are seen to be co-operative. Much of life is off the point; literature, where it is off the point, is not good, but bad. It is in this sense, and perhaps in this sense only, that literature is, in the phrase of a great writer, a criticism of life. Literature is always to the point. It does what life does not, what because we cannot do it for our lives makes them so hard, it eliminates the unessential.

You will see that, beginning from something very simple, we are now reaching towards a theme of some complexity. We have thrown a pebble; and on the waters of criticism it shapes a circle as wide as the world. A good test of a good book is to ask, Is it to the point? Are its parts a whole? Ask that of nine-tenths of the novels you read, of the plays you see, and you will know that, judged by the highest standards (though I do not say that a cheerful disposition will always insist on these), they are bad novels, bad plays. That is, I think, helpful in itself, it is a practical aid. But it opens, as you see, wide vistas of literary theory. A good book possesses organic unity; but in so far as it does so, it is a criticism of life.

Let us linger for a moment in what I may call the practicalities; and presently I will say something of the manner in which we may conceive a good book to criticize life. A good book speaks to the point. It studies what the French call 'l'art de ne pas tout dire', the art of not saying everything. It does not heap incident on incident, but combines only those actions which stand to one another in a relation of cause and effect. But that is not all. A book may so combine its actions or episodes that they constitute a unity, and yet not be a good book; it may, indeed, be less a good book than one in which this unity is less perfect, but in which another demand is satisfied, a demand of which the nature is, I think, easily explained. When you have read your novel, or seen your play, and have satisfied yourself that its actions present an organic unity, you must then proceed to a further question: Are these actions the actions of somebody? That has a cryptic ring. But the fact is that of most plays, and most novels, the actions are the actions of nobody at all. By that, I mean, as you guess, that the actions have no ground in character. If you met in real life the persons who performed them, you would not know them again— they have no gesture, no air, no sweetness, no human outline. They are just labels attached to their own behaviour. The question is sometimes asked whether in poetry, the drama, novels, and romance, character is more important than plot or action. Here—I would suggest—the good may be known from the bad, or at least the very best from the second best, by the fact that the question will not occur to you. At the top of fiction, the distinction of plot and character falls away. A man does what he is; and what he does is the man.

I have said nothing thus far of what is called style in writing, and of the ornament of words; yet by their style, it is commonly thought, books are most easily distinguished as good and bad. Of this I have said nothing, but I have, I think, implied something. The good book, I said, talks to the point. I used the expression in a different connexion—with reference to unity in the theme of a book. But it has a wider application; and, indeed, I am not sure that style can better be defined than by saying that a book that talks to the point has style. At once, you answer the question whether there is a language of literature which is different from that of real life; at once you solve the puzzle of the romantics, whether there is such a thing as poetic diction. When from the speech of common men you eliminate the unessential, the accidental, what is inexpressive, or less expressive than something else, Style arises. Poetry, after all, is called poetry because it is not prose; and equally truly, though Molière's Bourgeois Gentilhomme took a naïve pleasure in discovering that he had been talking prose all his life without knowing it, he was wrong; nobody talks prose; and that is why, when anybody does, we call him prosy. The fact is that very few of us talk to the point; very few of us, that is, truly relate what we say to what happens, or is, or to what we or others are, to character. I can recall, in the casual intercourse of life, but one occasion upon which I was witness to a supreme effect of style; and it is, I think, worth putting on record. In the first year of the war, I talked with a Belgian refugee, a man of education, whose acquaintance with the English language, however, was notably limited. He had come from Antwerp in the first days of its siege. He complained, no doubt with truth, that we, in England, did not know what war meant. 'But I', he said, 'I know. For I have seen the flight of old men, and it is terrible.' That has always stayed with me: an effect of style which you will hardly equal, as I think, outside Homer. And you can see for yourselves the conditions of it. Here was a man whose resources in our language were so confined in their scope as to throw him back upon bare essentials. Accident worked like art; everything unessential was eliminated; and, on a living theme, he spoke to the point.

Just now I acquiesced in the dictum, to which a good deal of objection has been taken, that literature, and particularly poetry, was a criticism of life. I acquiesced in it in the sense that that unity which is properly demanded of a work of art has for its corollary such a presentation of life as frees it from the tie of accidental circumstance, from the irrelevance, confusion, incoherence, which make up so much of what we call real life. But this is not to say that literature is, or should be, didactic, that it preaches, that it endeavours consciously to make men better. I should prefer to say, with a great man who in my time was Master of this college,[1] that literature is a criticism of life exactly in the sense that a good man is a criticism of a bad one. And good men, or at any rate wise ones, never preach. If you ask me whether art, or literature, must be moral, I can only answer you by a method not much liked by such persons as mostly ask the question, the method, that is, of common sense. It is hateful—I know—to carry common sense into the rarefied atmosphere of artistic discussion; and yet a man might as well ask, Should mankind be moral? A book of an unpleasant theme, or of an immoral tendency, may, as well as a man of like constitution, both exhibit talent and afford entertainment; and a prude in literature is as tiresome as a prude in life. But the fact is that, in the long run, in books and in life alike, morality can be trusted to look after itself. There are

[1] Edward Caird (the lecture was delivered in Balliol College).

periods of immoral literature, just as there are periods of
social convulsion. But the average citizen never dies; and
the good sense of the ordinary decent man, like charity,
never fails in the long run. Literature does not please by
moralizing us; it moralizes us because it pleases: and the
world is pleased by what is unpleasant only for a limited
time. I see no reason why literature should be moral,
except that people prefer it; nor any ground, out of faith,
why you and I should be moral, save that society insists
on making us so.

I have tried to put my finger upon some marks whereby
you may know the good book from the bad. I have not
travelled outside poetry, the drama, and the novel; but
with a little goodwill, and some not difficult adjustments'
what I have said is capable of being applied, I think, to
other departments; to history, for example, and to ora-
tory. One species of poetry, I am conscious, I have
neglected—the species called, rather inappropriately,
lyric. Here action and character, for the most part, stand
down; not the relations between these, but a certain relation of the writer to the reader, usurps the place of
primacy. To-day, it might almost be said, this species
alone lives; and it must be acknowledged to have an
amazingly developing life. Never perhaps was there an
equally bewildering exuberance of talent; and it is idle to
pretend that the poetry of to-day does not matter; it is
cowardly not to try and judge it. I can think of no greater
service that I could perform than to be able to turn you
loose into the wide and diversified field of what is called
absurdly 'Georgian' poetry, with a few plain rules for
distinguishing the good lyric from the bad. For myself
I know what I like, and why I like it. I like most in the
Georgian poetry what is least like the rest of it and most
like the poetry I know better; and that is why I like it.
I will hazard, indeed, one monition. Let everything be
done in order. It is no use to begin here: it is not safe
to begin here. We must begin farther back. We must
endeavour to be wise as Time is, which always works

forwards, never backwards. Albeit 'great spirits now on earth are sojourning', yet a sensible man will work from Milton to Masefield, and not the easier, the more delightful, way. And by this time you divine, no doubt, a lame and impotent conclusion to an inquiry which promised better things. I fear, indeed, that you came to this lecture with better hopes than I did—or you had not come at all. For to be wholly honest (since it has come to that), the only test—after all that I have said—the only test that I know of a good book is the best books. The highest scholarship is, in fact, the humblest pupilage. The masters of criticism are those who are still at school to Shakespeare, Milton, Wordsworth. Taste is still conditioned by the palate; and a safe diet makes a clean palate. Shakespeare and Milton and Wordsworth are a safe diet. The good book is not necessarily the book that is like the books of any of these three; but it is the book that savours well to a palate which these three have kept pure and sensitive.

More than once in this lecture I have said good things of bad books; and I seem to end now in what I most dislike, a dictum of the highbrows. It is too late (and it would be too uninteresting) to make myself consistent. The fact is that what is the matter with the highbrows is, not that they are wrong, but that they are irritating. To the good fortune of being right, they add the impudence of knowing it. They make also the mistake of supposing that our strength comes always from the hills; whereas the truth is that we are human creatures, and that we wilt sometimes in this fine mountain atmosphere, and pine for the coarse air of cities, the smoke of the plains. After all, literature is a part of life—else it were so dull that it died. There is nothing so good for us as the best books; but from the ambition to be the saints of literary study heaven shield us! I hope that you may all go away from this lecture with enough adventure left in you to want to rub shoulders with bad books.

M m

WALTER RALEIGH

BEYOND dispute Walter Raleigh was one of the great figures of the Oxford of his time. Nature had made him for a notable man in any society. His towering figure (he stood six foot six), his nobly-shaped and finely-poised head, his slow, swinging gait, his immense reach of arm (which had a generosity all its own when—as was his habit if he was at all moved—it was shot out for a sudden handshake), his long and lean but very mobile face, lighted by eyes expressing often an almost feminine tenderness—all these outward characters made him a man to look after in the street and to watch in a room. Wherever he went he was necessarily the most prominent person there, and another man to whom nature had given, as a setting for uniquely brilliant qualities of mind, so notable a physical endowment might have been tempted to dominate his company. But of Raleigh's great social charm, and of his vogue, a large part of the secret was a quick responsiveness to environment, an instinct for give and take, a genius for company conditioned by the need that other people should be at their best if he was to give them the best of himself. Certainly no one in Oxford, perhaps no one in England, was a better or more brilliant talker or better loved talking. Nor was Raleigh above a 'show performance': he liked being brilliant, and he liked being appreciated. But if he talked more and better than other people, he rarely failed to make other people talk more and better than themselves. The fact is that it was his nature to like people and to find them a good deal more interesting than they were. He liked the ordinary man; and he liked to catch up what he said and make it better than it was, and to illustrate by it something large in human nature. If he talked to dull and commonplace persons, there was always behind his conversation the assumption that they were as big and as human as himself. I fancy, indeed, that he thought that they were. For a cardinal element in his thinking was an intense belief in average human nature. It was this faith which attracted him so powerfully to the Elizabethans. He loved men in their casual strength, in what Emerson calls their 'peccant irregular passional force'. That was why the great English seamen were above all dear to him. That was why the last work upon which he was engaged was the history of the British Air Force. The present writer remembers well expressing one day to him some doubt whether that history would not use up too much of talents which could be more finely employed in other directions. But Raleigh had no doubts. 'No', he said; 'the best thing I have ever done was my *Hakluyt*, and this is on the same line, and it's really my line.' The men who made the Air Force held the same place in his imagination as Drake and Frobisher and Grenvile and the other great makers of English sea-power. Nothing appealed to him so profoundly as the big things done by what are called average men.

But this belief in ordinary men (which made Raleigh so fine a companion of men) he did not hold as ordinary men hold it. The fact is that, with his immense readiness to be ordinary, he had a temperament essentially romantic. These seamen and airmen, who were so dear to him, he saw in the mirror of a mind directed habitually by the sentiment of chivalry. And sometimes when he spoke of them one had the feeling that this man who sat with us so companionably, so responsive to the things and persons of the moment, was yet one who had strayed in from more spacious days, who in some strange fashion had drifted from the court, say, of Elizabeth to a decolorated and less noble world. This chivalrous and romantic element in his nature was brought into strong relief by the war; and the sense of what Oxford in particular owed to those of its young men who fought in the war was a kind of religion to him. But at all times he liked young men, and mixed with them in a fashion most natural and charming. They in their turn forgot to be shy; and Raleigh was perhaps

never seen to better advantage than when he presided at
a dinner of some undergraduate society. He was always a
great gentleman; but there was a specialized courtesy,
quite irresistible, in his dealings with persons either very
much younger or a good deal older than himself. Of the
quality of his conversation it is not easy to give any just
idea. He had a mind extraordinarily fertile of ingenious
images, and he was perhaps prone to suppose that he had
concluded a syllogism when he had invented a metaphor.
He was a master of inspired phrase, using epigram as other
men use respiration, to fill the intervals of more deli-
berated behaviour. He employed all forms of wit save
satire (a vein which the present writer, at any rate, never
remembers to have heard him use). His wit was always
informed by a large humanity, and he made the persons
to whom he talked genuine partners in it. He had a liking
for apophthegm, and his best utterances in this kind
played round large issues deftly and effectively. He had
some gift of denunciatory eloquence, but he exercised it
rarely, because he kept it for conduct which he thought
mean; and in general he thought of man as a creature,
not mean, but naturally magnanimous. He disliked cant.
But in other respects his tastes were catholic. He had
a particular tenderness for Dick Steele—and the Dick
Steeles of the world.

As a professor, Raleigh owed his success (for he was
successful beyond the expectations of those who knew
Oxford best) to the same qualities as those which made
him so fine a companion. He brought to letters the same
catholicity of taste which he carried into society, and a
temperament extraordinarily responsive to the note of
magnanimity. Other professors have been men of greater
learning (though it was possible to catch Raleigh possess-
ing much more learning than he owned to). But Raleigh
was a first-class lecturer and a first-class writer, for the
reason that his authors were men to him. He took fire
from them exactly as he took fire from talking to you.
They were just splendid people, and what they said ex-

cited him, and their manner of saying it; and he poured out, in books and lectures, a running commentary of inspired or ingenious annotation. It was all natural to him—both that they should be great, and that he should see wherein it lay, and that he should say notable things about them and find life in doing so. He loved, both in lectures and in private intercourse, to read aloud the great things of literature; and he read in a fashion finely interpretative. On such occasions, indeed, one might say of him what Hazlitt said of Coleridge: 'His voice was the music of thought.'

In connexion with his organization of the English Literature School two matters deserve special notice. Firstly, many persons, when the School began, affirmed confidently that we were founding a school of dilettantism; and they would have liked to see the Chair of Literature filled by one who was less a man of letters and more technically a scholar than Raleigh. But Raleigh knew the danger as well as any one, and it was largely his influence, exercised through colleagues between whom and himself there was complete confidence, which directed the School along the lines of a genuine scholarship. Secondly, Raleigh was profoundly sensible always of the continuity of literature and of the importance of watching its living development; and with this in mind he more than once invited to lecture for him in Oxford persons who represented the newer movements in poetry and criticism. But he was careful to impress upon his students what they might be apt to forget. 'Of these young poets,' he was fond of saying, 'those who survive a century hence will be found to be far more like the great poets of the past than they are like one another.' But he was always ready, in literature and in life alike, for experiment and adventure: always sympathetic towards anything in either which was free of pusillanimity and pedantism.

It was his sense for adventure, his flair for the romance of doing things, which took him on that expedition to the East in which he contracted the disease which cost him his life. The expedition was undertaken in connexion with his work upon the history of the Air Force. But he would have been the last person to wish that any one should think of him as a martyr of research, or even as a martyr of duty. Far rather he was the victim of his own indomitable youthfulness and of a romantic sympathy with the life of action. And probably he would not have asked to die in a better cause. It was perhaps this romance of temperament that made him so good a critic of books and of life. It was this certainly that lifted him out of the dullness of academic talent and that gave to whatever he did or said a singular chivalry and generosity. Personalities thus finely touched to fine issues are rarer than Raleigh himself was disposed to believe. Their advent is rare and their sojourn brief, but the memory of them is sweet in the dust.

PRINTED IN GREAT BRITAIN AT THE UNIVERSITY PRESS, OXFORD
BY JOHN JOHNSON, PRINTER TO THE UNIVERSITY

THE
PROFESSION
OF POETRY
AND OTHER
LECTURES

GARROD